ENGLISH
PHRASAL VERBS
IN USE

60 units of vocabulary reference and practice

Self-study and classroom use

Second Edition

Advanced

Michael McCarthy
Felicity O'Dell

CAMBRIDGE
UNIVERSITY PRESS

Shaftesbury Road, Cambridge CB2 8EA, United Kingdom

One Liberty Plaza, 20th Floor, New York, NY 10006, USA

477 Williamstown Road, Port Melbourne, VIC 3207, Australia

314–321, 3rd Floor, Plot 3, Splendor Forum, Jasola District Centre, New Delhi – 110025, India

103 Penang Road, #05–06/07, Visioncrest Commercial, Singapore 238467

Cambridge University Press & Assessment is a department of the University of Cambridge.

We share the University's mission to contribute to society through the pursuit of education, learning and research at the highest international levels of excellence.

www.cambridge.org
Information on this title: www.cambridge.org/9781316628096

First published 2007
Second Edition 2017

22   21

Printed in Malaysia by Vivar Printing

A catalogue record for this publication is available from the British Library

ISBN   978-1-316-62809-6   Paperback

Contents

The world around us

Key verbs

Acknowledgements English Phrasal Verbs in Use Advanced

Joy Godwin wrote two new units for the Second Edition: Unit 23, *Agreeing*, and Unit 33, *Lectures and seminars*. The publishers would like to thank Joy for her contribution to this edition.

The authors and publishers acknowledge the following sources of copyright material and are grateful for the permissions granted. While every effort has been made, it has not always been possible to identify the sources of all the material used, or to trace all copyright holders. If any omissions are brought to our notice, we will be happy to include the appropriate acknowledgements on reprinting and in the next update to the digital edition, as applicable.

Key: T = Top, B = Below, C = Centre, TL = Top Left, TR = Top Right, CL = Centre Left, CR = Centre Right, BR = Below Right, BL = Below Left.

Photographs

All the photographs are sourced from Getty Images.

p. 12 (TR): Plume Creative; p. 12 (CL): Jim Craigmyle/First Light; p. 12 (BR): diego_cervo/iStock; p. 13 (TL): DonNichols/iStock; p. 13 (TR): Colin Anderson/Blend Images; p. 13 (BL): Camilo Morales/Blend Images; p. 13 (BR): View Pictures; p. 26: Thomas Barwick/Digital Vision; p. 32 (T): Robert Harding; p. 32 (B): iStock; p. 40 (T): ivanastar/iStock; p. 40 (C): Wolfgang Ehn/LOOK-foto; p. 40 (B): michaeljung/iStock; p. 43 (TL): fstop123/E+; p. 43 (BR): Hill Street Studios/Blend Images; p. 45: Maskot; p. 50: Ezra Bailey/Taxi; p. 52 (TR): Phil Boorman/Cultura; p. 52 (BR) & p. 66 (photo 3): Hero Images; p. 55 (TR): PhotoAlto/Frederic Cirou; p. 55 (BL): Image Source; p. 56: gilaxia/E+; p. 58 (TR): Chris Ryan/The Image Bank; p. 58 (CR): omersukrugoksu/iStock; p. 58 (BR): Dougal Waters/DigitalVision; p. 60: Ezra Bailey/Iconica; p. 66 (photo 1): Sam Diephuis/Blend Images; p. 66 (photo 2): Colin Hawkins/Stone; p. 66 (photo 4): Blend Images/Trinette Reed; p. 66 (photo 5): Indeed; p. 66 (photo 6): Peter Dazeley/Photographer's Choice; p. 70 (TR): skynesher/E+; p. 70 (BR): monkeybusinessimages/iStock/Getty Images Plus; p. 76 (T): DmitriyOsipov/iStock; p. 76 (BR): RoBeDeRo/E+; p. 90 (TR): Chris Parker/Perspectives; p. 90 (BR): Betsie Van Der Meer/Taxi; p. 98 (photo 1): Thorsten Milse/robertharding; p. 98 (photo 2): ClaraNila/iStock; p. 98 (photo 3): EcoPic/iStock; p. 99: WLDavies/iStock; p. 101 (photo 1): Apriori1/iStock; p. 101 (photo 2): Walter Zerla/Blend Images; p. 101 (photo 3): Slava Bowman/EyeEm; p. 101 (photo 4): Anke Wittkowski/EyeEm; p. 101 (photo 5): Edwin Remsberg/The Image Bank; p. 101 (photo 6): mshch/iStock; p. 102: Robin Bush/Oxford Scientific; p. 109: Di_Studio/iStock; p. 110 (TR): tunart/E+; p. 110 (BR): Image Source/DigitalVision; p. 114 (fruits): 109508Liane Riss; p. 114 (vegetables): Teubner/StockFood Creative; p. 114 (pizza): Ed Nano/StockFood Creative; p. 114 (salad): Doram/E+; p. 120: StudioCampo; p. 121: Kirillica/iStock; p. 124: Yuri_Arcurs/DigitalVision.

Illustrations

Ludmila (KJA Artists), Katie Mac (NB Illustration), Martina (KJA Artists), Gavin Reece (New Division) and Miguel Diaz Rivas (Advocate Art).

Cambridge Dictionaries

Cambridge Dictionaries are the world's most widely used dictionaries for learners of English. The dictionaries are available in print and online at dictionary.cambridge.org. Copyright © Cambridge University Press, reproduced with permission.

Using this book

Why was this book written?

It was written to help you take your knowledge of phrasal verbs to a more advanced level. It is intended for students who already have at least an upper intermediate level of English. Many of you will have already worked with *English Phrasal Verbs in Use Intermediate* and this book builds on the work done there. However, it does not matter if you have gained your knowledge of phrasal verbs in a different way. We do not assume that you have used *English Phrasal Verbs in Use Intermediate*, although we do present and practise either different phrasal verbs in this book or, occasionally, more advanced uses of verbs that were presented in the lower level book.

How were the phrasal verbs in this book selected?

The approximately 1,000 phrasal verbs and related nouns and adjectives which are presented in this book were mainly selected from those identified as significant by the CANCODE corpus of spoken English developed at the University of Nottingham in association with Cambridge University Press, and the Cambridge International Corpus (now known as the Cambridge English Corpus) of written and spoken English. The phrasal verbs selected are accordingly also to be found in the *Cambridge Dictionary* online by going to the following website: http://dictionary.cambridge.org

How is the book organised?

The book has 60 two-page units. The left-hand page explains the phrasal verbs that are presented in the unit. You will usually find an explanation of the meaning of the phrasal verb, an example of it in use and, where appropriate, some comments on when and how it is used. The exercises on the right-hand page check that you have understood the information on the left-hand page and give you practice in using the material presented.

The units are organised into different sections.

First we start with important information about phrasal verbs in general (Units 1–4): what they are, how their grammar works and so on. We strongly recommend that you do these units first.

The next section looks at some interesting aspects of more advanced phrasal verbs, dealing with such important issues as collocation, register and metaphor. As these are themes that are returned to throughout the book, it is a good idea to work through these units before progressing to other more specific units.

After these two introductory sections, there is a section dealing with some of the most common particles used in forming phrasal verbs. Working on these units will help you to gain a feeling for the force of these particles and will help you have a feeling for the meaning of a phrasal verb you are meeting for the first time.

The next two sections deal with Concepts (e.g. Time) and Functions (e.g. Arranging things). These sections are followed by a large number of topic-based units focusing on different aspects of Work, Personal life and The world around us.

The final section looks at some of the most common verbs which are used to form phrasal verbs.

The book has a key to all the exercises so that you can check your answers. At the back of the book you will also find a useful Mini dictionary. This provides clear definitions of all the phrasal verbs and related noun and adjective forms that appear in this book. The Mini dictionary also indicates the unit number where you can find a particular phrasal verb.

How should I use this book?

It is strongly recommended that you work through Units 1–4 first so that you become familiar with the way phrasal verbs (and their associated nouns and adjectives) operate and with the terminology that is used in the rest of the book. Then we suggest that you move on to Units 5–8 and after that you may work on the units in any order that suits you.

What else do I need in order to work with this book?

You need a notebook or file so that you can write down the phrasal verbs that you study in the book as well as any others that you come across elsewhere.

You also need to have access to a good dictionary. We strongly recommend the *Cambridge Phrasal Verbs Dictionary* as this gives you exactly the kind of information that you need to have about phrasal verbs. Your teacher, however, may also be able to recommend other dictionaries that you may find useful.

So all that remains is to say **Go for it!** (Unit 30). We hope you'll find this an enjoyable as well as a useful way to keep up and extend your knowledge of English phrasal verbs in use.

1 Phrasal verbs: what are they and how are they used?

A What are phrasal verbs?

Phrasal verbs are verbs that consist of a verb and a particle (a preposition or adverb) or a verb and two particles (an adverb *and* a preposition, as in **get on with** or **look forward to**). They are identified by their grammar (more about that in Unit 2), but it is probably best to think of them as individual vocabulary items, to be learnt in phrases or chunks. They often – but not always – have a one-word equivalent. For example, you can **come across** a new phrasal verb or you can **encounter** it. You can **pick up** a language or you can **acquire** it. **Come across** and **pick up** sound less literary or formal than **encounter** or **acquire**.

B Why are phrasal verbs important?

Phrasal verbs are extremely common in English. They are found in a wide variety of contexts. You may have noticed them in songs, for example the Beatles' *I'll get by with a little help from my friends* or *Roll over Beethoven*, Bob Marley's *Get up, stand up* and Red Hot Chili Peppers' *Knock me down*. You find them in film titles such as *The Empire Strikes Back*, *Spirited Away*, *Along Came Polly* or *Cast Away*. They are very frequent in newspaper headlines. Here are just a few examples:

> Country's misplaced pride **holds back** its democracy

> Cricket: England **holds out** for a draw

> Inquiry points to a **cover-up**

> Turner **adds up** likely cost of pensions

Phrasal verbs are common in less formal English, but you will also hear or see and need to use them in more formal contexts. Register is discussed in more detail in Unit 6.

C Which phrasal verbs does this book deal with?

This book is based on information gained from the Cambridge International Corpus (a huge computerised database of present-day English) about phrasal verbs and how they are used in contemporary English. It focuses on phrasal verbs more advanced students need to know – but in general does not deal with the verbs in the lower level *English Phrasal Verbs in Use Intermediate*. It includes phrasal nouns such as **standby** or **onset** (see Unit 3) and phrasal adjectives such as **outgoing** or **worn out** (see Unit 4).

D What can I do to help myself master phrasal verbs?

Try to think positively about them! And, now you are at a more advanced level, try not just to understand them but also to use them in your own speaking and writing.

Keep an eye open for them whenever you are reading anything in English and make a note of any interesting ones you find. Write them down in a complete phrase or a sentence to fix in your mind how they are used.

Be aware that one of the special features of phrasal verbs is that some of them have many different meanings – for example, you can **pick** something **up** from the floor, you can **pick up** a language or bad habits, the weather can **pick up**, you can **pick up** a bargain, a radio can **pick up** a signal, the economy can **pick up**, you can **pick up** a story where you left it, you can **pick** someone **up** in your car. Sometimes the meanings are clearly related, some being more literal and some more metaphorical. Unit 7 deals with this in more detail.

In this book we may not present all the meanings of the verbs that are included. You may find others in *English Phrasal Verbs in Use Intermediate* and there are still more in the *Cambridge Phrasal Verbs Dictionary*.

Exercises

1.1 **Underline the phrasal verbs in these texts. Remember the particle or preposition may not be immediately next to the verb.**

1 I decided to take up gardening, so I took out a subscription to a gardening magazine and read up on the subject. I found out so many interesting things, such as the best time to plant flowers out for the summer and how to grow vegetables. I've really got into it now and spend hours in the garden every weekend.

2 The other day we went off on a hike in the mountains. We put our wet-weather gear on as the weather forecast wasn't good. We set off early to avoid the rush hour and soon reached the starting point for our walk. The whole walk took about four hours, and when we got back we were exhausted.

3 I have to catch up on my coursework this weekend as I've fallen behind a bit. I worked on it till midnight last night, but I still have loads to do. I have to hand one essay in on Tuesday and another one on Friday. I'm not sure whether I'll make it, but I'll try.

1.2 **Choose the correct particle to finish these song titles.**

1 Can't get you *off from* / *out of* / *away from* my head (Kylie Minogue)
2 Hold you *against* / *down* / *at* (Jennifer Lopez)
3 We can work it *with* / *across* / *out* (The Beatles)
4 Send *from* / *in* / *with* the clowns (Barbra Streisand)

1.3 **Complete the sentences in the right-hand column with a phrasal noun or adjective based on the phrasal verbs in the left-hand column. Use a dictionary if necessary, and remember that the particle may come at the beginning or end of the noun or adjective.**

1	The school took in some outstanding students last year.	Last year's .... included some outstanding students.
2	Some prisoners broke out of the local prison last night.	There was a(n) .... at the local prison last night.
3	It was an experience that put everyone off.	It was a(n) .... experience.
4	She always speaks out and gives her opinion.	She is very ....
5	A lorry which had broken down was blocking the road.	A .... lorry was blocking the road.

1.4 **Match the headlines with the sentences from the stories.**

1 **BIG SHAKE-UP EXPECTED IN EDUCATION**

2 MINISTER DENIES COVER-UP

3 **LOCKOUT CONTINUES AT AVIATION PLANT**

4 BREAKAWAY GROUP TO FORM NEW PARTY

5 **POWER PLANT SHUTDOWN LEAVES 5,000 HOMES IN DARKNESS**

a) The dispute is now in its fifth week.
b) Unity was no longer possible, a spokesperson said.
c) The event happened at 7.45 p.m. with no warning.
d) There will be major changes at all levels.
e) There was no attempt to hide the truth, claimed Pamela Harding.

2 Grammar of phrasal verbs

A Phrasal verbs with and without objects

Some phrasal verbs take an object (transitive); others do not take an object (intransitive).

with object (transitive)	no object (intransitive)
They're **knocking down** the old hotel.	The path **branched off**[1] to the river.
The plumber soon **sorted out** the shower problem.	The noise of the train **died away**.
She **tied** her hair **back** so she could swim faster.	In the winter the lake **froze over**.

[1] if a road or path branches off, it goes in another direction

Some verbs can be used both with and without an object, but the meaning may change. Use the context to decide if the verb has a different meaning from the one you are familiar with.

> Polly and Beth were so clever the teacher **moved** them **up** to a higher class. (with object)
> Polly and Beth **moved up** to a higher class. (no object = same meaning)
> I can **drop** you **off** at the station. (with object = drive you somewhere and leave you there)
> I was sitting in the armchair and I **dropped off**. (no object = fell asleep, different meaning)

Some verbs must have two objects, one after the verb and one after the particle.

> I always **associate** that song **with** our holiday in Jamaica.
> Playing tennis for three hours every evening after school **deprived** her **of** her youth.

B Position of the object

In many cases, the particle may come before or after the object.

> The teacher **marked** the student **down** / **marked down** the student because her bibliography wasn't up to standard.

Very long objects usually come after the particle.

> The accident **cut off** domestic and industrial water and electricity supplies.

When the object is a personal pronoun, the pronoun always comes before the particle.

noun object	personal pronoun object
I **picked** my parents **up** / **picked up** my parents and drove them to the airport.	I'll **pick** you **up** at 5.30. (Not: ~~I'll~~ **pick up** ~~you at 5.30.~~)

Some verbs (sometimes called prepositional verbs) must have the object after the particle, even if it is a pronoun. A good dictionary will tell you if this is so.

> We've had to **contend with** a lot of problems lately. (Not: ~~contend~~ a lot of problems ~~with~~) [deal with a difficult or unpleasant situation]

You probably already know some of these verbs (**look for**, **look after**, **cope with**).

C Three-part verbs

Some phrasal verbs have three parts – the verb and two particles. The object comes last.

> I will not **put up with** such bad behaviour. [tolerate]

Other examples include **look forward to**, **look down on**, **get on with**, **catch up on** [do something you did not have time to do earlier], **face up to** [accept that a difficult or unpleasant situation exists].

Exercises

2.1 **Look at A. Do these sentences need an object? If they do, add an appropriate one in the correct place.**

EXAMPLE   Last summer we knocked down.

Yes. *Knock down* is transitive; it needs an object.
Last summer we knocked down the old shed in our garden.

1 The sound of the violin slowly died away.
2 If you're ready to leave now, I can drop off at your office.
3 The river in St Petersburg freezes over for several months each year.
4 My son is so good at English that I think the teacher should move up to the advanced class.
5 I associate with that evening we spent together in Rome.
6 I was so tired that I dropped off in front of the TV.

2.2 **Put the words in the correct order to make sentences. If you can do it in two different ways, then do so.**

1 pick / off / you / work / the / I / and / can / at / you / from / airport / up / drop / then
2 from / that / put / teacher / she / The / not / would / said / with / such / up / class / rudeness / her
3 villages / The / off / several / have / mountains / in / cut / the / floods
4 your / doesn't / the / improve / down / If / will / spelling / mark / examiners / you
5 always / Margot / to / with / all / seems / her / cheerfully / problems / cope

2.3 **Rewrite each sentence using the verb in brackets in an appropriate form.**

1 I'll have to ask my daughter to get my Internet connection working. (SORT)
2 I was so tired after work that I fell asleep in the train on the way home. (DROP)
3 I was given a lower mark because my essay was over the word limit. (MARK)
4 Jason has no right to despise me – he's no better than I am. (LOOK)
5 Lara doesn't have a good relationship with one of her flatmates. (GET)
6 You have to accept the fact that you will probably never see each other again. (FACE)
7 Maria has got a new job taking care of an old lady. (LOOK)
8 If you don't let the children get enough sleep, they won't be able to concentrate at school. (DEPRIVE)
9 In Lapland we had to manage in some difficult driving conditions. (CONTEND)
10 The road to our house leaves the main road just after the service station. (BRANCH)

2.4 **Write answers to these questions using the phrasal verb in brackets.**

1 What are your plans for the summer holidays? (LOOK FORWARD TO)
2 What homework have you got to do this weekend? (CATCH UP ON)
3 If you've been away somewhere by train and arrive back late, how do you usually get home from the station? (PICK UP)
4 What is your favourite album and why do you like it? (ASSOCIATE WITH)
5 What sorts of things make you feel stressed? (CONTEND WITH)
6 How easy do you find it to fall asleep at night? (DROP OFF)

> ### Over to you
>
> Look up these verbs in your dictionary: *associate with, deprive of, contend with* and *face up to*. How does your dictionary give information about the structures that these verbs require? What nouns do these verbs typically combine with according to the examples in your dictionary?

3 Phrasal nouns

A   What are phrasal nouns?

Like phrasal verbs, phrasal nouns consist of a verb combined with a particle. The particle may come before or after the verb.

phrasal noun	meaning	example
standby	ready to be used if necessary	My wife's a pilot and she's on **standby** over the weekend.
		We're keeping the old equipment as a **standby**, in case of emergencies.
letdown	disappointment	I had been looking forward to the concert for weeks, but it turned out to be a terrible **letdown**.
back-up	support	Nicholas can provide technical **back-up** if you need it.
warm-up	preparation	The comedian who did the **warm-up** for the studio audience before the TV programme started was excellent.
onset	start (of something unpleasant)	The match was halted by the **onset** of torrential rain.
input	contribution	Try to come to the meeting – we'd value your **input**.
overkill	more of something than is needed	Shall I add some more decorations to the cake or would that be **overkill**?

Some such nouns have a corresponding phrasal verb, but some don't. For example, there is no phrasal verb ~~to kill over~~. The phrasal verb **set on** exists but it means attack. The verb related to **onset** is **set in**: We couldn't continue playing after the rain **set in**.

If the particle is in first place, then the phrasal noun is never written with a hyphen. If the particle comes second, then there is sometimes a hyphen between the two parts of the phrasal noun, particularly if that particle is *in* or *up* or if the phrasal noun is relatively infrequent, e.g. **walk-on** [small part, with no words, in a play], **stand-off**.

B   When are phrasal nouns used?

Phrasal nouns are used frequently in newspapers and informal conversation.

> **STOWAWAY**[1] FOUND ON PLANE

> **STAND-OFF**[2] IN TRADE TALKS

> **WALKOUT**[3] AT CAR FACTORY

> SINGER STAGES A **COMEBACK**

> **BREAKDOWN** IN STRIKE TALKS

> MANAGEMENT **BUYOUT** FOR HIGH STREET CHAIN

> HELP FOR BUSINESS **START-UPS**

> MILITARY **BUILD-UP**[4] CONTINUES

[1] person hiding in order to travel
[2] failure to reach agreement
[3] strike
[4] increase in size or strength

Annie	Who do you think will get the job – Paul or Elsa?
Finn	I don't know. It's a **toss-up**. [(informal) both seem equally likely]

Lily	Did you have a good time at football last night?
David	Yes, but we didn't have a real game, just a **knockabout**.

> **Tip**
>
> The stress is on the first syllable in these nouns regardless of whether this is the verb or the particle.

Exercises

3.1 **Complete these sentences using a phrasal noun from A opposite.**

1 The .... of winter meant that there was less food for the animals and birds.
2 I thought having a 45-piece orchestra at their wedding really was .... , personally.
3 The police officer radioed for .... before entering the bank.
4 Let's ask Joel what he thinks. I always find his .... very useful in these matters.
5 TV producers find that studio audiences react better if they have a .... to watch before a live programme.
6 Our holiday in the Mediterranean was a bit of a .... The hotel was second-rate and the food was awful.
7 Although Cameron usually rides his new road bike to school now, he's kept his old bike as a ....

3.2 **Rewrite these sentences, starting with the cues given, using phrasal nouns from the opposite page instead of the underlined words.**

1 Two men who had <u>stowed away</u> in the container were arrested when police opened it.
   The police opened the container and ....
2 Negotiations with union members <u>broke down</u> after a couple of hours.
   There was a ....
3 The management <u>bought out</u> the company in 2014.
   There was a ....
4 Last night all the workers <u>walked out</u> and the factory was forced to close.
   There was a ....
5 Military forces are continuing <u>to build up</u> on both sides of the border.
   The military ....

3.3 **Correct the mistakes with the phrasal nouns in these sentences.**

1 There has been a stand-up for several days now in the talks between the government and the rebels. Neither side will make any concessions.
2 Last year there were 15,000 new Internet business start-offs, most of which only survived for a few months.
3 After years without releasing an album, Madeleine Flame has staged a comeagain with her new collection of love songs.

4
| Holly | Have you decided where you're going this summer? |
| Flora | Not really. It's a toss-over whether it'll be Italy or Greece. |

5 I met Nasser and we just had a knockover on the college football pitch for half an hour.

3.4 **Choose the correct phrasal noun in each sentence. Use a dictionary if necessary.**

1 *Putout / Output* has increased this year and the factory is doing well.
2 One of the robbers acted as *lookout / outlook* while the others robbed the bank.
3 There was a sudden *pourdown / downpour* and we all got very wet.
4 The *breakout / outbreak* of war in 1914 changed Europe for ever.
5 *Lift-off / Off-lift* is scheduled for 07.00 on Friday and the astronauts will arrive at the space station later that day.
6 There was *a break-in / an in-break* at our office last night. Two computers were stolen.

4 Phrasal adjectives

Some phrasal verbs have related adjectives. Make a note of these as you meet them.

phrasal verb	adjective	meaning	example
go on	**ongoing**	one which continues	We've had an **ongoing** problem with the computer system.
wear out	**worn out**	weak, damaged through much use	She was wearing old, **worn-out** shoes.
break down	**broken-down**	one that has stopped working	In our garage we've got an old **broken-down** fridge.

However, this is not the case for all such adjectives. We can say 'that way of thinking is very **outdated**', but there is no related verb ~~to date out~~; we can say 'the restaurant was really **overpriced**', but there is no phrasal verb ~~to price over~~ (the verb is 'to overprice').

Note the phrasal adjectives in these extracts from people talking about their dreams and ambitions.

 I'm an **outgoing** sort of person, so I want a career where I mix with people. To be honest, I find the idea of a desk job quite **off-putting**[1]; I just don't think I'd like it at all. I'd love to do something new, something completely different.

[1] makes you not like it or not want to do it

I've always been very **outspoken**. I'm never afraid to express my opinion, so I think a job campaigning for an environmental organisation would suit me. I would never accept any **watered-down**[2] proposals and would make some very direct demands of our political leaders.

[2] made less strong in order to make more people agree with them

I always feel completely **tired out** at the end of the day in my present job and just want to sleep. Instead of feeling cheerful after a good weekend, I always feel quite **downcast**[3] every Monday when the new week starts, so I want something new and more stimulating, preferably with a more **go-ahead** company which will bring interest and excitement into my work.

[3] sad and depressed

Here are some more examples in small advertisements and announcements.

Forthcoming[4] events at the City Stadium

Live-in nanny wanted for 3-year-old.

Caravan for sale: **built-in** fridge, freezer and satellite TV

[4] happening in the near future

Fold-up picnic chair for sale. As new.

For rent, cosy one-room flat with **foldaway** bed. Ideal for student.

> ### Tip
> When you come across a phrasal adjective, check to see whether it has a 'matching' verb and, if so, learn the two together.

Exercises

4.1 **Replace the adjective in each sentence with a phrasal adjective with the opposite meaning.**

1 There was a new carpet on the stairs.
2 The newsletter has a list of recent activities at the tennis club.
3 What's happened? You're looking very cheerful!
4 Unlike her sister, Emily is very introverted.
5 I find the cover of this novel very attractive, don't you?
6 It doesn't matter what time of day it is, Polina always looks fresh.
7 We are not in the habit of going to such cheap restaurants.
8 When you meet my boss I think you'll find her surprisingly uncommunicative.

4.2 **What do these pictures show?**

1 a .... chair
2 a .... car
3 a .... oven
4 a .... bed

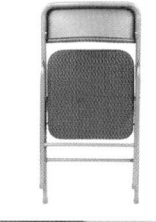

4.3 **Answer these questions about the words on the opposite page.**

1 Can you think of one advantage and one disadvantage for parents of having a live-in nanny?
2 In what kind of room might it be particularly useful to have a foldaway bed?
3 What kind of job would not be suitable for a very outspoken person?
4 When might you want to give a watered-down version of something that happened to you?
5 What kind of job requires you to be outgoing?
6 What kind of problem tends to be ongoing?
7 What might you find off-putting if you are having a meal in a restaurant?
8 What sorts of things do you think are often overpriced?

4.4 **Match the pairs of synonyms in the box below.**

broken-down	candid	continuing	diluted	downcast	dynamic
exhausted	extrovert	forthcoming	future	go-ahead	miserable
not working	obsolete	off-putting	ongoing	outdated	outgoing
outspoken	repellent	shabby	tired-out	watered-down	worn out

4.5 **Here are some more phrasal adjectives. Work out from the context what they mean and rewrite the sentences replacing the underlined words with a word or phrase that means the same.**

1 If the union doesn't accept our terms, what should we have as <u>our fallback position</u>?
2 Clara always feels <u>left out</u> when her brother's friends come round to play.
3 Julian is usually chatty but his sister is not very <u>forthcoming</u>.
4 You shouldn't get <u>so worked up</u> about every little thing.
5 Zack met me at the airport with <u>outstretched</u> arms.

5 Collocation and phrasal verbs

Why is collocation important?

Collocation means the way words combine with one another. When learning a phrasal verb, it is important to note what kinds of words the verb is typically used with. For example, can it be used for both people and things, or only for people, or only for things? Is it typically used with negative things or can it be used for both positive and negative things?

Look at this chart for the verb **pore over** [study or look carefully at something] and note how the objects it is used with refer especially to books or documents.

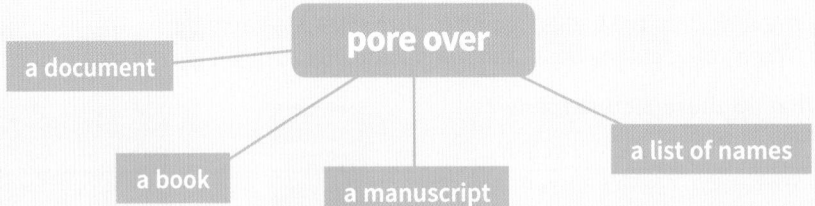

a document — pore over — a list of names

a book — a manuscript

Making a note of collocations in this way will help you remember the meaning of the phrasal verb. It is a good idea to learn the verb and its typical collocations as chunks of language. This will help you to speak and write more fluently.

Collocations with positive or negative/problematic things

Make a note if a phrasal verb collocates especially with positive or negative things.

☑ typical/correct collocation   ☒ untypical/wrong collocation

The plan was **riddled with** problems ☑ good ideas ☒.
The rain ☑ The traffic ☑ The fine weather ☒ has **eased off/up** now.
After hours of discussion, we **hit on** a good idea ☑ the solution ☑ a stupid plan ☒.

Collocations with objects denoting people or things

Make a note if a phrasal verb collocates especially with objects denoting people or things, or both.

I've really **gone off** Sienna ☑ cheese ☑ recently.
I'd advise you to **keep in with** the boss ☑ Andrew ☑ the exam system ☒.

Collocations with subjects denoting people or things

Make a note if a phrasal verb collocates especially with subjects denoting people or things, or both.

As we opened the door, **water streamed into** the room. ☑
People were streaming into the meeting. ☑
I have to dash off. I have a meeting in ten minutes. ☑
The car dashed off along the motorway. ☒ [**headed off / drove off at high speed** would be more typical]

Collocations with particular situations

Make a note of particular situations a phrasal verb typically refers to.

He just **sailed through** his exams ☑ the interview ☑ his breakfast ☒. [**sail through** is used with challenging things and situations]
I was always **hankering after** an easier life ☑ sweet food while I was on a diet ☑ passing my exams ☒. [**hanker after** is most often used with things we cannot or should not have]

Exercises

5.1 Answer the following questions.

1 What does the word *collocation* mean?
2 Which of these are correct collocations?
  a) pore over a book
  b) pore over a view
  c) pore over a manuscript
  d) pore over a flower
  e) pore over a list of names
3 What do the nouns that collocate with *pore over* have in common?
4 Why is it helpful to learn phrasal verbs in collocations?
5 What sorts of things might you note down about what a phrasal verb collocates with?

5.2 Do the sentences below show appropriate collocations or not?

1 When we took our old dog to the vet, she discovered he was riddled with disease.
2 The pain in his leg seems to be beginning to ease off now.
3 You can always rely on Joseph to hit on an idea that will never work.
4 I used to enjoy that TV series but I've gone off it a bit now.
5 It's usually a good idea to keep in with your bank account.

5.3 Complete these sentences using the correct particles.

1 There is no point in hankering .... your lost youth.
2 When her housemate rang to say that water was streaming .... the basement, Maria dashed .... to the station to catch a train home.
3 I always find job interviews really difficult, but my brother seems to sail .... them.
4 We'll have to cut down that tree – it's riddled .... disease.
5 When my sister was pregnant she drank a lot of milk, but she completely went .... tea and coffee.
6 Liam was bullied a bit when he started school, but it seems to have eased .... now.
7 You should apologise to Juliette's mother. It's sensible to keep .... your future in-laws.

5.4 Rewrite each sentence using the verb in brackets in an appropriate form.

1 Helena easily passed her driving test. (SAIL)
2 I really don't like coffee any more. (GO)
3 The wind is less strong than it was now. (EASE)
4 If I have a problem, I find a walk by the sea often helps me to find a solution. (HIT)
5 Masses of people entered the shop as soon as it opened, hoping to find a bargain in the sale. (STREAM)
6 There are a lot of holes in his argument. (RIDDLE)

Over to you

Look back at any other phrasal verbs you have recently written in your vocabulary notebooks. Write them down in some typical collocations. You will find these in the example sentences of a good dictionary, e.g. the *Cambridge Phrasal Verbs Dictionary*.

Register

Phrasal verbs in the English lexicon

The word *register* is often used to refer to whether a word is formal or informal. It can also be used to refer to the language associated with a particular job or interest.

English vocabulary is particularly rich because it combines a large vocabulary originating from Anglo-Saxon roots with a large vocabulary originating from Latin or French. This means that English often has words with very similar meanings from each of these sources. To give a phrasal verb example, you can **put forward** or **propose** an idea, where **put forward** (like the majority of phrasal verbs) has a typical Anglo-Saxon etymology, whereas **propose** is of Latin origin. It is interesting to note that **propose** comes from the Latin prefix *pro-* [= forward] added to the Latin root *-pose* [= put]; there are many other examples of where the Latin etymology parallels the etymology of its phrasal verb equivalent. Words of Latin or French origin tend to be more formal and so 'proposing an idea' is found more frequently in formal written English than in informal spoken English.

Although phrasal verbs are typical of more informal English, many – like **put forward**, for example – will also be found in neutral or formal as well as informal contexts. Most phrasal verbs are like this. Some phrasal verbs, however, are only used in either informal or formal situations. We indicate throughout the book when this is the case.

Informal phrasal verbs

Serge	How's things, Jessie? Is work OK these days?
Jessica	Not really. Sophie's **gunning for**[1] me. I think she's after my job. I **mucked up**[2] an important deal yesterday and she was so thrilled!
Serge	Don't pay any attention to her.
Jessica	I know, but the trouble is Tim's **ganged up with**[3] her now too. So it's got much worse. They **hang around**[4] together in every break and after work too. If Sophie doesn't **shoot down**[5] one of my ideas, Tim does.
Serge	Well, they're **asking for**[6] trouble, aren't they? You know your boss respects you, don't you?
Jessica	Yes, I **couldn't ask for**[7] a better boss, that's for sure. But she's got more important things on her plate than sorting out petty office squabbles.

[1] (only used in continuous) trying to cause trouble for somebody
[2] did very badly with
[3] formed a group to act against me
[4] spend a lot of time (with)
[5] criticise strongly
[6] (only used in continuous) behaving in a way that is sure to create problems for them
[7] couldn't ever find, because this person (or thing) is the best of their kind

Formal phrasal verbs

In the first five examples below, the base verb is in itself formal. The base verb here is of Latin rather than Anglo-Saxon origin. In the final three examples, it is the specific usage rather than the base verb which is formal.

The authorities finally **acceded to** his request for a work permit. [agreed to]
We will **attend to** your request in due course. [deal with]
He **ascribes** his success **to** hard work in his youth. [explains]
The presence of the gene may **predispose** a person **to** heart disease. [make more likely]
James Hansen is to **preside over** the government inquiry. [be in charge of]
Some new facts have emerged which **bear on** the Smith case. [are connected to]
The castaways had to **call on** all their strength to survive. [use]
All her life the princess had never **wanted for** anything. [needed]

Exercises

6.1 Replace the phrasal verbs in the letter with verbs from the box to make it more formal.

meet	continue	complain	respond	remedy	investigate	achieve

●●●   ✉   Reply   Forward

Dear Mr Janes,

Thank you for your letter of 23 May going on about the bad service you experienced at this hotel. I promise you we will look into the problem at once and get back to you as soon as possible. We always try to go for the highest standards of service, and if we have failed to live up to those standards we will immediately seek to sort out the situation. Meanwhile we hope you will go on making Miromana Hotels your first choice for all your business and leisure travel.

Yours sincerely,

G. H. Logan (General Manager)

6.2 Now do the opposite with these sentences. Use phrasal verbs from the box to make the sentences less formal. Use a dictionary if necessary.

go into	fall through	put out	go over to	look after
call in on	buy up	get by	take on	ask out

1 Will you attend to Aunt Elsie while I go and get the children's supper ready?
2 He explored the subject in great detail in his lecture.
3 When the president died his son assumed the title of Great Leader.
4 I like her. Do you think I should invite her to go out with me?
5 During the war he defected to the enemy side and was killed in action.
6 She purchased all the shares in the company last year.
7 The local newspaper published a story about a strange animal seen in the city park.
8 I think I'll visit my grandfather on the way home from work.
9 The deal collapsed at the last minute.
10 I managed to survive on about €70 a day when I was travelling.

6.3 Which professional registers are these phrasal verbs associated with? Put each of them into one of the three categories below. Use a dictionary if necessary.

sell up	sum up	log in	take over	put forward
back up	gloss over	scroll down/up	base on	hack into
turn over	bail out	carry forward	square up	print off

computers and technology	academic lectures/writing	money and business

6.4 Rewrite each sentence using the word in brackets in an appropriate form.

1 Despite his family's poverty, Alfie always has everything he needs. (WANT)
2 You must inform the police if you have evidence relating to the case. (BEAR)
3 Jack will have to use all his ingenuity to resolve the situation. (CALL)
4 The president believes his party's victory is due to his leadership. (ASCRIBE)
5 The manager will deal with your enquiry without delay. (ATTEND)

A Multiple meanings

Many phrasal verbs have more than one meaning. Often, the basic meaning relates to some physical action, while other meanings are metaphorical (i.e. they are figurative, not literal). For example, the meanings in the grey boxes below are literal and the others are figurative.

phrasal verb	definition of phrasal verb	example
run over	hit sth/sb with a moving vehicle and injure or kill them	I **ran over** a rabbit as I was driving home. It really upset me.
	go on after its expected time	The meeting **ran over** so I missed my train.
	read quickly to make sure something is correct	Could we just **run over** the schedule again to make sure it's all going to work?
brush sth/sb **off**	use a brush (or hand) to remove something	I **brushed off** the dust from my shoes.
	refuse to listen to what someone says, or refuse to think about something seriously	The boss just **brushed** him **off** and told him to get back to work.

B Examples of metaphors based on quick or violent actions

The price of petrol has **shot up** this year. [gone up rapidly and sharply]

I don't want to just **dive into** a new job without carefully considering it. [start doing something suddenly and energetically without thinking about it]

The leader of the opposition party has **hit out at** the government's new proposals on tax. [strongly criticised, typical of journalism]

My success in the exam **spurred** me **on** to study even harder. [spurs are worn on the ankle and are used to make a horse go faster; here the meaning is 'encouraged me']

C Metaphors and context

The context will usually tell you that a verb is being used in a metaphorical way. Look at these extracts from the advice column of a magazine which use phrasal verbs metaphorically rather than literally.

> Don't just **stand by** and let others have all the fun. It's time to **strike out** on your own and do something completely different. **Sweep aside** all your inhibitions and start living life to the full. It all **boils down to** whether you are prepared to take control of life or let life control you.

> You must find the strength to **drag** yourself **away** from your domestic responsibilities for a short while and stop feeling **sandwiched between** your family and your career. Doing everything single-handed is **eating into** all your free time and you need time to think. You can't be expected to **soldier on** on your own any longer.

D More examples of phrasal verbs used metaphorically

She searched in her bag and **fished out** an old photograph.
We wandered round the old market, just **drinking in** the atmosphere.
He spends hours **glued to** his computer every evening.
We found this vase when we were just **nosing around** in an antique shop.
People were **flooding into** the stadium two hours before the concert.

Exercises

7.1   **Look at A and B opposite. Read the email and then answer the questions below using your own words rather than the phrasal verbs in the email.**

Hi Bella

Sorry to miss you this morning – the budget meeting ran over and I just couldn't leave. We had to try to find some ways to cope with the way that our transport costs have shot up over the last few months. Luke was finding fault with all my ideas and I had to stay and try to defend them as best I could. He always takes any opportunity to hit out at me – I don't know why. Anyway, could we meet later today to run over the agenda for tomorrow's meeting? My problems today have spurred me on to succeed tomorrow. We mustn't just dive into our proposal without preparing the ground carefully. It'd be a disaster if the boss just brushed us off after all that work!

Rory

1. When did the budget meeting end?
2. What has happened to transport costs recently?
3. How does Luke usually behave towards Rory?
4. What does Rory want to do with Bella this afternoon regarding tomorrow's agenda?
5. Has today's meeting made Rory more or less determined about tomorrow's meeting?
6. What does Rory not want to do with their proposal at tomorrow's meeting?
7. What is he afraid that the boss might do to them?

7.2   **Rewrite the underlined parts of these sentences using a phrasal verb from C or D opposite.**

1. It's not good for children to spend too much time <u>just watching</u> a screen.
2. Choosing a university course <u>is a matter of</u> deciding what you want to do with your life.
3. I arrived at the stadium early and watched the other spectators <u>entering in large numbers</u>.
4. Laura <u>reluctantly left</u> the window and returned to her desk.
5. Sam was staring at Megan, <u>listening intently to</u> every word she said.
6. George <u>dismissed</u> all objections to his plan, saying they were unimportant.

7.3   **Complete these sentences with a phrasal verb from the opposite page.**

1. It is terrible how the world just .... and lets such terrible things happen!
2. Despite all his difficulties, Douglas does his best to bravely ....
3. William reached into his pocket and .... his passport.
4. When I go to a new town I love .... the back streets.
5. You mustn't let your social life .... your study time.
6. The politician simply .... the allegations being made against him.
7. When he was 30 Mario left his uncle's business and .... on his own.
8. Our little house is .... a bank and a supermarket.

7.4   **Here are some more phrasal verbs which can be used metaphorically. How are their literal and metaphorical meanings connected? Use a dictionary if necessary.**

1. I've left you some soup which you can **warm up** when you get home.
   A fantastic singer **warmed up** the audience before the main programme started.
2. The boy wasn't looking where he was going and **fell into** a hole in the ground.
   Alexander **fell into** his first job as soon as he had left university.
3. The cat got up the tree but didn't seem able to **climb down**.
   Molly always wants to win an argument – you'll never get her to **climb down**.

English Phrasal Verbs in Use Advanced   **19**

8 Idioms using phrasal verbs

A Problems at work and home

● ● ●

✉ Reply   Forward

Hi Millie,

How's your awful new boss? Still planning a total reorganisation of the office or have you persuaded her not to **throw the baby out with the bathwater**[1]? Let me know if you need an evening out to **let off steam**[2] – it's about time we met up again.

We've been told at our company that we won't be getting a salary increase this year. They **took the sting out of it**[3] by giving us a Christmas bonus, but people are not happy.

My boss is still as difficult as ever. Her personal assistant's resigned, but I think that might be **cutting off her nose to spite her face**[4] as she'll find it hard to find anything else as well-paid. She can usually **run rings round**[5] anyone, so it must have been a shock for her to get a boss she couldn't manipulate.

I badly need your advice. Joey's beginning to **turn up the heat** in our relationship – he's dropping hints about marriage. He invited me to meet his parents last weekend. We **got on like a house on fire**[6] but I just don't feel ready to **put down roots** yet. Should I stop seeing him? I don't want to but maybe it'd be kinder? I can't **make up my mind**. Let me know what you think.

Lydia

[1] get rid of the good parts of something as well as the bad parts
[2] talk or act in a way that helps get rid of strong feelings
[3] make something that is unpleasant less so
[4] doing something because you are angry though it may cause you more problems
[5] outwit, be cleverer than
[6] immediately liked each other

B Progress meeting

Oscar Well, Anna, you've been here for a month now and it's time we had a little chat.

Anna OK. Well, I know I **got off on the wrong foot**[1] by deleting all last year's client information, but I hope you'll agree I've **got my act together**[2] now?

Oscar Erm, not exactly. I've tried my best to show you where you're going wrong, but I just appear to **be going round in circles**[3]. Nothing ever seems to get any better. You **dig your heels in**[4] and don't make any effort to change.

Anna Oh, I don't think that's fair. I'm sure Stan would **put in a good word for me**[5]. I've helped him out with one of his projects.

Oscar Hmm, well Stan needs to **clean up his act**[6] too. If you don't start **making up for lost time**[7] soon, we're going to have to let you go.

Anna Oh, no, please. Just give me a bit more authority and I'll **come into my own**[8].

Oscar Oh, Anna. **Wake up to the fact**[9] that you won't get any more authority unless you **pull out all the stops**[10] and your work improves significantly.

[1] started badly
[2] (informal) organised myself more effectively
[3] using a lot of time and effort with no results
[4] refuse to do what others try to persuade you to do
[5] say good things about me to someone in authority
[6] (informal) start to behave better
[7] doing something to compensate for not doing it previously
[8] be very successful
[9] be realistic
[10] do all you can

Exercises

8.1 Answer these questions.

1 What should you not throw out with the bathwater?
2 What expression uses a burning house as a metaphor for a good relationship?
3 What expression uses steam as a metaphor for strong feelings?
4 According to the idiom, why might people cut off their own nose?
5 What idiom means 'ease an unpleasant situation' and refers to what bees can do?
6 Which two phrasal verb idioms refer to circular motion?

8.2 Complete these sentences using expressions from 8.1.

1 Refusing that job offer just because you're annoyed about the interview would be cutting .... your .... to .... your ....
2 When she came back to the UK, Harriet decided it was time she .... down .... and she bought a little cottage not far from here.
3 The robbers .... round the police. It took two years to catch them.
4 The extra day's holiday we offered should take the .... out .... the pay cut.
5 I felt as if I was just going .... in .... and getting nowhere.
6 We should keep the better parts of the old system when we move over to the new system. We don't want to .... the .... out with the bathwater.
7 Isaac and Matthew .... on like a .... on fire; they're great friends.
8 I don't think she was really angry with you; she was just .... steam.

8.3 Cross out the five mistakes in this text and write the correct form in the box next to that line.

After a year of travelling, I decided to put my act together and get

a job. A friend who worked for a bank put in some good words

for me. In fact he pushed in all the stops and arranged for me to

have lunch with the CEO. I got on the wrong feet by saying I wasn't

ready to plant down roots yet; I think they were looking for

someone to make a long-term commitment. I should have kept quiet!

1	*get*
2	....
3	....
4	....
5	....

8.4 Complete these dialogues using phrasal verbs from the opposite page so that the second speaker agrees with and repeats more or less what the first speaker says.

1 **Michael** Alice seems determined not to agree to the new plan.

    Juan Yes, she really seems to be digging ....

2 Sarah Wow, my Uncle Joshua is 75 and he's getting married for the first time!

    Amelia Really? He's obviously trying to make up ....!

3 Luis Charles lives in a fantasy world. He thinks he can make a living writing poetry.

    Ava That's crazy! He should wake up .... that poets never make any money!

4 **Eva** Teddy has been very successful in his new career.

    Gabriel Yes, he really seems to have come into ....

5 Robert The boss seems to be getting very serious about the new sales campaign lately.

    Dan Yes, he's really turning up ....

6 Franck I think it's time I made a decision.

    Daisy Yes, it's time for you to make up ....

9 Around and about

Around and about are often (but not always) interchangeable in phrasal verbs. A good dictionary will tell you whether they can both be used. The only verbs on this page where both are not possible are marked *.

A Basic meaning of around and about in phrasal verbs

Around and about keep a lot of their basic meaning in many phrasal verbs. They often indicate activities and situations taking place in various locations, often without having a clear direction or order.

> There were books **lying around** everywhere in the room.
> The children were **running about** in the garden.

Phrasal verbs with around and about are often informal. Look at this conversation between two teachers.

Holly	Rumours have been **flying around** the staffroom lately that you're leaving. Is it true?
Jake	It amazes me how news **gets around** in this place! I did say to one or two people that I was tired of being **bossed around** by you-know-who, and, I have **asked around*** here and there to see if they need any full-time teachers, but I haven't made a decision yet.
Holly	Oh, right. I heard the other day that Eleanor is sick of **running around* after** you-know-who sorting out problems he's caused. So she might leave too. By the way, do you have a copy of that new grammar book? I want to show it to my students. My copy's **floating about** here somewhere but I just can't find it.
Jake	Yes, I think I have a copy **lying around** here somewhere ... Yes, here you are.
Holly	Thanks very much. So, what are you up to this weekened?
Jake	Nothing much, just **pottering about** at home, really. Oh goodness! Is that the time? I have a class now.
Holly	OK, see you later. Don't forget that we **switched** our classrooms **around** this afternoon. You're in Room 2.

Note that in **boss around**, around emphasises the fact that the person is *frequently* being bossed by someone else, not the fact that this occurs in different places.

B Other uses of around and about

Here are some other phrasal verbs which use around and about.

> Children! Stop **playing around**! Sit politely. [behaving stupidly]

> The neighbours have been **banging about** next door all morning. I wonder what they're doing. [making loud noises, for example hammering or moving heavy objects]

> Theo was **clowning around** at the party last night. It got very irritating. [acting in a silly way]

> Politicians often **skirt around*** the truth and don't give direct answers to questions. [avoid discussing a difficult subject or problem]

> It's a problem, but I'm sure we can **work around*** it in some way. [organise our activities to ensure that the problem does not prevent us from doing what we want to do]

Exercises

9.1 **Choose the correct word to complete these sentences.**

1 I couldn't get to sleep because of Owen .... around upstairs.
   a) banging   b) lying   c) switching
2 Wait a moment – the document you need is .... about here somewhere.
   a) flying   b) floating   c) running
3 I think we should stop the car and let the children .... around for a bit.
   a) get   b) lie   c) run
4 The room looks different. Have you .... the furniture around?
   a) pottered   b) switched   c) banged
5 If you .... around, you might be able to find someone with a car for sale.
   a) ask   b) boss   c) play
6 I hate the way rumours .... around the office.
   a) run   b) fly   c) lie
7 You really shouldn't leave such important papers .... about.
   a) clowning   b) lying   c) playing
8 Yanis made the children laugh by .... around with pieces of fruit.
   a) banging   b) getting   c) clowning

9.2 **Complete each dialogue using a verb from the box with _around_ or _about_.**

boss	get	ask	clown	lie

1 **Isla**   I need to find a flat to rent in London. Do you know of anything available?

   Katie No, but I'll ....

2 Sara   Do you know where the extension lead is?

   Milo   Yes, I think it might be .... in my study somewhere.

3 **Adam**   How did Hugo know we're getting married?

   Zara   Well, news like that .... very quickly.

4 Ava   Do you get on well with your sister?

   Ella   Yes, on the whole, though she .... me .... a bit too much.

5 Amber   What do you think of Freddie?

   Louis   I find the way he always .... a bit childish.

9.3 **Complete these sentences with phrasal verbs from the opposite page. Put the verb in the correct form. Sometimes more than one verb is possible.**

1 I thought Alex was just .... in his bedroom today, but in fact he's been really busy. He's tidied up all the books and papers that were .... on the floor. He's also .... his bed and his desk, which makes the room feel bigger.
2 When I was a child I used to hate visiting Great Uncle Edward. He wouldn't allow us children to .... in case we broke anything, and he was always .... us .... , getting us to .... after him, doing odd jobs for him.
3 Do you think we could find a way to .... the problem of having to get written permission from everyone to use the photographs in our book?
4 I think we should be honest with everyone and not try to .... the issue.
5 We hear people .... every night in the flat upstairs. All sorts of rumours have been .... among the neighbours as to what is going on up there.

```
Over to you
```

Look up these words in your dictionary: _crowd around, knock_ sth _about/around, knock_ sb _about/ around, turn around, turn_ sth _around, roll about/around, blunder about/around_. Make a note of the meanings of these words and record them with an example sentence.

10 Down

A *Down* meaning lower

Lottie   Well, did he **come down**[1] on the price?

Tom   I **knocked** him **down**[2] by £100 but he wouldn't go any lower.

Lottie   Oh, so that's why you **slammed** the catalogue **down**[3] when you finished?

Tom   No, that was because I was distracted by the music and annoyed. Why didn't you **turn** the volume **down**[4]? I could hardly hear a word he was saying!

[1] suggest or agree to a lower price
[2] persuaded him to reduce the price
[3] put down with a lot of force
[4] reduce the amount of sound

B *Down* suggesting preventing or restraining

phrasal verb	definition of phrasal verb	example
shout down sb or **shout** sb **down**	shout in order to prevent someone who you disagree with from being heard	I couldn't hear what the prime minister was saying because some people at the front were **shouting** him **down**.
pin down sb or **pin** sb **down**	force someone to stay in a horizontal position by holding them	Two police officers **pinned** the robber **down** while the third handcuffed him.
tie down sth/sb or **tie** sth/sb **down**	use ropes to fasten someone or something in a particular position	The tent is secure, but make sure you **tie down** anything else that might blow away in the storm.
tie sb **down**	(metaphorical meaning of the previous verb) prevent someone from having the freedom to do what they want to do	My brother prefers to take temporary work because he hates the idea of being **tied down**.

C Other meanings of *down*

Not working
The computer system is always **going down**. We need a new one. [stopping working]
Don't forget to save your documents before you **shut** the computer **down**. [turn off]

Depressed or sad
This rain is **getting** me **down**. [making me feel depressed]

On a list
Freya asked me to **put** her **down** for a copy of the report when it's published. [put on a list to arrange for her to have something]
You can **put** me **down** to organise the refreshments. [put on a list to arrange for me to do something]

Killed/injured
The terrorists mercilessly **gunned down** their victims. [shot and killed or seriously injured]
We had to have our poor old dog **put down** last week; she was very sick. [put to death]

Surviving through time
The legend has **come down** to us from the ancient records of the Quilhoa people. [passed from generation to generation]

Be considered or remembered
This will **go down** in history as the most important event of the century. [be remembered]
My workshop **went down** really well. [was well-received]

Exercises

10.1 **Read these sentences and then answer the questions below by writing the correct name in the box.**

Harry Irving felt he had lost his freedom when he and Antonia had their first baby.
Oliver Reece was forced to the ground and held there by two security guards.
People protested so loudly that no one could hear what Heidi Knight had to say.
Mia Calvo persuaded the man to reduce the price by £500.
Lucas Hind was shot dead yesterday by terrorists.

1 Who was shouted down?
2 Who was gunned down?
3 Who felt tied down?
4 Who was pinned down?
5 Who managed to knock someone down?

10.2 **Rewrite the underlined parts of these sentences using a phrasal verb from the opposite page. Make any other necessary changes.**

1 The computer system suddenly <u>stopped working</u> this morning, so we're doing everything manually at the moment.
2 I'm sorry I'm so irritable. Things have been <u>depressing me</u> lately.
3 Shall I <u>write your name on my list</u> to sponsor me for the charity walk?
4 This event will <u>be remembered</u> in history as the worst catastrophe this country has ever suffered.
5 The company had to <u>stop</u> all their machines during the 24-hour strike at the factory.
6 The salesman <u>agreed to a lower price</u>, and after that we even managed to <u>persuade him to reduce the price</u> by a further 10%.
7 Many everyday remedies for minor ailments have <u>reached us over time</u> from our ancestors.

10.3 **Answer the following questions using a phrasal verb from the opposite page.**

1 What might someone do if they get very angry during a phone call?
2 What might you do to a very old and sick dog or cat?
3 What would you do to stop a tent from blowing away?
4 If work is making you depressed, what is it doing to you emotionally?
5 If your radio was too loud, what would you do?

10.4 **Which of the meanings given are possible or likely interpretations of the phrasal verbs in these sentences? More than one interpretation may be possible. Use a dictionary if necessary.**

1 I think you should take this down.
   a) write it
   b) drink it
   c) dismantle it
2 The house has come down.
   a) has been rebuilt
   b) is for sale at a lower price
   c) has been demolished
3 She turned it down.
   a) reduced the heat
   b) refused the offer
   c) put the collar of her coat in its normal position
4 They watered it down.
   a) extinguished a fire using water
   b) added water to make a liquid less strong
   c) made an idea, opinion or argument less strong

11 In

The particle *in*, when used with phrasal verbs, keeps a lot of its basic meaning, often referring to things which move towards being, or are already, 'within something' or are 'included in something'.

Look at this transcript of a meeting at a computer software company. Dominic, the Chief Executive, who chairs the meeting, speaks first. Note the phrasal verbs with *in*.

Chair   Well, I think we should begin. One of our colleagues from Manchester has been delayed, but I've asked David to **show** her **in** when she gets here, so she'll join us later, I hope. Now, first item is the Musicmatch software suite, which, I like to think, has helped to **usher in**[1] a new era in music production. It's been **bringing in** good profits, and we've certainly been able to **cash in on** the recent crash of one of our major rivals, as we all know, but with an economic recession **setting in** now, we may want to rethink our pricing so that it **fits in** better **with** the rest of our range. We also need to **factor in**[2] the loss of a major client – we lost the *Popmaster* **contract this year**.

Grace   Can I **come in** here, Dominic? Ben and I are already looking at this and we'll have something to report next week. Basically we hope to **build in** an automatic upgrade system so that customers will find it easier to stay with us. Ben's looking at the cost. I said I'd **pitch in**[3] so that we can get it moving faster.

Chair   OK, well, maybe we can leave that. But I'd just like to say, remember, we need flexibility – we don't want to become **boxed in**[4] by our own systems. We'll come back to it.

David   Sorry to **cut in**, Dominic. Amy Peckham is here.

Chair   Ah, good. Our colleague from Manchester has arrived. Hello, Amy. You're very welcome. Can you **squash in** there somewhere? Sorry the room is a bit small. Amy Peckham, everyone. Some of you know her already. Right, I suggest we move to Chloe's presentation. I believe you're going to use the projector, Chloe?

Chloe   Yes. Could we close those blinds? Thanks. Oh dear, they're still **letting** a lot of light **in**. Never mind. I'll begin. I'd like to use this presentation as a **lead-in**[5] to our general discussion about the future.

[1] (formal) begin or cause a period in which new things or changes happen
[2] include something when making a calculation or when trying to understand something
[3] (informal) help with work that needs to be done
[4] restricted
[5] something that introduces something else

> ## Tip
>
> Take note of the context when you meet new phrasal verbs. For example, the context on this page is a fairly informal business meeting. Spoken business English is often less formal than the spoken language of business in some other languages and cultures. The same is often true for other contexts, such as spoken academic language.

Exercises

11.1 **Find phrasal verbs or phrasal adjectives from the opposite page which mean the following:**

1 benefit from
2 interrupt (two answers)
3 help
4 introduce
5 unable to act freely

6 introduction
7 take into consideration
8 find a space
9 include
10 start

11.2 **Correct the mistakes with the phrasal verbs in these sentences.**

1 My new curtains are excellent – they don't bring any light in.
2 Alba, can you pitch Mr Hill in as soon as he arrives, please?
3 Having the meeting on the 28th would squash in better with our plans than the 30th.
4 Our office in Buenos Aires has cashed in a lot of new business this year.
5 When you are planning the course, make sure you set in enough free time.
6 It's rude to factor in when someone else is in the middle of speaking.
7 If everyone shows in, we'll soon get the job done.
8 If I move up, then Rachel should be able to box in at the end of the bench.

11.3 **Complete this paragraph with verbs from the opposite page.**

My ten-year-old daughter Rosie had some friends
to sleep over last night. Eight of them managed
to sleep on her bedroom floor. I don't know how
they .... (1) themselves in as it is a
very small room. Rosie's birthday had been the
previous week, but we had her party yesterday as
that .... (2) in better with other plans.
In the evening we had a barbecue and we made
lots of different salads and puddings. Rosie and her
friends all .... (3) in, and they enjoyed
helping as much as eating. Later in the evening rain
.... (4) in, so they went indoors and
watched a film. I was afraid the girls would wake up
ridiculously early, but we've had new blinds fitted
and they don't .... (5) any light in, so no
one stirred till half past eight.

11.4 **Cross out the item which does not normally collocate with the phrasal expression in bold. Use a dictionary if necessary.**

1 **bring in** customers / profits / a loss / business
2 a **lead-in** to a discussion / a bargain / a lesson
3 a recession / rain / a new product **sets in**
4 **usher in** a price increase / a new era / changes

```
Over to you
```

What other phrasal verbs with *in* do you have in your vocabulary notebook? Do they also have a
connection with the basic meaning of *in*? As you learn other new ones, think about how the idea
conveyed by *in* might help you remember the meaning of the phrasal verb.

12 Off

A *Off* suggesting get rid of

My feet were hot, so I **kicked off** my shoes. [removed with my feet]

The robbers drove faster and faster to try and **shake off** the police car. [lose]

I went for a long walk to **work off** my frustation. [get rid of a feeling (often unpleasant) by doing something energetic]

Archie doesn't worry about anything – he'll **shrug off** any problem. [treat something as unimportant]

B *Off* suggesting separation

phrasal verb	definition of phrasal verb	example
be cut off	be unable to see many other people	My office is in a different building from my colleagues, so I am quite **cut off**.
cut off sth/sb or **cut** sth/sb **off**	stop providing something, e.g. aid, electricity, supplies	They **cut off** our electricity / **cut** us **off** because we hadn't paid the bill.
split off	form a separate group	Two of the climbers **split off** from the group and went off on their own.
back off	(slightly informal) stop being involved in a situation, especially in order to allow other people to deal with it themselves	She was interfering, so I told her to **back off** and let me deal with it on my own.
have sth **off**	spend time away from work	I **had** a week **off** last June.
cordon off sth or **cordon** sth **off**	put something, e.g. a rope, a barrier, around an area in order to stop people from entering it	The police have **cordoned off** the area the president will be visiting.

C *Off* suggesting starting or finishing

I'll fill in the first line of this spreadsheet to **start** you **off**, and then you can do the rest yourself. [help you to start]

The weekly meeting usually **kicks off** around 2 p.m. [(informal) starts]

We **rounded off** the meal with freshly brewed coffee. [finished]

That boring meeting just **finished** me **off**. I think I'll go home; I've had enough for one day. [made me feel so weak, tired or unhappy that I couldn't continue]

It's nice to just **switch off** at the weekend and forget about work. [stop giving your attention to someone or something]

D Other verbs with *off*

Ben told his little brother to **leave off** playing his new guitar. [(informal) stop]

William told his younger sister to **shove off** out of his room. [(informal) something that you say when you are angry to tell someone to go away.]

Layla wanted to **show** her new bike **off** to her friends. [show someone or something that you are proud of to a group of people]

The boss gave the receptionist a **ticking off** for making private calls to friends. [telling someone that you are angry with them because they have done something wrong]

Exercises

12.1 **Replace the underlined words in these statements with a phrasal verb from the opposite page.**

1 Eliza's father to Eliza's mother: Eliza's 18 now and should make her own decisions. I think we should <u>stop getting involved</u> and let her run her own life.
2 Newsreader: The prime minister has <u>treated as unimportant</u> leadership threats from within his party, saying that they are only rumours.
3 Mother to father: I think we should let the kids run round in the garden for a bit and <u>get rid of</u> some of their energy so that they sleep tonight.
4 Mother to Imogen: Imogen, you MUST pay your electricity bill. If you don't, they'll <u>stop providing it</u> and you won't have any heating.
5 Louis to Callum: Oh no! Seth wants to come back with us to Nikita's house. He's such a drag! How can we <u>get away from him</u>?
6 Chairperson: I'd like to just <u>conclude</u> the meeting by giving a vote of thanks to the committee for all their work this year.
7 The last 100 metres to the top of the hill just <u>made me so tired I couldn't continue</u>. I had to sit down and rest for an hour.
8 I don't want you in my room any more, so just <u>leave</u>!

12.2 **Cross out the five mistakes in this text and write the correct form in the box next to that line.**

When I come home from work, I love to just kick ~~away~~ my
shoes and relax for the evening. It's great to let off worrying
about work and round up the day with a nice meal. If I
have off a couple of days it's even better. I usually go off to
our country cottage. I can just light off completely. I love it.
I never stay there long because after a while I feel a bit stood
off from all my friends and social life back in the city.

	...........off...........
1	....
2	....
3	....
4	....
5	....

12.3 **Complete the word puzzle.**

Across
1 The boss .... me off with a simple task to get me used to the job.
3 The police decided to .... off the scene of the crime.
4 What time does the meeting .... off?
5 She always loves to .... off her latest technological gadget.
6 Look, just .... off playing with my phone, will you? You're getting on my nerves.

Down
2 The director gave him a .... off for arriving late at the meeting.
5 A group of youths .... off from the rest of the demonstrators and started causing trouble.

Some phrasal verbs with *on* share a meaning of dependence/reliance, e.g. **depend on***, **rely on***, **count on***, **hinge on***, **hang on***, **ride on**.

REFERENDUM RESULT CRUCIAL, SAYS PM

The prime minister said, 'Everything **hinges on** the result of next week's referendum. The future prosperity of the nation **hangs on** this crucial day of decision.' Politicians of all parties agree that everything **rides on** the government securing a Yes vote.

On can also convey the idea of continuing in an irritating or boring way, for example, **harp on** [talk repeatedly about something in a way that others find boring or irritating], **keep on**, **go on (and on)**, **ramble on** [talk or write for a very long time in a boring way] and **drone on** [talk for a long time in a very boring way and in a monotonous voice].

> Don't **keep on** about the garden! I'll mow the lawn tomorrow.
> We had a tedious lecture from the boss. She just **went on and on** about punctuality.
> He **droned on** for hours about ancient civilisations; everyone fell asleep.

Read on, **press on**, **live on** and **dwell on*** [think or talk about a particular subject for too long] also emphasise continuation over time.

HOUSING MINISTER HONOURS
CHAMPION OF THE POOR

'Her death is a great loss to society, but her memory will **live on**', said the minister.

Grouping verbs in this way can help you to remember them.

Now look at these news items which contain some of these and other examples of phrasal verbs with *on*.

80%   4:21PM

headlines

CURATOR FINDS LOST MEDIEVAL MANUSCRIPT

The curator, Mr Jackson Bedgrove, **happened on*** the lost manuscript while searching the museum's archives for some missing 18th century letters. As he **focused** his attention **on*** the text, he said, he could hardly believe what he was reading. As he **read on**, he realised the importance of what he'd found...

EDUCATION EXPERT EXPRESSES CAUTION ON HOME SCHOOLING

Phoebe Garrett stated that home schooling was often **frowned on*** by politicians, and she herself had some doubts as to its effectiveness. However, to **spring** a new piece of legislation **on** parents successfully educating their children at home was not right, she said. The education secretary insists that she will **press on** with plans to introduce a new law...

CHILDREN'S PRANK TURNS TO TRAGEDY

A 13-year-old girl who stole a car and took it for a joyride admits that friends **led** her **on**. The prank resulted in the serious injury of a 25-year-old mother of two...

The verbs marked with * on this page are all transitive.

Exercises

13.1 In the following sentences, mark each phrasal verb according to whether it has predominantly a dramatic feeling (write D), a negative feeling (N), a feeling of boredom (B), or a feeling of irritation (I).

1 Professor Taylor was droning on about the Ancient Greeks in his lecture this morning.
2 The success of the peace talks hinges on both sides maintaining the present truce.
3 Uncle Alex goes on and on about his broken chair. I've told him a hundred times I'll mend it.
4 Dwelling on the past all the time is no way to live your life. Think of your future.
5 If you ask Beatrice about beekeeping she'll ramble on for hours.
6 I wish you wouldn't keep on about money. Let's just enjoy life.
7 The championship now rides on Saturday's crucial game against Real Madrid.

13.2 Choose the correct word to complete these sentences. Sometimes there is more than one possible answer.

1 You can always .... on Daniel. He's totally dependable.
   a) rely   b) count   c) hinge   d) hang
2 I wish Georgia would stop .... on about Kian. It's so tedious!
   a) riding   b) droning   c) going   d) harping
3 Do make up your mind soon. So much .... on what you decide.
   a) hinges   b) presses   c) rides   d) hangs

13.3 Correct the mistakes with the phrasal verbs in these sentences. There is one mistake in each sentence.

1 Try to focus what is really important on and to ignore what is not essential.
2 Now we've had a bit of a rest, it's time to spring on again.
3 I'm hingeing on you to let me know when my talk has gone on for long enough.
4 Your grandmother will always happen on in your memory.
5 This is a quiet neighbourhood where noisy behaviour is counted on.
6 After the first few pages of the book, I decided I couldn't be bothered to ride on.
7 Please stop focusing on about Lena. Your relationship is over, so just forget her.
8 I am worried about my son's behaviour. He is so easily relied on by his friends.

13.4 Complete each sentence with a verb from the opposite page.

1 Don't try to remember every sentence of the text. Just .... on the main points.
2 Elizabeth is going to .... the news on her parents over lunch. I hope they'll be happy for her.
3 Try to look to the future rather than .... on the past.
4 We've got a lot of work to finish today so we'd better .... on.
5 Julia's not usually naughty herself, but her brothers tend to .... her on.
6 In most schools, wearing big, colourful jewellery and dyeing your hair bright colours would be .... on or even forbidden outright.
7 Whether we go for a picnic tomorrow or not will .... on the weather.
8 I wish he'd stop .... on and on about his ex-wife.

13.5 Rewrite these sentences using phrasal verbs from the opposite page.

1 James is a reliable person.
2 Dad will talk monotonously for hours about European history.
3 Many political reputations are about to be crucially affected by the outcome of next week's election.
4 Josh never stops complaining about the litter in the office car park. It irritates me.
5 While tidying my room, I found an old diary of mine from 2001.

14 Out

A Basic meanings of *out* in phrasal verbs

A very frequent meaning of *out* is the opposite of *in*.

> I don't want to leave my job but I suppose they may **kick** me **out**. [(informal) force me to leave]
>
> I've had enough of working for such a difficult organisation and I **want out**. [want to leave]
>
> **Count** me **out**! I'm far too tired to join the skiing trip today. [don't include me]

Another meaning is when something or part of something extends from its surroundings.

> The chalet roof **juts out** (over its walls) to help prevent snow from blocking the doors. [sticks out beyond the edge]
>
> The rocky peninsula **juts out** into the bay.

Another meaning is separate.

> The woman **picked out** a kitten to take home. [chose one from a large group]
>
> We **spread** our wet clothes **out** on the grass so they could dry in the sunshine.

Another meaning is distribute.

> Don't eat all the sweets yourself, Ollie. **Share** them **out** among all the children. [give one to each person in the group]

B Other meanings of *out* in phrasal verbs

phrasal verb	definition of phrasal verb	example
go out	(of a fire) stop burning	When we woke up in the morning, the campfire still hadn't **gone out**.
clean out sb or **clean** sb **out**	steal or take everything from a person	The burglars completely **cleaned** us **out**.
test out sth or **test** sth **out**	see how it works in a practical situation or find out what other people think of it (the *out* stresses testing something in the environment in which it is intended to be used, not, for example, in a laboratory)	We need to **test** the product **out** in the market before launching it.
drop out	not do something that you were going to do, or stop doing something	The runner **dropped out** halfway through the marathon.
lash out (usually + **at** sth)	criticise someone or something in an angry way	Sofia **lashed out at** me yesterday for wasting her time.
yell out sth or **yell** sth **out**	suddenly shout something in a loud voice, especially to get someone's attention	As I walked past the room, I heard someone **yell out**.
draw out sth or **draw** sth **out**	make something continue for longer than is usual or necessary	I wish Thomas wouldn't always **draw** meetings **out** by talking so much.
sort out sth or **sort** sth **out**	solve a problem or restore order to something which has become disordered	A management consultant was hired to **sort out** the personnel problems in the company.

Exercises

14.1 **Answer the questions using phrasal verbs with _out_.**

1 Naomi gave two apples to each of the four children. What did she do with the apples?
....
2 Clément took control of the situation and soon everything was OK and back to normal. What did Clément do? ....
3 Evie looked at all the oranges on the stall and put the best ones in her basket. What did she do with the oranges? ....
4 The manager forced Sam to leave the restaurant because he was behaving badly. What did the manager do? ....
5 The roof extends over the terrace and provides a bit of shade from the midday sun. What does the roof do? ....

14.2 **The verb in each of these sentences sounds a little formal in the context. Find a phrasal verb from the opposite page to replace the one-word equivalent in each sentence.**

1 I don't have any money so you can <u>exclude</u> me from the shopping trip.
2 I <u>distributed</u> the mints among my friends in the car.
3 We need to <u>resolve</u> this mess about the misprinted tickets pretty soon.
4 He really <u>criticised</u> me when I suggested he'd got it wrong.
5 Look at those big rocks <u>protruding</u> from the sea.
6 <u>Select</u> the good strawberries and leave the rotten ones in the box.

14.3 **Rewrite the underlined parts of these sentences using a phrasal verb with _out_ that means the opposite of the underlined words.**

1 I opened the door and heard somebody <u>whisper</u> from the staircase below.
2 My position as regards the committee is that I <u>would like to continue as a member</u>.
3 He always <u>shortens</u> the discussion with arguments about political ideology.
4 When we got back to our campsite, the campfire had <u>started burning</u>.
5 <u>Put</u> the leaflets <u>together in one place</u> on the table.
6 The burglars <u>stole absolutely nothing at all from us</u>.

14.4 **Match the headlines 1–4 with the stories a–d below.**

1 **RECORD NUMBERS OF STUDENTS DROP OUT**

2 **DAVID BLAKE LASHES OUT AT CRITICS**

3 **GOVERNMENT TO TEST OUT NEW SPEED CAMERAS**

4 **WILSON SAYS COUNT ME OUT OF OLYMPIC TEAM**

a) After a trial period of six months, a decision will be made as to whether they will be installed throughout the country.
b) She said she did not wish to take part as she had found the pressure too great in the last Games.
c) More than 6,000 withdrew from a range of programmes, almost 1,000 more than last year, according to the minister.
d) He said he was sick of the hypocrisy of people who had never done anything themselves to help the poor.

15 Up

Basic meanings of *up* in phrasal verbs

You are probably familiar with verbs such as **eat up** and **write up**, which carry a meaning of completion. Here are some more examples:

> Come on, children, **finish up** your breakfast. It's time to go.
> Well, let's **wrap up** the discussion now and vote. [(informal) finish an activity]

Up can also carry the meaning of upward movement or relating to an upper position.

> Could you **lift** the table **up** while I put the rug under it?
> Teddy, **pick** all your toys **up** from the floor and put them in your toy box.

Another meaning of *up* in phrasal verbs is maintain in an upright position or strengthen, prevent from falling down or failing.

> Victoria was lying **propped up** on a pillow. [supporting herself in an upright position]
> The minister announced new measures to **shore up** the economy. [strengthen or improve an organisation or system that is not working effectively or that is likely to fail]

Up can also mean increase or improve.

> This sauce is tasteless. I'll add some garlic to **pep** it **up** a bit. [(informal) make something more interesting, lively or energetic]
> We **jazzed up** our all-white kitchen by adding red tiles and doorknobs here and there. [(informal) make something more attractive or interesting]

B

Other phrasal verbs with *up*

Read these TV programme previews and note the phrasal verbs with *up*.

The Man Who Hated Dogs DDC
Tuesday 9pm

The hero of this comedy, played by Nathan Farr, finds himself playing daddy to three homeless dogs, but **lands up**[1] in trouble with his girlfriend when the local press publishes a story about him which is **blown up**[2] to make him look like a pitiless animal-hater.

[1] (informal) finally does something, especially without having planned to
[2] made to seem much worse than it is

History File Thursday 8.30pm

An archaeologist notices some strange, pointed stones **sticking up** from the surface of a lake during a drought. Suspecting they may mark the site of an ancient tomb, she takes infrared photographs from the air. What **shows up**[3] in the images deepens the mystery. After a long investigation she concludes that theories about the ancient Mosa people no longer **stand up**[4].

[3] becomes visible
[4] appear correct when examined

Nation on the Move GlobalNews TV
Friday 10pm

Phrasalia, once a country closed to the rest of the world, has **opened up** since the death of its long-time ruler President Particulos. But will the new-found freedoms ultimately lead to the country **splitting up** into chaotic, rival republics as tensions emerge in its five provinces?

Chips with everything HNTV
Friday 7.30pm

Documentary-maker Elliot Warcross **picks up on**[5] recent rumours in the press that an ultra-rich business tycoon has attempted to **buy up** the world's supply of silicon, **opening up** the terrifying possibility of a world monopoly in computer chips. Warcross tries to **set up** an interview with the mystery tycoon but receives death threats in return.

[5] reacts to something that he has noticed

> **Error warning**
>
> We say 'I went into the garden and **picked** some flowers.' Don't say 'picked up some flowers'; **pick up** is used for things which are on or have fallen to the ground.

Exercises

15.1 Complete these sentences using a phrasal verb from A opposite. Put it in the correct form and, if necessary, add a pronoun as object.

1 Zoe, if you don't .... your spinach, you can't have any pudding.
2 We can .... the asparagus with a nice oil and vinegar dressing.
3 The prime minister appointed three new ministers in an attempt to .... his failing administration.
4 You've just dropped some of your papers. Let me .... for you.
5 I noticed Tim's bicycle .... against a wall outside Hannah's apartment.
6 Your black dress is a little plain – why don't you .... a bit with a colourful scarf?
7 I think we should try and .... the meeting by 4 p.m.
8 Can you .... that plant pot? I need to put a saucer under it to catch the water.

15.2 Complete these dialogues using phrasal verbs from the opposite page so that the second speaker agrees with and repeats more or less what the first speaker says.

1 Aaron   I just don't think his theory is correct when you look at it very carefully.

   Leo   No, I agree. It just doesn't .... up when you examine it closely.

2 Salima I think we should ask the students to form small groups.

   Martha Yes, we should .... them up into groups of two or three.

3 Keira   I think we should try to arrange a meeting with the whole team.

   Zac   You're right. We should try to .... one up.

4 Nazir   I just knew Patrick's son would get into trouble with the police one day.

   Anna   Yes, it was inevitable he'd .... up in serious trouble.

5 Jake   She said they'd sold all the tickets for the concert in one go.

   Ruby   Yes, apparently some mystery person .... them all up over the Internet.

6 Sam   Oh look, Sebastian freckles are really visible in this photo, aren't they?

   Tyler   Yes, they really .... up, don't they?

7 Harvey I think the newspapers have greatly exaggerated the story.

   Aisha   Yes, they've .... it up out of all proportion.

8 Megan   There's a big nail protruding from that floorboard; be careful.

   Fellix Yes, I noticed one .... up the other day but forgot to mention it.

15.3 Which phrasal verb fits into each of these sets of collocations?

1	a photo	3	a business
to	a balloon	to	an interview
	a story		a meeting
2	a political system	4	unlimited possibilities
to	an ailing economy	to	an opportunity
	the foundations of a building		a new line of investigation

16 Time

A How time passes

Diana	The sales conference will be **coming around**[1] soon. We'd better start **hurrying** those sales reports **along**[2].
Paul	I can't believe that the conference is **coming up**[3] again already. This last year seems to have **slipped away**[4]!
Diana	I know! There's an awful lot to do **leading up to**[5] the conference, especially as it's going to be held in our branch this year.
Paul	Oh well, at least it **breaks things up**[6] and makes life a bit more interesting, I suppose.
Diana	It hasn't been that bad a year, surely. There was all the excitement over the new marketing campaign.
Paul	Oh, that completely **passed me by**[7]. It didn't really affect me in my department.
Diana	OK, Paul. Time's **getting on**[8] a bit now. I need to head home. Let's talk about what we need to do tomorrow.

[1] (of a regular event) happening at its usual time
[2] making someone do something more quickly, making something happen more quickly
[3] will be happening soon
[4] passed very quickly
[5] preparing in the period before an event begins
[6] makes a period of time more interesting by being different from what you are doing for the rest of the time
[7] went unnoticed
[8] (mainly British and Australian informal) it's getting late

B Spending time

Right, I'm not going to **spin** this **out**[1]. I just have one thing to say. You only have two weeks now till the exams start and you're going to have to **pull your socks up**[2] if you want to pass. We're going to **set aside**[3] the next fortnight just for revision. In other words, we're going to **free up**[4] some time by cancelling all non-exam lessons like sport. All school sports matches will be **held over**[5] until the exams are finished. We felt that would be better than trying to **fit** revision **in**[6] around sport commitments. The sports staff agree that **putting back**[7] these matches won't cause any major problems, but we mustn't **set** schedules **back**[8] by more than two weeks or we won't be able to fit in all the matches before the end of term. So now, put everything else out of your minds and concentrate on your revision. No more **frittering** time **away**[9] – get down to some serious work.

EXAMS START JUNE 14

[1] make something continue for longer than necessary
[2] make an effort to improve, an idiom using a phrasal verb (see Unit 8 for more)
[3] use time for one purpose and no other purpose
[4] make time or money available for a particular use by not using it another way
[5] delayed and arranged for a later date
[6] do it between other activities
[7] causing something to happen later than it should happen
[8] make something happen more slowly, or make something happen later than it should
[9] wasting time by using it for unimportant things

> ### Tip
> The following verbs can be used about money as well as time – *free up* and *fritter away*.

Exercises

16.1 **Match the beginning of each sentence with its ending.**

1 There was a lot of excitement	a) getting on now.
2 My birthday seems to be	b) hurrying people along?
3 The annual meeting will be	c) leading up to the final match.
4 I'd better go as it's	d) coming up some time next month.
5 It's getting late – can you start	e) coming around more quickly every year.

16.2 **Read these remarks by different people and then answer the questions below.**

> **Mary** I'm 63 and I've never had an interesting job or done anything exciting.
>
> Jack I feel I'm wasting a lot of time on useless and unimportant things.
>
> **Leah** I'm trying to improve my performance. I know I've been lazy and inefficient.
>
> Jude I feel the days are passing very quickly and we need to solve the problem now.
>
> Adriana I'm cancelling my meetings next week so I can take time off to decorate my flat.

1 Who is trying to free up some time?
2 Who feels that time is slipping away?
3 Who feels life is passing them by?
4 Who is trying to pull their socks up?
5 Who feels they are frittering away their time?

16.3 **Complete this text with the correct particles.**

My staff often spin things .... (1) much longer than they need to so that they don't
get asked to do any more work. As a result they sometimes set the schedules .... (2)
by days or even weeks, and then I have to hurry them .... (3) so that the work gets
done on time. And not only do I have to keep an eye on the staff, I also have to find time to
fit .... (4) consultations with management and the unions, and inevitably meetings
have to be put .... (5) because of some unexpected emergency, or important tasks
have to be held .... (6) till the more immediate problems can be sorted out. I try to set
.... (7) at least one hour every day for planning, but it's not easy. I like to take a proper
lunch break and get out of the office. I find that breaks the day .... (8) nicely.

16.4 **Correct the mistakes with the phrasal verbs in these sentences.**

1 You'd get far more done if you didn't fritter out so much time.
2 The children tried to spin their game off so they didn't have to go to bed.
3 Cameron might lose his job if he doesn't pull his collar up.
4 We must discuss what we need to do leading up the opening of the new branch.
5 Let's try to make some time apart next month to discuss progress on the project.

16.5 **Rewrite each sentence using a phrasal verb from the box in an appropriate form. Make
any other necessary changes. You may need to use a dictionary to help you.**

eke out	drag out	bring forward	space out	creep up on

1 We've had to reschedule the meeting for this Tuesday as Austin will be away next week.
2 Francesca always makes any discussion last longer than necessary.
3 I think we should have longer intervals between our meetings.
4 I thought I had ages to prepare for my exams, but they have arrived in no time at all.
5 I think we should try to make the printing paper last as long as possible.

English Phrasal Verbs in Use Advanced **37**

Cause and effect

Many of the phrasal verbs in this unit are usually used in quite formal contexts. Using these phrasal verbs will help you to improve your style when writing formal correspondence, giving presentations and writing reports and essays.

Look at these formal letters to the editor of a newspaper and note the phrasal verbs connected with cause and effect.

● ● ●   ✉   Reply   Forward

Dear Sir/Madam,

Recent events in Herean City **point to**[1] a failure of central government to control spending by local and regional authorities. This failure can be **put down to**[2] a long-standing reluctance to tackle local corruption, which has **resulted** in a situation where certain powerful local politicians feel free to act outside the law. This then **contributes** to a general atmosphere in which all politicians are mistrusted.

Yours sincerely,

G. Johnson (Ms)

● ● ●   ✉   Reply   Forward

Dear Sir/Madam,

Arthur Power's explanation for the growth of crime in our cities just does not **add up**[3]. He **attributes** recent rises in crime to a decline in leisure facilities for young people and the economic recession. But the problem in fact **stems from**[4] a longer-term neglect of the cities, and dealing with the problem **depends** on accepting this fact first and foremost. We have been talking about rising crime rates for decades and after the last general election the government set up an inquiry into inner-city crime, but as yet nothing seems to have **come out of**[5] this enquiry.

Sincerely,

A. H. Lowe

● ● ●   ✉   Reply   Forward

Dear Sir/Madam

No one should be surprised that the recent education reforms have **rebounded on**[6] the government. The reforms were **rooted in**[7] a deep-seated elitism, which **accounts for**[8] the fact that inequality has grown rather than diminished, as your report showed (13 November). As always, the effects have **impacted** most **on**[9] poorer families, where the new system has **led to** parents being unable to afford a good education for their children. It all **adds up to**[10] more misery in our schools and fewer opportunities for our young people, especially in the inner cities.

Yours sincerely,

D. Mitchell (Prof.)

[1] make it seem likely that something is true

[2] thought to be caused by (used for problems and bad experiences)

[3] (slightly informal) constitute a reasonable or likely explanation for something

[4] is caused by

[5] if something comes out of a process or an event, it is one of the results

[6] had a bad effect on the person who did it with the result that they did not achieve what they were trying to achieve

[7] based on, or caused by

[8] explains the reason for

[9] had a noticeable effect on

[10] results in

Tip

Always make a note in your notebook if a phrasal verb is formal or informal.

Exercises

17.1 **Match the beginning of each sentence with its ending.**

1 Aidan's new job will undoubtedly impact
2 How the situation develops will depend
3 Isabelle's behaviour may well rebound
4 Freddie's interest in botany stems
5 Her attitude to foreigners is rooted
6 It is impossible to point
7 The new education reform should result
8 Professor Bukowsky attributes the crisis
9 The situation in the country may lead

a) to one clear cause of the crisis.
b) from a childhood spent in the rainforest.
c) in ignorance.
d) in significant social change.
e) to the changes in the country's leadership.
f) on the reaction from the USA.
g) to a civil war.
h) on his family.
i) on her if she is not careful.

17.2 **Correct the mistakes with the particles in these sentences. There is one mistake in each sentence.**

1 Theodore puts the problems down to the government, but I attribute them for the general world economic situation.
2 To a large extent, how a person accounts for the problems in their lives seems to depend largely of their own parents' attitudes to difficult situations.
3 I believe the new legislation will contribute to a general improvement in the standard of living, but Ben thinks it will result from increased poverty for most people.
4 The desire for reform has come off a general desire to improve the situation, but I suspect the proposed changes may rebound on the government.
5 The proposals are rooted in an appropriate awareness of the problems that exist, but I do not feel that what is proposed adds up a coherent programme of action.

17.3 **Rewrite each sentence replacing the verb with a phrasal verb expression based on the word in brackets.**

1 The school's rituals and traditions have originated from its long history. (ROOT)
2 My mother attributes the problem to a decline in moral values. (PUT)
3 How do you think the changes will affect your business? (IMPACT)
4 The economic recession inevitably led to increased unemployment. (RESULT)
5 How would you explain the recent increase in violent crime? (ACCOUNT)
6 Joel's criticism of Erica may have a bad effect on him now that she's his boss! (REBOUND)
7 I do not feel that the writer's analysis of the problem makes sense. (ADD)
8 Some unforeseen problems have resulted from the change in legislation. (COME)

17.4 **Answer these questions using full sentences.**

1 What would you put global warming down to?
2 What do you think has led to the current increase in violent crime in most societies?
3 How would you account for the fact that teenage girls tend to do better at school than teenage boys?
4 What would you attribute the success of social media sites to?
5 What would you point to as the main cause of social problems today?
6 What would you say your own interest in English stems from?
7 Do you think that mobile phones have resulted in more or less communication between people?
8 What do you think is the main thing that contributes to the difficulty of phrasal verbs?

In this unit, some phrasal verbs can be grouped by the meaning given by the particle. For example, *up* means uppermost in your mind in **summon up**, **conjure up**, **call up** and **stir up**. *Up* in **store up** memories carries a different meaning in that it means gather or collect. *Back* in **come back**, **flood back** and **flashback** carries a sense of a returning memory. *Behind* and *out* occur with verbs which describe things we don't want to remember (**put** something **behind** somebody, **block** something **out** / **block out** something). Grouping the verbs by the meaning carried by the particle will help you to remember them.

Look at this conversation on social media between Bethany and her two cousins about old family photos.

Bethany Wells

When I look at these old photographs I've just found in our grandmother's desk, memories come **flooding back**[1]. This one here, of Granny's mother just before she died, **stirs up**[2] sad memories of how she suffered. It **reminds** me **of** how different life was then. But we can't let bad memories **eat away at**[3] us; we should **put** bad experiences **behind**[4] us. It's important to live in the present and live for the future.

[1] one suddenly remembers very clearly a lot of things about an experience or period in the past
[2] makes one remember events in the past, usually ones that make you feel sad
[3] make us unhappy because we think about them too much
[4] not think about them any more so that they do not affect our life

George Wells

We **store up** so many memories over the years, good ones and bad ones. I **associate** this photo that you found **with** our early childhood. Looking at the picture, it **came back** to me how we used to feed the animals on our grandparents' farm. It **summons up**[5] lots of happy memories, and some sad ones, too, like when my favourite old pony died. We tend to **block out**[6] sad memories, but sometimes you might get a **flashback**[7] to an unpleasant experience. The happy ones can **stick with**[8] you forever. I still remember the picnic we had on the farm for my sixth birthday.

[5] makes you remember something or think about something
[6] stop yourself from thinking about something unpleasant because it upsets you
[7] an occasion when you suddenly remember something vividly that happened to you in the past
[8] you remember them

Toby Wells

For me this photo you sent me that Granny took **conjures up**[9] a series of crazy events. I got this diploma, then fell down the steps as I left the stage. As I fell, I grabbed the curtain and all the curtains came down on top of me and the professor! Then all the lights went out! It's amazing how one picture can **call up**[10] an event in such detail. When I look at it, my thoughts always **flash back**[11] immediately to that moment.

[9] makes a picture, image, memory, etc. appear in my mind
[10] make one remember or think about a particular memory or idea
[11] get a sudden vivid memory of something

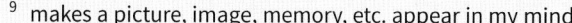

Exercises

18.1 **Choose the best word to complete each sentence.**

1 I was sitting in a train looking out of the window, when my mind suddenly .... back to that amazing trip we made to India.
   a) put   b) flashed   c) stirred   d) associated
2 Close your eyes and try to .... up a picture of a place where you feel at peace.
   a) store   b) eat   c) conjure   d) stick
3 Ivan has an excellent memory – he can .... up precise details of things that happened when he was a small child.
   a) come   b) flood   c) flash   d) call
4 Please don't talk about that day – I want to .... it all behind me.
   a) put   b) stir   c) block   d) summon
5 Pablo should try not to let his regrets for what he has done .... away at him.
   a) come   b) eat   c) stick   d) flood

18.2 **Complete this dialogue with phrasal verbs from the opposite page.**

Maya   I've just found this old dress at the back of my wardrobe. It .... (1) me of that party at Anna's. Do you remember? It must be at least 20 years ago!

Rory   Goodness me! That certainly does .... (2) up some memories. I hadn't thought of it for years, but it's all .... (3) back now! Do you remember all those roses she had everywhere?

Maya   That's right. I always .... (4) the smell of roses with Anna.

Rory   We spent all evening dancing together. We had such a lovely evening.

Maya   Actually, I don't know if we did. It's all .... (5) back to me now. Don't you remember, as we were leaving the party, Anna's brother came running out accusing you of stealing his wallet? He got really violent and started pushing you.

Rory   Oh yes! That was awful. I'd just completely .... (6) the memory out.

Maya   Well, I'm glad you did. If you hadn't .... (7) it behind you, then we wouldn't be friends with him now.

Rory   That's right. Anyway, it's the good memories that you want to .... (8) with you. Those are the ones to .... (9) up for the future.

Maya   Well, we've got plenty of those we can .... (10) up when we need them.

18.3 **Explain the play on words in these titles of newspaper articles.**

1 **COOK STIRS UP MEMORIES OF 1950s SCHOOL DINNERS**

4 **HAPPY MEMORIES OF LIFE AT GLUE FACTORY STICK WITH WORKERS**

2 **MAGICIAN CONJURES UP MEMORIES OF VICTORIAN ENGLAND**

5 **MEMORIES OF 1963 BURST PIPES COME FLOODING BACK**

3 **FILM CALLS UP OLD SOLDIERS' MEMORIES OF CONSCRIPTION**

18.4 **Answer these questions using full sentences.**

1 What colour do you associate with your childhood and why?
2 Is there any particular smell that reminds you of your childhood?
3 What music conjures up memories of your youth?
4 Is there any particular memory of your schooldays that you would like to block out?
5 Which makes memories come back to you more powerfully – music or smells?

19 Making progress

A Beginning and ending

phrasal verb with collocations	definition of phrasal verb	example
new businesses / political movements / buildings **spring up**	suddenly appear or begin to exist	At the turn of the century, new left-wing political movements **sprang up**.
new buildings / factories / cafés **sprout up**	suddenly appear or begin to exist	Pavement cafés have suddenly **sprouted up** all over the town.
open up opportunities/ possibilities or opportunities/ possibilities **open up**	make possible or become possible	The new shopping centre will **open up** all sorts of job opportunities.
break up a meeting/party or a meeting/party **breaks up**	end, people start to leave	I'm sorry to **break up** the party, but it's getting very late.
finish with magazine/ scissors/salt	no longer need	Can you let me have the magazine when you've **finished with** it?
trend/business/price **bottoms out**	reach a low level and stay there	The share price fell steadily last year but has now **bottomed out**.
game/match/anger/protest/ conflict **peters out**[1]	gradually become less strong and then stop completely	The crowd started shouting and protesting, but the protests soon **petered out** when they saw the armed police.
wind up a business/interview/ meeting	end	Jack intends to **wind up** his business soon.

[1] an interesting phrasal verb in that, unusually, *to peter* does not exist as a verb on its own

B Helping and hindering progress

We couldn't continue when our cheap supply of materials **dried up**[1].

We had some staffing problems but the new HR person has **magicked** them **away**[4].

Things've been **falling apart**[2] since the new manager arrived.

How's progress with your business?

We **got up to** the third stage of our plan but haven't made much progress since.

We can't do anything at the moment because the money's **run out**.

My PA has really improved things recently, so I hope we can **hang on to**[5] her.

We're **pressing on**[3] though we've had lots of problems. We can't do anything at the moment because the money's **run out**.

The CEO's **whittling away (at)**[6] the authority of middle managers.

[1] came to an end
[2] not working well
[3] continuing in a determined way

[4] made them disappear, as if by magic
[5] keep
[6] gradually reducing

English Phrasal Verbs in Use Advanced

Exercises

19.1 **Answer these questions.**

1 Would you be happy or unhappy if the exchange rate between your currency and the US dollar bottomed out?
2 Which two verbs from the opposite page could you use to complete this sentence?
  Wind farms seem to be .... / .... up all over the countryside these days.
3 *Open up* and *break up* can both be used with or without an object. True or false?
4 If someone whittles away your confidence, do you feel more or less confident?
5 If your anger peters out, does it become more or less strong?

19.2 **Complete the film blurbs below, using the correct verb or particle from the opposite page.**

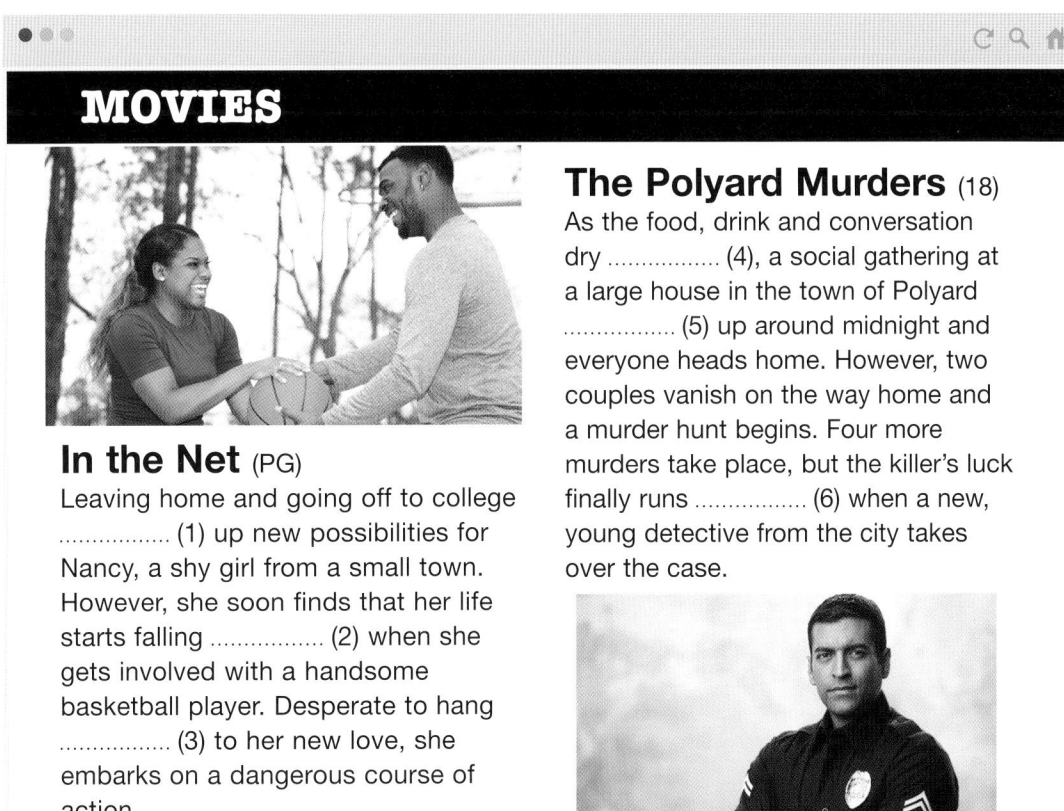

● ○ ○   ⟳ 🔍 🏠

MOVIES

In the Net (PG)
Leaving home and going off to college .... (1) up new possibilities for Nancy, a shy girl from a small town. However, she soon finds that her life starts falling .... (2) when she gets involved with a handsome basketball player. Desperate to hang .... (3) to her new love, she embarks on a dangerous course of action.

The Polyard Murders (18)
As the food, drink and conversation dry .... (4), a social gathering at a large house in the town of Polyard .... (5) up around midnight and everyone heads home. However, two couples vanish on the way home and a murder hunt begins. Four more murders take place, but the killer's luck finally runs .... (6) when a new, young detective from the city takes over the case.

19.3 **Rewrite these sentences to make them sound less formal using phrasal verbs instead of the underlined words.**

1 When you <u>no longer need</u> the scissors, could you pass them to me?
2 They <u>terminated</u> the business in 2014 after a year of low sales.
3 OK, so who's <u>made</u> the bottle opener <u>vanish</u>? It was here a minute ago!
4 We've had some setbacks but we'll <u>continue undeterred</u>.
5 I only <u>reached</u> page 12 of the book before I got bored and stopped reading it.

19.4 **Explain the play on words with the phrasal verbs in these sentences.**

1 Mr Bellamy decided to wind up his clock-making business after 35 years.
2 Three new greengrocers' shops have sprouted up in the town centre recently.
3 Even though the dry cleaner's was not getting much business, the owners decided to press on.
4 A new trampoline factory has sprung up on the outskirts of the town.
5 The *Speedyheels* training shoe company has run out of money.

A Particles in phrasal verbs connected with conflict and violence

Some of the phrasal verbs in this unit have the particle *up* (**smash up**, **flare up**) where *up* suggests extreme or complete. In **come at** and **fly at** *at* indicates the direction of the violent action. *Off* suggests remove in **bump off** [(informal), kill] and **fight off**, and *out* suggests remove completely in **wipe out** [completely destroy]. Thinking about the meaning the particle adds will help you learn the verbs in groups and remember them better.

B Talking about conflict and violence

Faisal	Why couldn't you buy a ticket?
Emma	**The ticket office was closed and vandals had smashed up the machine on the platform.**
Fatima	What happened to you? Are you hurt?
Alex	A man **pushed** me **over** and tried to steal my bag. He **came at** me from behind.
Fatima	Oh, that's dreadful! Did he take your bag?
Alex	No, I managed to **fight** him **off**, then some people came and he ran off.
Camille	What did the boss say when you all complained?
Albert	Well, he just **flew at**[1] me and said I was irresponsible, then he **rounded on**[2] the others and ordered them to get back to work. I've never seen him **flare up**[3] like that before, you know, he just **flew into**[4] a rage as soon as I opened my mouth.
Camille	So relations are not good now?
Albert	No. It's the biggest **bust-up**[5] we've ever had with him. But we're not going to let him **push** us **around**[6].

[1] suddenly spoke to me very angrily
[2] suddenly turned and attacked them or shouted at them angrily
[3] suddenly become very angry
[4] if someone flies into a particular state (e.g. rage, panic), they are suddenly in that state
[5] (informal) an angry argument
[6] tell someone what to do in a rude or threatening way

Jade	I hear your neighbours have been fighting one another!
Ben	Yes, Luke said Arthur had stolen some plants from his garden, so he **set** his dog **on**[7] him. Arthur kicked the dog, then punched Joss and almost **knocked** him **out**. The police had to come and **break** it **up**!

[7] attack someone, or make a person or animal attack someone

Eloise	What happened at the end of the film?
Maisie	Well, they caught the man who'd been **bumping** everyone **off**, of course.

C Metaphorical uses of phrasal verbs to suggest conflict or violence

The verbs in this group are particularly typical of newspaper language because they have metaphorical meanings, which is good for word play.

The government promised to **wipe out** poverty. [make it disappear completely]

The minister is **fighting off** calls for her resignation.

Some newspapers are trying to **drag** the prime minister **into** the scandal. [talk about or bring someone or something into a difficult or unpleasant situation, especially when that person or thing is not seen as being connected with the situation]

He published an article in a national newspaper as a way of **striking back at** his critics. [attacking someone who has attacked you (the literal meaning of striking is hitting)]

Exercises

20.1 Complete these sentences by adding one word to the end of each one.

1 I couldn't get anything from the vending machine because some hooligans had smashed it ....
2 When Charlotte told her mother she had scratched her car, she flew into a ....
3 He's terribly bossy, so make sure you don't let yourself be pushed ....
4 Tom hit the man so hard that he knocked him ....
5 Don't interfere in the fight yourself – wait for the police to come and break it ....
6 Robyn did her best, but she didn't manage to fight her attacker ....
7 If someone criticises you unfairly, it is better to ignore them than to strike ....
8 My neighbour went to jail for trying to bump her boss ....

20.2 Correct the six mistakes with phrasal verbs in this paragraph.

There was a terrible bust-off at work today. The departmental manager came into the office in a terrible temper. She flew on her PA and when people tried to calm her down, she rounded at them. I don't know what had got into her. She pushes everyone over a lot, but she's not normally quite so aggressive. I tried not to get dragged onto it at first, but she started shouting really loudly at Jessica, so I stepped in to try to break things out.

20.3 Do the phrasal verbs in these sentences need an object? If so, add an appropriate object in an appropriate place.

1 When I tried to enter the house, the dog flew at.
2 Ellis can seem quite happy one moment and then the next he'll flare up.
3 They threatened to bump off if he told anyone about the robbery.
4 Because she had learned some judo as a child, Lauren found it much easier to fight off.
5 I was completely taken by surprise when someone suddenly came at from behind.
6 After only ten seconds in the ring, Henry's opponent had knocked out.

20.4 Rewrite these sentences using the word in brackets.

1 Paul tried to involve me in the argument, but I managed to stay out of it. (DRAG)
2 The old man thought the boys were trying to break into his house, so he told his dog to attack them. (SET)
3 The aim of the organisation is to completely abolish cruelty to children. (WIPE)
4 Although he is small, James is strong and he quickly managed to hit his attacker so hard that he became unconscious. (KNOCK)
5 Uncle Ronnie can lose his temper very quickly if you say the wrong thing. (FLARE)
6 The witness saw the thief attack the woman just as she was opening her car door. (COME)
7 The robbers came running out of the bank, knocking down an old lady who was in their path. (PUSH)
8 Older people often find it harder to get rid of colds and other infections than younger people do. (FIGHT)

> ### Over to you
>
> Find a story in a newspaper dealing with conflict or violence in some way. Note down any phrasal verbs that it contains in their context.

21 Sound

Loud or unpleasant sounds

● ● ●   ✉   Reply   Forward

Hi Finn,

Thanks for your email.

I've more or less settled in to my new cottage. It's lovely – except for the neighbours. They are just so noisy! I can hear their sound system **blasting out**[1] at all hours of the day and night and one of them plays the trumpet – he's **belting out**[2] jazz most evenings. At least he plays well, so that noise doesn't **grate on**[3] me as much as it might! Much worse is the fact that one of them has a very loud voice and is also very bad-tempered. When she's angry she **bangs** things **down**[4] and her voice **booms out**[5] and sometimes the arguments even **drown out**[6] my own music. I've asked them nicely if they could **keep** the noise **down** a bit, but they have ignored me. And I thought I was moving to a quiet village where the only loud noise would be bells **pealing out**[7] on a Sunday morning!

Hope all goes well with you.

Cheers,

John

[1] producing a lot of noise, especially loud music
[2] (informal) playing a musical instrument or singing very loudly
[3] (of sound or behaviour) annoy
[4] puts down with force because she is angry

[5] makes a very loud noise
[6] prevent from being heard
[7] ringing loudly (of bells)

Sounds starting and finishing

● ● ●   ✉   Reply   Forward

Hi John,

Interesting to hear about your new cottage. I'm attaching an ad for some earplugs which claim to help you **shut** anything **out**[1]!

I moved into a new flat a month or so ago, too. It's next to the football stadium. I can't see the matches, but I can follow what's going on from the sounds I hear. A cheer **goes up**[2] whenever the home team shoots. But the sound quickly **dies down**[3] if the ball doesn't go in. Every time there's a match I find myself **listening out for**[4] the cheers. When I told my girlfriend that I wanted to stay at home to listen to the sounds of a football match, she **burst out**[5] laughing, thinking I was joking, and started talking about how we could decorate the flat. When another cheer went up from the stadium, though, her voice **trailed off**[6] and she rushed to the window in excitement. Then she stayed in the flat with me and spent all afternoon at the window watching spectators going in and out of the stadium.

Cheers,

Finn

[1] prevent a sound from being heard (can also be used about preventing a sight from being seen)
[2] if a shout (e.g. cheer, cry, groan) goes up, a lot of people make that noise at the same time
[3] becomes less loud or strong and then stops
[4] making an effort to hear a noise which you are expecting

[5] (of a sound) suddenly started (collocates with *laughing, crying, with a comment/remark*)
[6] gradually became quieter and then stopped

Exercises

21.1 Put these phrasal verbs into two groups, a 'noisy' group (making noise) and a 'not noisy' group (reducing noise).

| belt out | boom out | die down | trail off | keep down | blast out |

making noise	reducing noise

21.2 Complete these sentences with phrasal verbs from 21.1. Use each verb only once.

1 She was telling us about how angry Simon had made her, but her voice .... off when he entered the room.
2 As we entered the club, the singer was .... out his latest song.
3 Rock music was .... out from an open window as I passed the house.
4 Children, please .... the noise down – Grandpa's having a rest.
5 Major Frogshort's voice .... out across the square as he issued orders to his men.
6 At 6 p.m. the noise of the machines .... down and the workers went home.

21.3 Choose the correct particle to complete these sentences.

1 Suddenly a cheer went .... as the president appeared on the balcony.
  a) out b) up c) on
2 I'll listen .... for your call and come down to the street so you don't have to park.
  a) with b) to c) out
3 Faye was so angry she banged her phone ....
  a) down b) on c) away
4 These ear defenders shut .... 90% of external noise.
  a) down b) away c) out
5 When she heard how the story ended, she burst .... laughing.
  a) into b) out c) in
6 I love to hear the bells pealing .... at New Year.
  a) out b) on c) off
7 The noise of a plane passing overhead drowned .... the radio and I missed the news.
  a) down b) off c) out
8 She has such an awful voice; it just grates .... me every time she sings.
  a) to b) at c) on

21.4 Answer these questions. Use a dictionary if necessary.

1 If someone's voice drones on, are you likely to enjoy listening to them or not?
2 If birds are chirping away and if a person is chattering away, *away* suggests a continuing sound. True or false?
3 What particle would be best here?
  The cheers of the crowd built .... to a roar as the runners approached the finish line.
4 What particle would be best here?
  The noise of the train died .... as it headed towards the distant coast.
5 What phrasal verb with *ring* can be used for all of these things?
  church bells   a cry   a shot   a shout   applause
6 What phrasal verb with *come* would fit in this sentence?
  Suddenly an announcement .... the public address system warning everyone to evacuate the building.

22 Supporting and opposing people or views

A

In these television interviews, Members of Parliament (MPs) are defending their positions.

Interviewer	Recently you seem to have **come out against**[1] those in your party who want stronger anti-terrorist laws. Why?
MP	I haven't changed my position at all, and I **stick by** what I've always said. Those who **side with**[2] the terrorists or support them in any way must be opposed. But we need a mature debate about the causes of terrorism.

[1] stated publicly that you opposed an issue (opposite: **come out in favour of**)
[2] support a person or group in an argument

Interviewer	You said you were determined to introduce higher fuel charges, but after the opposition from the trucking companies you seem to have **caved in**[3]. Why?
MP	We are a listening party and we always **defer to**[4] expert opinion. We were advised that higher charges would have a negative economic effect in the long term, so we have decided to **go with**[5] that advice.

[3] agreed to something that you were against before, because of persuasion or threats
[4] (formal) accept someone else's opinion because they know more or are more important
[5] accept a plan or an idea

Interviewer	You seem to be **leaning** increasingly **towards**[6] more conservative policies. Is there any truth in the rumour that you are about to **cross over**[7] to the Conservative Party?
MP	No. The values I **stand for**[8] are liberal values, but I see no point in **siding against**[9] the Conservative Party on those issues where I agree with them.

[6] support or begin to support a particular set of ideas or a particular political party
[7] start to support a different, often opposing, person or group
[8] support
[9] opposing a person or group in an argument

B

Note the phrasal verbs for supporting and opposing people or views in these newspaper extracts.

17-year-old boy claims he was **egged on**[1] by his friends to steal cars.

[1] encouraged to do something, often something that is wrong, stupid or dangerous

Cheered on[2] by her supporters, Sadie Hinds beat the world record.

[2] received encouraging shouts

Mrs Gilmore, who celebrated her 104th birthday, when asked what her secret was, said she **swears by**[3] a glass of hot milk with a little sugar every night before bed.

[3] believes that something is very effective and that it will always work well

Mr West said the club would **not hear of**[4] letting children attend the event.

[4] not allow something, or not allow someone to do something (always in the negative)

The peace campaign was **buoyed up**[5] recently by a donation of €1,000,000.

[5] supported and made more successful

He was someone who always **stuck up for**[6] the rights of the poor and the homeless.

[6] (informal) defended or fought for something important

Exercises

22.1 **Look at A opposite. Complete these statements from a political manifesto.**

This party .... for equality for all.

We do not hesitate to .... out strongly against any case of injustice.

We .... by our principles at all times and never .... in to threats or pressure from the opposition.

We .... with the underdog and do not .... to those who are wealthy and powerful.

22.2 **Look at B opposite. Put the words in the correct order to make sentences.**

1 runners / The / cheered / line / on / the / were / as / they / spectators / for / the / by / finishing / headed
2 rely / sister / Tim / You / to / on / stick / little / can / his / for / up
3 grandfather / by / My / garlic / a / of / raw / himself / as / way / from / colds / protecting / swears / catching
4 bungee / My / have / mother / would / tried / we / never / hadn't / her / jumping / on / egged / if
5 all-night / to / wanted / to / go / mother / party / an / it / her / wouldn't / but / of / She / hear
6 of / discovery / the / years / British / gas / the / North / The / up / buoyed / in / economy / Sea / some / for

22.3 **Which word from the opposite page could fit into all the sentences in each set? Note any new meanings of the word which you come across.**

1 If a politician doesn't .... by what he has said, he will lose the voters' trust.
Don't forget to .... a stamp on each of your postcards.
It is not always easy to .... up for what you believe in if others are attacking you.

2 I cannot believe that you would .... with the government on the issue of the war.
Peter was warned not to .... against the minister if he wanted to have a successful career in politics.
You will find a lot of interesting phrasal verbs on the left-hand .... of the page.

3 Please come and .... me on in the tennis match.
Josie is a bit miserable, so we really should go round and try to .... her up.
A .... went up as the prince entered the stadium.

4 Harry Carr's investment should help to .... up the company.
We always try to .... each other up before giving important presentations.
You must try to sail the yacht round that red ....

22.4 **Are these sentences correct? If not, correct them.**

1 My preferred course of action would be to get with what Ivan has recommended.
2 He began his political life as a Conservative but crossed across to the Labour Party when he realised that he would be more likely to get a seat in Parliament that way.
3 Many people start to lean more towards right-wing ideas as they become middle-aged.
4 Either side with the prime minister or against him – don't abstain from voting.
5 I shall have to defer on your superior knowledge of the situation.
6 My mother promises by a daily spoonful of honey to keep healthy all year long.
7 Josh is not usually naughty himself but he is quick to egg others off.
8 The headteacher said she would not hear of pupils coming to school with hair dyed a bright colour.

23 Agreeing

A Coming to an agreement

Toby	So the first thing on the agenda today is **nailing dow**n[1] the plan for next month's launch party.
Magda	Well, what happened at the senior management meeting? Did our budget request **go through**[2]?
Toby	Yes, it did. A couple of them didn't want to **agree to** it at first, so I had to explain about the plans to invite local business leaders and other influential people. I had to leave before the end, but apparently they arrived at a unanimous decision and approved the budget.
Kate	Great. Well, Jon and I have already **hammered out**[3] a deal with a venue just down the road. The boss at the Olive Bistro can give us a great price.
Magda	Shouldn't it be somewhere a little more upmarket?
Kate	I don't think you should **rule** it **out**[4] until you see it. It doesn't look like much from the outside, but they have done a great job with the recent refurbishment.
Toby	We don't have to **settle on**[5] the venue right now. We just need to **come to** an agreement by the end of the week. Maybe a couple of us should go and have a look at the Olive Bistro tomorrow morning. Magda, can I **count** you **in**[6]?
Magda	Yes, OK. And what about entertainment? At the last meeting Nigel was very keen on having a DJ. Do we all want to **go along with**[7] that?

[1] making a decision about all the details of something
[2] be approved by an official authority
[3] reached an agreement after a long discussion
[4] say no to something
[5] agree on
[6] include a person in a plan or activity (opposite: **count** someone **out**)
[7] agree with someone's idea or opinion

B Agreeing after disagreeing

At first only Tania and I liked the blue design best, but we gradually **won** the others **round**[1].

Ben wasn't sure about joining the special project team at the beginning, but I managed to **talk** him **round**[2] in the end.

It took a while to persuade my line manager to send me on the business management course, but she **gave in**[3] eventually!

When we first moved to an open-plan office, I didn't really like it. But I've **come round to**[4] it now, as it has improved communication in the team.

The Board have finally **backed down**[5] over their proposals to restructure the department.

The management had to **bow to**[6] pressure from the unions and give the pay rise they promised.

She wanted to work in London originally, but in the end she had to **settle for**[7] the regional office.

Two of the team had a big disagreement and weren't talking to each other for a few days. Fortunately, they seem to have **smoothed** things **over**[8] this morning.

[1] persuaded (can also be **win over**)
[2] persuade
[3] agree after initially refusing
[4] changed my opinion
[5] admitted they were wrong and changed their minds
[6] do something you don't want to do (another way to say this is **bend to**)
[7] agree to something which isn't your first choice
[8] made a problem less serious

> ### Tip
> If we persuade someone <u>not</u> to do something, we **talk** them **out of** something. *He wanted to have a party while his parents were away, but I **talked** him **out of** it.*

English Phrasal Verbs in Use Advanced

Exercises

23.1 Match the beginning of each sentence with its ending.

1. The Marketing Director refused to go
2. Although it's very unlikely that we'll get the contract, I wouldn't rule it
3. I'd like to settle
4. I really want to smooth things
5. The application for my credit card went
6. Lucy was very resistant at first, but we eventually managed to win her
7. After a very difficult meeting with the shareholders, the Board finally bowed
8. Dominic's very good at talking people

a) through last week, and it arrived in the post this morning.
b) to pressure and agreed to increase the annual dividend.
c) along with our suggestions about the new product design.
d) round to his way of thinking. That's why he's such a good negotiator.
e) on a date for the interviews as soon as possible.
f) over with Roger, as we have to work together every day.
g) out completely.
h) over. Now she loves the idea!

23.2 Choose the correct particle to complete these sentences.

1. We've booked the venue and the caterers. Now we just need to nail *down / up / round* the rest of the details.
2. I've explained why we should update the website, but he just refuses to give *up / in / back* and let me do it.
3. We spent ages discussing the new logo, and we eventually came *to / through / up against* an agreement.
4. Can we settle *on / for / down* a paint colour for the walls first, and then start looking at furniture?
5. Polly agreed *to / out / up* the new schedule initially, but then realised that it didn't give her enough time to finish her work.
6. Despite the fact that Mark was clearly in the wrong, he refused to back *up / round / down* and apologise.
7. We need some volunteers to help organise the charity fundraiser. Can we count you *on / in / into*?

23.3 Rewrite each sentence using a phrasal verb based on the word in brackets in an appropriate form.

1. After two weeks of strikes, the company finally changed their mind and increased the overtime rate. (GIVE)
2. Our application for planning permission was approved without any problems, so we can start building next month. (GO)
3. We've got a general agreement, but it will take some time to work out the details. (HAMMER)
4. Chris always just agrees with what the manager says. He never thinks for himself. (GO)
5. It's going to be difficult to finalise all the details of the training day until we've chosen a date. (NAIL)
6. Charlie said he didn't like the new website design, but I think he'll change his opinion about it when he sees the latest version. (COME)

23.4 Answer these questions.

1. If someone says they'll go along with you when you make a suggestion, do they mean a) they agree b) they have changed their mind c) they disagree with you?
2. If someone gives in too easily to their children, are they a) very strict b) easily persuaded c) always arguing with them?
3. If your boss rules out an idea you suggest, does that mean she a) wants to do it b) isn't sure whether to do it c) definitely doesn't want to do it?
4. If you hear on the news that a government is bowing to international pressure, does it mean a) they are keeping the same opinion b) they agree with other countries c) they are changing their mind?
5. If someone says they want to smooth things over after an argument, does it mean a) they don't want to talk to you again b) they want to make a problem less serious c) they want to agree with you?

Understanding

As a maths teacher I find it interesting to see how pupils cope with my subject. Some **pick up** every new topic very quickly, while others take rather longer to **catch on**[1]. Some have to **grapple with**[2] the topic for a long time but eventually understand it very well. Some find it **goes in** better if they are presented with the whole picture right from the beginning, whereas others like me to **break** a topic **down** into small bite-sized chunks. Then they gradually **piece** it all **together** for themselves. Although some find it harder than others to **keep up**[3] with what I tell them, everyone usually **cottons on**[4] in the end.

[1] (informal) understand
[2] try hard to deal with
[3] be able to understand something that is happening or changing fast
[4] (informal) begins to understand

Having ideas

phrasal verb	definition of phrasal verb	example
occur to sb	come into your mind	It suddenly **occurred to** me that he hadn't told me his name.
hit on (an idea)	have a good idea (especially one that solves a problem)	We weren't sure how to celebrate our anniversary until James **hit on** the idea of spending the weekend in Paris.
rough out	write or draw the outline of an idea without going into details	The novelist said he always **roughs out** several plots before he decides which one to use.
reflect on	(slightly formal) think very hard about something	We all need to take some time to **reflect on** what has happened.
think up sth or **think** sth **up**	create an idea or plan using your imagination and intelligence	Can you help me **think up** an idea for my presentation?
play with (an idea)	consider an idea but usually do not do it	The headteacher **played with** the idea of introducing compulsory lessons in good manners.
leap out at	be immediately obvious	I couldn't solve the crossword clue last night, but this morning the answer **leapt out at** me.

Discussing ideas

I have some great colleagues. Whenever I have a problem at work, I **talk** it **through**[1] with my supervisor. She always **comes at**[2] problems from a slightly different angle, and **thrashing** an issue **out**[3] with her helps me to see the problem more clearly and to find a solution. Then there is my marketing team. I am very proud of them. In our regular meetings to discuss new promotional activities, we **bounce** our ideas **off**[4] each other until we find something that we all like. We find that **batting** our ideas **around**[5] like this is really productive and results in great campaigns.

[1] discuss something in order to understand it better
[2] approaches
[3] discussing something in order to find a solution
[4] (informal) tell someone about an idea to find out what they think of it
[5] (slightly informal) discussing different ways of dealing with an issue

Exercises

24.1 Complete this conversation using verbs from the box.

| reflect | break | rough | cotton | thrash | hit | grapple | occur | piece | bounce | talk |

Student I've been .... (1) with this idea you talked about in your lecture, that written language is becoming more like spoken language these days, but I'm finding it difficult. I've been trying to .... (2) out some chapters for my dissertation and I like this topic, but I think I need to .... (3) it through with you first.

Lecturer Well, why don't I .... (4) a few ideas off you? Then you can see if they make sense. When you write emails to your friends, how formal are they?

Student Pretty informal usually.

Lecturer Let's just .... (5) on that for a moment. What makes them informal?

Student I suppose it's grammar for one thing. I use contractions like 'I'm' or 'it's' instead of 'I am' or 'it is'. And slang words and so on.

Lecturer Yes, and hasn't it .... (6) to you that what you're doing is sort of talking to people rather than writing to them?

Student Ah. I see. I think I've .... (7) on now. Things like email and text messages and chat rooms and so on are changing the way we write, is that it?

Lecturer Exactly. Go away and think about it a bit more and I'm sure you'll .... (8) on a few more ideas. Look at a few newspapers and magazines. Try and .... (9) the topic down into different themes, like grammar and vocabulary.

Student OK, thanks. I'll probably be able to .... (10) it all together now.

Lecturer Yes, and come back if you need more help and we can .... (11) it out together and try and clarify it more. OK? Bye.

24.2 Choose the correct particle to complete these sentences.

1 I've been trying to think *about / up / over* a plan for a surprise birthday party for Theodore, but I haven't hit *on / out / up* the right idea yet.
2 I thought about the problem for ages, but then the solution just leapt *over / away / out* at me.
3 Some of the trainees are very good at picking *on / over / up* new techniques, while others take a long time to catch *on / across / in*.
4 It's hard to keep up *to / with / for* all the reading for my literature course.
5 We formed a committee to bat a few ideas *over / up / around* for the college open day.
6 For a while we played *with / on / at* the idea of making all the courses compulsory, but we dropped it because it would be so unpopular.
7 I think we should try and come *into / on / at* the problem from a different angle.
8 I tried to explain it to him, but new information takes a long time to go *on / in / off* sometimes!

24.3 Find phrasal verbs from the opposite page which seem to treat ideas as if they are:

1 balls that can be played with
2 parts of a puzzle
3 things that you need physical strength to deal with

Max stared at the crossword for ages, but then the answer suddenly leapt out at him.

25 Arranging things

A group of students are organising things for a college open day. Note how they use phrasal verbs to talk about arranging things.

Ben	We need something to **prop up**[1] the video camera. Maybe we could use that big box?
Anna	Or we could rest it on the bookcase. That could **double up as**[2] a camera support.

[1] make something stay in a particular position by putting something underneath or against it
[2] also be used as

Tim	Let's **gather up** all those brochures and **stack** them **up** in one pile over here.
Elodie	OK, then I'll have to **see about**[3] an extra table; we've got too much stuff.

[3] deal with something, or arrange for something to be done

Sacha	We need to **space out** the tables a bit; they're too close together at the moment.
Lizzie	Yes, and we should **line** them **up** a bit better too so that it all looks neat.
Paul	Why don't we **separate off**[4] all the student work displays and put them all together in the other room?
Jake	Yes, OK. I'll **round up**[5] some more helpers; it's going to be quite a big job.
Paul	Yes, and then **separate out**[6] the first-year students' work, the second-year students' work and the third- and fourth-year students' work and make a special display of it. That would be nice.
Jake	OK, but how will I **know** the first-year stuff **from** the rest?
Paul	The name and the year are on the back of each piece of work.

[4] remove something from a large group of things
[5] find and gather together a group of people or animals
[6] divide a group of people or things into smaller groups

Kelly	Hey everyone, if you could **pile up** all your rubbish in the corner there, I'll get someone to take it all away at once.
Paul	OK, but I think we should **sift through**[7] everything before we throw it away in case we're throwing away things we should keep.

[7] examine a large collection of something, especially papers, usually in order to discover something or to decide what is important

Other verbs connected with organising and arranging things

We **hoarded away** dozens of bottles of water as we knew there would be a shortage in the hot weather. [put a supply of something in a safe place so that it can be used in the future]

I've been trying to **fix up** a meeting with our local MP so we can get to know her better. [(informal) arrange]

He **folded up** the scarf, wrapped it in gold wrapping paper and **did** it **up** with a red bow, ready to give to his grandfather on his birthday. [fasten or tie something]

The headteacher **geared** his speech more **towards** the parents than the pupils. [designed something so that it was suitable for a particular purpose, situation, or group of people]

Norton College **ranks among** the best in the country. [has a particular position in a list arranged in order of quality]

Exercises

25.1 **Answer these questions about the verbs in A.**

1 What other things can someone round up, apart from people?
2 What might you prop your head up with if you're reading on the sofa?
3 Which other verb in A is close in meaning to *stack up*?
4 If you sift through papers, what are you doing?
5 Does the particle *up* seem to have any similar meanings in the verbs in A?

25.2 **Choose the correct phrasal verb to complete these sentences.**

1 We had to *stick up* / *stock up* / *stack up* the chairs after the meeting and lock the hall.
2 Could you *round in* / *round up* / *round off* some people to help move the furniture?
3 Let's *separate off* / *separate away* / *separate out* the blue forms, the green forms and the white forms so that they don't all get mixed up together.

25.3 **Complete the gaps in the texts with a particle from B opposite.**

My nine-year-old son is so untidy. I'm tired of trying to get him to fold his clothes .... (1) and put them neatly into drawers. The trouble is, his drawers are full of other things – toys and games, stones and pieces of wood that he has hoarded .... (2) for some reason or another.

I've just done a presentation of our company's products with a major firm we'd like to do business with. It's ranked .... (3) the biggest in the country, so we could make a lot of money if they agree to let us supply them with our boxes. I geared my presentation .... (4) the quality of our boxes, and at the end of it I presented their team with one of our boxes done .... (5) in specially-designed paper in their company colours and filled with information about our company. I think they may be interested. They've certainly agreed to fix .... (6) another meeting.

25.4 **Answer these questions using a phrasal verb based on the verb in brackets in your answer.**

1 What would you do if you wanted to discuss a business idea face-to-face with your bank manager? (FIX)
2 If students are taking an important written exam, what are schools usually required to do with the desks where they sit to write their exams? (SPACE)
3 If one leg of a table is shorter than the others, how might you use a book? (PROP)
4 If you recycle your rubbish, why might you need several different containers? (SEPARATE)
5 For a school photo, how does the photographer typically arrange the pupils? (LINE)
6 If you are a student living in one room and you often have friends and family to stay with you, why might it be useful to have a large sofa? (DOUBLE)
7 If you have a lot of papers on the floor and you want to tidy your room, what do you do with the papers? (GATHER)
8 If you are going to meet someone who you've never met before at a crowded café, why might you each agree to wear something distinctive? (KNOW)
9 You are arranging a party and want to ask an artistic friend to deal with decorating the room where the party is to be held. What could you say to your friend? (SEE)
10 You have a pile of papers that you think it may be all right to throw away, but what is it a good idea to do with them first? (SIFT)

A   Increasing and totalling

phrasal verb	definition of phrasal verb	example
build up (sth) / **build** (sth) **up**	increase in amount, size or strength, or make something increase	Paula has been doing a lot of long-distance running to try to **build up** her stamina.
bump up sth / **bump** sth **up**	(informal) increase the size or amount of something, e.g. price, by a large amount	Hotels in this town always **bump** their prices **up** when the film festival is on.
round up sth / **round** sth **up**[1]	increase a number to the nearest whole number	The taxi fare came to £29.25, but we **rounded** it **up** and gave the driver £30.
push up sth / **push** sth **up**	increase the amount, number or value of something	The TV series about Caitlin Cliff's pottery **pushed up** the value of her work.
put on sth / **put** sth **on**	if a person or animal puts on weight, they become heavier	Bobby's **put on** six kilos since he stopped playing football.
amount to sth	become a particular amount	When we added living costs to the fees, the cost of the course **amounted to** £34,000.
add up	(informal) increase and become a large number or amount	Bringing up children is an expensive business. Clothes, shoes, food, toys, – it all **adds up**!

[1] (opposite: **round down** sth / **round** sth **down** = reduce to nearest whole number)

B   Decreasing

Ice cream sales are high in summer but **tail off** as winter approaches. [decrease in amount]

Since they employed a new chef, the quality of the food has really **fallen off**. [become smaller or lower]

We'll never be able to get out of the car park now. Let's wait till the football crowds **thin out** a bit. [become fewer in number]

Laura was so keen to get rid of her old car that I was able to get her to **knock** the price **down** a bit. [(informal) reduce]

I'm afraid we have no choice but to **slim** the business **down** and some redundancies will be announced next week. [make it smaller in size, often by employing fewer people]

C   Staying the same

Exam results out: Differences narrowing between boys and girls

This year 16-year-old girls have again done much better than boys in their school exams. However, the differences in grades between the sexes now seem to be **levelling off**[1] by the time pupils reach 18. At 18, boys' results now **average out at** 66% per exam, whereas the equivalent figure for girls is 67%. Several years ago there was concern at the rapidly rising rate of academic success among girls in comparison with boys, but this rate has clearly now **flattened out**[2]. It is believed that greater use of technology in the classroom is helping to **balance** things **out**[3], reviving boys' interest in their schoolwork.

[1] becoming more similar (can also be **level out**)
[2] stopped increasing or decreasing and begun to stay at the same level
[3] make things equal

Exercises

26.1 Correct the mistakes with the phrasal verbs in these sentences.

1 The total cost of our holiday amounted at nearly £500.
2 The bill came to £22.20 each, so we rounded it over to £25 to include a tip.
3 Helena has pushed on a lot of weight recently.
4 It will take Joe some time to build on his strength again after such a long illness.
5 The college hoped that the advert would push off enrolments for its new course.
6 The new fertiliser claims to dump up agricultural yields considerably.

26.2 Match the statements 1–6 with the illustrations a–f.

a   b   c   d   e   f

1 Sales levelled out at £600.
2 The prices averaged out at £600.
3 The price was rounded down.
4 They knocked the price down.
5 Sales tailed off later in the week.
6 The price was bumped up.

26.3 Answer the questions.

1 The new manager has decided to slim the business down.
  What does the new manager intend to do?
2 We picnicked in the forest in a place where the trees were beginning to thin out.
  Why might this have been a good place for a picnic?
3 The graph showing hits on our website begins to flatten out in May.
  How many hits did the website get in June?
4 Interest in politics seems to be falling off now, particularly among young people.
  Are young people more or less interested in politics than they used to be?
5 Joseph's lack of interest in housework is balanced out by his love of gardening.
  How does the speaker probably feel about Joseph and what he does at home?

26.4 Complete this email with phrasal verbs from the opposite page.

Dear Gordon,

Sorry I haven't been in touch for a while. I'm not finding it so easy running my own business. We've had to .... (1) our prices because of strong competition, so our profits are beginning to .... (2). They still .... (3) a pretty sizeable sum, but even so, it's a bit worrying to see them .... (4). I'm planning to close one of our factories. I hope that by .... (5) the business in this way, I may be able to .... (6) our profits again. All the worry has made me .... (7) a lot of weight too because I tend to eat snacks to make me feel better. And as you know, it all .... ! (8)

Esther

27 Talking about success and failure

The chief executive of a company is making a speech to the staff. Note the phrasal verbs connected with success and failure.

This year has been an eventful one. We've been able to **capitalise on**[1] the publicity we got in the new year with the launch of our new lines, and we've **come out** stronger than ever, despite strong competition. We've **succeeded in** reversing the downward trend we were suffering last year. What's more, we've managed to **win back** customers from the competition. We had been **losing out to**[2] international players, but now we can **pride** ourselves **on**[3] being able to offer better quality products at lower prices. In the middle of the year, we faced a hostile takeover bid from *Diotecnics*. We fought hard against it and finally **won through**[4], as I knew we would. That bid **fell through**[5] and we are now stronger than ever. So I want to thank you all.

[1] use a situation in order to achieve something good for yourself
[2] being less successful than
[3] be proud of
[4] succeeded after trying hard to achieve something
[5] failed to happen

Two students are talking on the phone about studying for exams.

Harry I don't think I'll **get through**[1] the end-of-term exam this time.

Libby Oh, really? Why?

Harry Well, I've been really busy with the drama club, that's the problem. I wish I could be one of those people who **sail through**[2] exams and still manage to **pack in**[3] a huge amount in their spare time.

Libby Yes, me too. But never mind, you did your presentation the other day and you managed to **carry** that **off**[4] quite well.

Harry I managed to fool everyone, you mean! I **got by**[5] only because I found some useful stuff on the Internet the night before.

Libby Well, that's OK. That's what the Internet's for. As long as you didn't just copy it!

[1] pass
[2] easily pass
[3] (informal) manage to do a lot of activities in a period of time
[4] succeed in doing or achieving something difficult
[5] (informal) had just enough or knew just enough of something to deal with a difficult situation

Other verbs connected with succeeding and failing

I couldn't really afford the time to go to a lecture on bees, but my curiosity **won out** and I went. [(informal) was stronger than other, competing emotions]

The general lack of enthusiasm **doomed** the plan **to** failure. [made it sure to fail]

The support of my friends and family helped to **pull** me **through** a very difficult time. [succeed in dealing with a difficult period of your life, or to help someone else to do this]

You have to learn to **rise above** negative criticism if you want to succeed. [not allow something bad that is happening or being done to you to upset you or to affect your behaviour]

Did you see the match on Saturday? We've **fallen behind** Liverpool by three points now. [failed to score as many points as another team or player in a competition]

Exercises

27.1 **Rewrite each sentence using a phrasal verb based on the word in brackets in an appropriate form.**

1 Some people were going to buy our flat, but at the last moment the sale failed to happen. (FALL)
2 Steve is very proud of his organisational skills. (PRIDE)
3 The company was able to take advantage of the unusually wet weather by promoting its inexpensive umbrellas. (CAPITALISE)
4 The England team lost the trophy in 2014 but regained it the following year. (WIN)
5 It's been a difficult year for us, but we have emerged from it with renewed vigour. (COME)
6 Leila managed to pass her driving test at her first attempt. (SUCCEED)
7 Hassan was beaten by his brother in the finals of the tennis tournament. (LOSE)
8 They had a long battle in court to prove their innocence, but finally they succeeded. (WIN)

27.2 **Complete the text below using the correct verbs.**

Home   About   Blog   Contact me

A French Adventure

13 MARCH

Richard was very pessimistic about my plans to ride my bike from the very north of France to the south. He was convinced the project was .... (1) to failure despite all my attempts to persuade him that I would be able to .... (2) it off. He said I would never be able to .... (3) in so many miles in the short period of time I had at my disposal. I knew I'd be unlikely to .... (4) through the trip without any problems, but I made a great effort to .... (5) above all his negative comments. I am so glad I did! It wasn't an easy ride, and my French isn't great, but I managed to .... (6) by using gestures and a translation app. My determination .... (7) me through, and in the end I .... (8) in reaching my destination just one day later than planned. I'm glad to say Richard was there to congratulate me.

27.3 **Say whether the people in these sentences (a) succeeded in doing something, (b) succeeded in doing something but only in the face of difficulty or (c) failed to do something.**

1 He was so nervous when he stood up to sing, but I think he carried it off rather well.
2 She sailed through the interview and was offered the job immediately.
3 I lost out in the job interview to another woman who had more experience than me.
4 I'd hoped to go to Peru in March but the trip fell through.
5 We packed in such a lot on our trip to Korea – we saw all the main cities and sights.
6 The college authorities ignored our protests at first, but we won through in the end.

27.4 **Correct the ten mistakes with phrasal verbs in this paragraph.**

Oliver has always wanted to become an engineer, but it was quite difficult for him to get a place at college. He didn't get in at his first attempt, losing off to applicants with better exam grades. However, at his second try he succeeded to win a place. He then sailed over all his first-year exams but failed some of his exams in the second year, as he started spending a lot of time on the rugby pitch, playing for the college first team, rather than in the library. Then his team fell back in the college league after three games, so he wasn't too happy and did even less work, and as a result he failed three exams. However, he's always prided himself for being able to revise very efficiently when he's really under pressure, and in the third year he did enough to pull himself across. His friends were amazed that he managed to carry it out, as they were sure he could not have packed up enough study in such a short time to get by the exams. But Oliver knew that he had only just got over and he resolved to organise his life much better after leaving college.

Describing problems

Rosie   How's life with you, Kate? Is everything going OK?

Kate   Not really. They're threatening to make some redundancies at work, so that's **hanging over**[1] me. All because senior management **botched up**[2] and lost the company millions of pounds last year! My daughter's relationship with her boyfriend of five years has **broken down**[3] because pressures they were both having at work began to **spill over**[4] into their private lives and they just couldn't cope. Then my son, the journalist, was in Phrasalia and got **caught up in**[5] the revolution there – he **ran into**[6] difficulties when he was trying to leave and we don't know when he'll get home. He even **landed in**[7] prison for a few days.

Rosie   Oh dear! And how are you **bearing up**[8]?

Kate   Oh, it's hard, but I'm OK. But how about you, what's going on in your life?

Rosie   It's quite stressful, too, as we've just learned Leo's sister is **riddled with**[9] cancer …

[1] making us worry about what is going to happen
[2] (informal) spoiled something by doing it badly
[3] failed
[4] have an unpleasant effect on another situation
[5] involved in an activity or situation which prevented him from moving
[6] began to experience
[7] found himself in a difficult situation or unpleasant place
[8] dealing with a sad or difficult situation
[9] full of something unpleasant or bad

Dealing with problems

We must all **resign ourselves to**[1] the fact that we will encounter problems throughout our lives. We cannot **safeguard against**[2] all unpleasant events. Nor can we **walk away**[3] from every difficult situation that comes along. We have to find ways of **living with**[4] the bad situations that we inevitably face from time to time and find ways of **ironing out**[5] difficulties. We should not be too proud to **fall back on**[6] our parents for advice – we may be surprised at how helpful they can be. If the problem is a disagreement, then we may be able to **smooth things over**[7]. Explaining how we feel will sometimes be all that is needed to **clear up**[8] a misunderstanding. If we have behaved badly, then we should apologise and find a way to **make up for**[9] our actions. The important thing is not to **resort to**[10] behaviour that we know is wrong even if it seems to offer a temporary solution. Don't just **grasp at**[11] the first chance of an easy way out – it may not be the right thing to do.

Annette Berg, Therapist and agony aunt

[1] accept that something we do not want to happen will happen
[2] do things to stop something unpleasant happening
[3] stop being involved in a situation that is difficult to deal with
[4] accepting a difficult situation and continuing with our life while it exists
[5] doing something to resolve a problem
[6] use something when other things have failed, or when there are no other choices
[7] make a disagreement or problem seem less serious or easier to deal with, especially by talking to the people involved in it
[8] give or find an explanation for, or deal with, a problem or disagreement
[9] do something good so that the bad thing seems less important and does not cause a problem any more
[10] do something that you do not really want to because you cannot find any other way of achieving something
[11] quickly use or accept an opportunity to do or have something, especially because you are unhappy with the present situation

Exercises

28.1 Complete these emails between Isabella and Nicole using phrasal verbs from the opposite page.

● ● ●   ✉   Reply   Forward

Hi Nicole,

Life's never easy, is it? I've had a big misunderstanding with my colleague Blake and I want to
.... (1) it up, but I'm not sure how. It's been .... (2) over me for a week now,
and I don't want relations to .... (3) down between me and him as I have to meet with him
once a week. He thinks I told people he took time off when he wasn't really sick and as a result
he .... (4) in trouble with the boss. All I had said was I was glad to hear it wasn't anything
serious. What should I do? Advice greatly appreciated!

Isabella

● ● ●   ✉   Reply   Forward

Dear Isabella,

Well, you're right not to try to .... (5) away from the situation. It's bound
to .... (6) over into your professional dealings with him. It sounds like you've got
.... (7) up in some malicious office gossip. Invite him out to lunch, explain, and
apologise for causing him any problems. That should .... (8) things over a bit.
Tell him what a wonderful colleague he is. At moments like this you have to .... (9) to
flattery! It's usually the only way to .... (10) up for saying or doing something you wish
you hadn't. Most people can't resist being flattered!

Hope that helps.

Love,

Nicole

28.2 Rewrite the underlined parts of these sentences using a phrasal verb from the opposite page.
Make any other necessary changes.

1 When the doctors examined the dead man, they found his body was <u>full of</u> disease.
2 I just <u>quickly accepted</u> the first opportunity to get out of my boring job and do something more
   exciting. I wasn't prepared to just <u>continue to accept</u> it; I had to make a change.
3 I <u>was forced to use</u> my knowledge of map reading from my days as a scout to help us find a way
   out of the valley.
4 I'm sorry, I've <u>done things the wrong way</u> and caused a lot of problems for everyone.
5 A healthy diet and plenty of exercise is the best way to <u>protect yourself from</u> heart disease.
6 His life is difficult. His parents died last year when he was only 16. Now he just has to <u>be brave and
   determined</u> and try to carry on as best he can.
7 I'm afraid we just have to <u>reluctantly accept</u> the fact that we are going to have to sell the house.
8 She tried very hard to <u>resolve</u> the misunderstandings between the two groups.

Over to you

Look at the problem page of any English language magazine or newspaper and see how many phrasal
verbs are used to talk about problems. Make a note of any you find, especially any not practised in this
unit. There are also many problem pages in English on the Internet. Try doing a search for 'problem page'.

29 Deciding and influencing

A

Note the phrasal verbs for making decisions and influencing people and events.

It's time for me to **decide on** that interesting offer I had last week. I've **mulled it over**[1], but I still don't know whether to say yes or no and the deadline is tomorrow. I just want to be careful not to **tie myself down**[2] to something I might regret later.

[1] thought carefully about something for a long time
[2] stop yourself from being free to do what you want to do

For a long time I've been **toying with**[3] the idea of doing something completely different with my life. The opportunity has finally come, but I need to **size up**[4] the situation before I make my decision.

[3] considering (doing) something, but not very seriously and without making a decision
[4] carefully examine a situation or person in order to make a judgement

Have you heard the rumours about the changes that are going to be **pushed through**[5] at work? I know you've been **singled out**[6] for praise recently, but so has your rival for promotion and I get the feeling that management are trying to **play you off against**[7] each other. I'm worried that the changes may result in her **doing you out of**[8] the promotion you deserve.

[5] made officially accepted
[6] chosen from a large group of people or things, usually in order to criticise or praise them
[7] encourage you to compete/argue with another to get some advantage from this situation
[8] (informal) stopping you from getting or keeping something, in a dishonest or unfair way

I'm sorry to hear about your disagreement with your colleague. It's clear that it's very difficult to **reason with** her, but don't let her **play on**[9] your good nature and don't give in. Do your best to try and **work things out**[10] with her, but if you can't, I think you should consult your boss.

[9] use your fears/weaknesses to make you do what they want, often in an unfair way
[10] think carefully about how you are going to do something and make a plan or decision

B

In these dialogues the second speaker uses a phrasal verb to paraphrase what the first speaker says.

Ahmed	I might say no to the Berlin trip and go to Moscow instead, but I'm not sure.
Julian	So you're **tending towards** the Moscow trip? I thought you might.
Lucy	I think I now agree with you that we should postpone the new product launch.
Stan	Ah-ha! So you've finally **come round** to my way of thinking.
Ryan	That's it. I've decided. I'm going to take the job in Madrid.
Daniela	Good! I'm glad you've **arrived at** a decision at last. You won't regret it.
Dan	So who's going to have the extra ticket? I've got a coin, if you like.
Evan	OK, let's **toss for**[1] it. 'Heads' – you get it, 'tails' – I get it.

[1] throw a coin into the air to see which side lands facing upwards. For British coins, 'heads' means the side with the Queen's head on it; 'tails' is the other side.

Manon	We need to encourage people to join the campaign and work with us.
Charles	Yes, we need to **drum up** more support.

Tip

Do sb **out of** sth is not the only informal phrasal verb with *do*. We also find it in **do in** sb [kill], **do out** sth [decorate], **do** yourself **up** [make yourself look more attractive] and **do without** [manage without something]. Where verbs form groups like this, record them together.

English Phrasal Verbs in Use Advanced

Exercises

29.1 **Find phrasal verbs in A that match these definitions.**

1 play with an idea, consider it but not very deeply ....
2 try to discuss something rationally with someone ....
3 consider something carefully over a period of time ....
4 make up your mind about something ....
5 unfairly deprive someone of something ....
6 evaluate someone or something ....
7 restrict or limit someone ....
8 select one person from a large group ....

29.2 **Answer these questions about the verbs in B.**

1 What do you need if you and a friend agree to make a decision by tossing for it?
2 If someone is tending towards something, have they made a definite decision?
3 What is a *drum* and why do you think it is used metaphorically in collocations like *drum up support* or *drum up business*?
4 If someone comes round to a decision, how quickly did they arrive at that decision?

29.3 **Complete these sentences with a phrasal verb from the opposite page.**

1 If we talk about the problems between us properly, I'm sure we'll be able to ....
   things ....
2 I thought it was very unfair of Mrs King to .... you .... for criticism in front
   of everyone else like that.
3 Although the redevelopment plans are unpopular, the government is determined to ....
   them ....
4 Clara is very keen that her daughters should not .... themselves .... by
   getting married too young.
5 I hope it won't take you too long to .... a decision.
6 If we don't manage to .... some more business soon, we may have
   to close down.
7 Sometimes children seem to be able to sense a new teacher's weakness and they ....
   .... it to their own advantage.
8 If you can't agree on which film to go and see, we'll have to .... it.
9 You don't need to made a decision immediately – take time to .... it ....
10 Saif is only two, but he is already very good at .... his father ....
   .... his mother.

29.4 **Correct the mistakes in these sentences. If there are no mistakes, put a tick at the end of the sentence.**

1 Everyone is trying to dissuade me from taking the job, but I'm tending for accepting it.
2 You'll need to take time to shape up the situation before you decide what to do.
3 Wicked Uncle Fred succeeded in making his brother out of his rightful inheritance.
4 Erica is toying with the idea of going to live in Australia, but I don't think she'll do it.
5 It took Lily ages to get her father to go round to the idea of her training as a bus driver.
6 The careers teacher helps pupils in their final year decide on a career.
7 The advert plays off people's desire to appear young and attractive.
8 I don't want to do the washing-up either. Get a coin and we'll throw about it.

The exclamations on this page are all informal. Be careful with the ones marked * as you risk insulting the person you are speaking to.

A Encouraging others

Eat up!

Take it away!¹

Drink up!

Can I look at your paper?

Sure, go ahead!

Go on then!

Go for it!

Keep it up!

¹ a command used in musical contexts, meaning 'Start playing/singing!'

B Expressing impatience

expression	possible context	you say this in order to …
Roll on (Friday)!	You are in the middle of a very busy week at work.	show that you are looking forward to a time or event
Dream on!	A not very musical friend is telling you about their plans to become a famous rock star.	tell someone that what they hope for is not possible and will not happen
Grow up!*	A member of your family refuses to speak to you.	tell an older child or an adult to stop acting like a small child
Hang on! **Hang about!**	A friend is telling you about a problem when you suddenly think of something that might solve their problem.	tell someone to stop doing or saying something, to wait a minute
Go on!	A friend has just told you that he's been invited to appear in a Hollywood film.	tell someone that you do not believe what they just said (Note: spoken with a falling intonation)
Come on! **Come off it!**	A friend is claiming he plays better chess than you – and you pride yourself on your play.	tell someone you don't believe them or disagree or are angry with them
Wake up!	You are telling someone how to do something but they are clearly daydreaming.	tell someone not paying attention to listen to what you say
Shut up!*	Your two brothers are arguing when you are trying to concentrate.	tell someone to stop talking

Exercises

30.1 **Using exclamations from the opposite page, what could you say to a family member who …**

1 was about to start a race in the hope of breaking a record?
2 was acting in a childish way which was annoying you very much?
3 told you a very surprising bit of news?
4 told you he/she had just seen a flying saucer? (give two possible answers)
5 was in a long-distance race and who was looking very tired and about to give up?
6 was daydreaming and had not listened to something important you just said?
7 said he/she intended to be an astronaut?

30.2 **Complete these sentences with a verb from the opposite page.**

1 .... on the end of term! I'm sick of studying.
2 Oh, ... on! I've just found her number; we can ring her straightaway.
3 .... up, everyone! Your glasses are still half-full. We have to leave now if we're to catch the film!

4
Tim	Can I print something out on your printer?
Mariam	Of course, go ....! You don't need to ask!

5 (Older brother to younger brother) .... up Tom, will you! I'm trying to work out this maths problem.
6 (Emma is standing at the side of the pool)

Emma	Mum, watch me dive in!
Mum	OK, ... on then, but be careful, darling!

7 Come on, ... up, children! Grandma has cooked us a delicious meal.
8 (Singer to guitarist) OK, ... it away! One, two, three!

30.3 **Which exclamations from the list would fit these situations? Use a dictionary if necessary.**

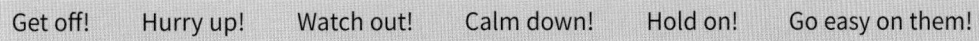

Get off!	Hurry up!	Watch out!	Calm down!	Hold on!	Go easy on them!

1 You think a teacher should treat some students less severely. What might you say?
2 Someone is starting to lose their temper. What might you say?
3 A child is pulling at the clothing of another child, who is getting annoyed. What might the second child say?
4 Someone is about to cross a busy road without looking. What might you say?
5 You are waiting for a friend to arrive to go to the cinema, but he calls you to say he is running late. What might you say?
6 A friend calls with some important information that you need to write down, but you don't have a pen. What might you say to the caller while you find one?

Read these statements by different people talking about their jobs.

The boss

I'll be retiring next year. I already find that I can **farm out**[1] tasks I used to do myself. I'm slowly **easing off**[2] now so that I can **step aside**[3] next year knowing I've left everything in good hands.

[1] give work to other people instead of doing it yourself
[2] starting to work less or do things with less energy
[3] leave a job or position, especially so that someone else can do it

The union representative

We never like to **call** people **out**[4] on strike, but when we do, we have to be determined to **see** it **through**[5] to the end. We have to keep talking constructively and try not to get **bogged down**[6] in lengthy negotiations which only prolong the strike.

[4] order workers to strike
[5] continue doing a job until it is finished, especially when it is difficult
[6] (informal) become so involved in the details of something that you cannot achieve anything

The assembly-line worker

My job is monotonous. I just **slog away**[7] day after day. People like me **get passed over**[8] for promotion, so we're not motivated. I often feel like **packing** this job **in**[9] and finding something else. One day I'll just **hand in** my notice and go.

[7] (informal) keep working very hard, usually for a long time
[8] are not given a higher position because it is given to someone else
[9] (informal) stopping doing something, especially a job

The administrative assistant

In this job you just have to **fling** yourself **into**[10] your work and **beaver away**[11] to get things done each day. I spend a lot of time **running round** helping other people. It's not a bad job, and sometimes I'm allowed to **get off**[12] early if I've stayed late the day before.

[10] start to spend a lot of your time and energy doing something
[11] (informal) work hard at something for a long time, especially something you are writing
[12] leave the place where you work, usually at the end of the day

The scientist

I decided to **go in to** research, as I wanted to do something exciting. I don't think I'm **cut out for**[13] teaching. University was fun, but now I've got to **knuckle down**[14] and build my career.

[13] have the right qualities for something, especially a job
[14] start to work or study hard, especially if you have not been working very hard before can lt find 'buckle down'

The office worker

Well, in this job you just **plug away**[15] and hope the day will pass quickly. If I have to write a report, I do what I can to **cobble** something **together**[16], but I don't ever feel that I achieve anything worthwhile. Most people in my position just **coast along**[17] and dream of the summer holidays.

[15] (informal) work hard at something for a long time
[16] make something quickly and not very carefully
[17] do only the things that you have to do without trying to go faster or be more successful

Exercises

31.1 **Answer these questions about the phrasal verbs in this unit.**

1 Which verb focuses on working with enthusiasm?
2 Which three verbs focus on stopping work?
3 Which two verbs focus on working without using too much energy?
4 Which four verbs focus on working hard?
5 Which verb is based on an animal metaphor?
6 Which two verbs are based on metaphors connected with the land?

31.2 **Rewrite the underlined parts of these sentences using the word in brackets in an appropriate form. Make any other necessary changes.**

1 Louise always <u>approaches</u> her work <u>with great enthusiasm</u>. (FLING)
2 I really think that it is time you <u>applied yourself much more seriously</u> to your studies. (KNUCKLE)
3 As a research scientist, you just have to keep <u>working hard</u> at your experiments <u>over a long period of time</u> and eventually you'll get results. (PLUG)
4 If this morning's meeting goes smoothly, I should be able to <u>leave work</u> by 1 p.m. (GET)
5 The meeting was going well until we got <u>really involved with</u> the details of the sales conference party. (BOG)
6 I'm not sure exactly what I'm going to say in my speech, but I'm sure I'll be able to <u>get something ready</u> by tomorrow morning. (COBBLE)
7 There comes a time when it is best for an older manager to <u>withdraw</u> and let a younger person take over. (STEP)
8 I always say that if you start a job, you should <u>make sure you finish it</u>. (SEE)

31.3 **Correct the six mistakes with particles in this paragraph.**

I'd hate a job where I could just coast about without needing to think about what I was doing. I'd far rather keep busy and really don't mind how much I have to slog off each day. I'd soon pack off any job that didn't keep me working hard. I fling myself onto everything I do. Even when I was at school, I used to beaver up at my homework as soon as I got home from school. My sister certainly never used to knuckle into work in the way I did.

31.4 **Complete these sentences using verbs from the box and the correct particles. Put the verbs in the correct form and make any other necessary changes.**

call	cut	ease	farm	go	hand	pass	run

1 I can't stand the sight of blood, so I'm not really .... nursing.
2 If you hate your job so much, why don't you just .... your notice?
3 When several workers were unfairly dismissed, the trade union official decided it was time to .... on strike.
4 As a PA I spend most of my time .... after my boss.
5 We've had a very busy few months at work, but things are beginning to .... now.
6 Liam is very good at his job, so I can't understand why he always gets .... while less able people get promoted.
7 Our company has started doing a lot of outsourcing, which means that we .... jobs that we previously used to do ourselves.
8 Ever since she was a child she has wanted to .... medicine.

32 Study

A Going through college

Sam and Ben are twin brothers. They have a very rich grandfather who offered to **put** them **through**[1] university. Sam **sailed through**[2] his exams at school and easily **got into**[3] a good university. Ben wanted to go to the same university, but it was harder for him to **get in**. However, in his last few months at school, he managed to **get through**[4] all the necessary exams. Both brothers wanted to **major in**[5] law. Sam had worked in a law firm in several summer holidays and this experience was able to **count towards**[6] his degree. Ben spent his holidays playing sport. Sam continued to study hard and soon **left** most of the other students in his group **behind**[7]. At the end of six months, the professor **creamed off**[8] the best students and **moved** them **up** to the next class. Sam was in this group but Ben was not. The professor felt he was more interested in rugby than law and this **counted against**[9] him. He was **marked down**[10] for careless mistakes in a number of his essays and by the end of the year he had **fallen behind**[11] the rest of his year. His tutor says he'll be lucky if he even **scrapes through**[12] his exams. His grandfather has arranged to come and visit him and Ben is feeling a little nervous.

[1] pay for them to study at university
[2] easily passed
[3] succeeded in getting a place (at a school, college or organisation)
[4] succeed (in an examination or competition)
[5] (US, Aus) study something as their main subject at university
[6] be part of what was needed in order to complete something

[7] made much faster progress than others
[8] separated the cleverest or most skilful people from a group and treated them differently
[9] contributed to his bad marks
[10] given a lower mark
[11] failed to remain level with a group of people that was moving forwards
[12] (informal) passes but only just

B In the library

Let me try to describe this scene in a university library. A girl with long hair is **poring over**[1] a map. Next to her a boy is **skimming through**[2] some books, looking for some information on wind energy for his thesis. At the same table is a girl with short hair, who has **buried** herself **in**[3] a journal. Next to her a boy is **ticking/checking off**[4] names on a list – he's **crossed off**[5] one of them. There is a busy and studious atmosphere in this library and I hope this has **come across**[6] in my description.

[1] studying carefully
[2] reading quickly without studying the details
[3] given all her attention to
[4] writing something next to each item on a list in order to make sure that everything or everyone on it is correct, present, or has been dealt with

[5] removed a word (e.g. name) from a list by drawing a line through it
[6] been expressed clearly enough for the reader to understand it

Exercises

32.1 Match each sentence on the left with a sentence which follows logically on the right.

1 He took three weeks off in the middle of term.   a) He got through all the exams.
2 He didn't read the book thoroughly.   b) He was marked down.
3 He searched the manuscript carefully.   c) He just skimmed through it.
4 He was very successful at college.   d) He fell behind with his work.
5 He didn't keep to the set topic for his essay.   e) He pored over it for hours.

32.2 Complete these sentences using the correct particles.

1 It cost Oscar and Nina a huge amount of money to put three children .... college.
2 Artem sailed .... all his exams at school but found things much harder at university and only scraped .... his final accountancy exams.
3 I'm afraid you'll have to cross my name .... the list for the trip next Saturday.
4 The college basketball team always seems to cream .... the best athletes and other sports suffer as a result.
5 She was so brilliant, she left all the other students ....
6 The end-of-semester marks in each year all count .... your final degree.
7 I like Professor Watson's lectures; they're so clear. His ideas don't come .... nearly as well in his books.
8 He was on the borderline between pass and fail, but his poor attendance on the course counted .... him and they failed him in the end.

32.3 Rewrite each sentence using a phrasal verb based on the word in brackets.

1 As each person arrived she asked their name and put a tick on her list. (check)
2 She picked up her favourite novel and became completely absorbed in it. (bury)
3 He decided to take economics as the main subject for his degree. (major)
4 His tutor transferred him to a higher class. (move)
5 What sort of grades do you need to be given a university place in your country? (get)
6 I applied to Oxford University but I wasn't accepted. (get)

32.4 Make suitable questions which could come before these answers. Use a dictionary if necessary.

1 I'd like to go on to university.
2 I just wanted to take up a new subject; that's why I gave it up.
3 No, she dropped out at the end of the first year.
4 I can't – I'm snowed under. I've got two essays to do for tomorrow.

32.5 Answer these questions about your own experience of study.

1 At school did you usually sail through or scrape through your exams?
2 Have you ever fallen behind with your work?
3 Do you think a teacher has ever marked down your work unfairly?
4 What other things apart from exam results can count towards getting into a good university in your country?

In a lecture

In today's lecture, I'd like to **look at**[1] Sonda's explanation of this phenomenon.

To **start with**[2], I think we need to consider the importance of geographical location.

Hanes has an interesting theory about the relationship between culture and language which **draws on**[3] the results of Kaminsky's research.

Traynor **set out**[4] to test the theory using a range of new technologies which were not previously available.

Because the results are based on a very small sample, we have to **allow for**[5] a significant margin of error.

A study was **carried out**[6] with 152 diabetic patients over a three–year period.

I want to **round off**[7] my talk by returning to the question I asked at the beginning.

To **finish off**[8] today, I'd like to spend some time looking at a couple of previous exam questions.

Finally, I want to **point out**[9] that there is a list of additional sources on this topic on the second page of your handout.

If you didn't **get down**[10] all that information, don't worry. I'll be emailing the list of assignments to you later today.

[1] focus on
[2] begin
[3] uses information from
[4] intended to
[5] take into consideration

[6] done
[7] finish in a satisfactory way
[8] end, complete
[9] highlight
[10] manage to write down

Seminars

● ● ●   ↻ Q ⌂

University help: what you need to know before you go   Campus Freshers Week Student Union Personal Tutor Seminars

Seminars

Seminars are classes with small groups of students and give you the opportunity to **look into**[1] a topic in detail. You can also **bring up**[2] any questions you might have and discuss them with the tutor and other students. Seminars often involve **weighing up**[3] different ideas that were mentioned in your lectures, so it's a good idea to **go over**[4] your lecture notes and other research just before you attend.

Sometimes a student will be asked to **put together**[5] a short presentation, which will be used to start the discussion. If you are presenting, then it's important to carefully **think through**[6] the points you want to make. You don't want to **end up**[7] with nothing to say! However, it's always better to **sketch out**[8] your ideas with rough notes, rather than **writing out**[9] every word of the presentation.

If you are not presenting, you should still try to **read up on**[10] the subject before the seminar in order to **get** the most **out of**[11] it. During the presentation, try to **jot down**[12] any new ideas or key points. And don't forget to **type** them **up**[13] later. You might also make a note of any questions that you want to **follow up**[14] later, either during the seminar or through research afterwards.

[1] investigate
[2] start to talk about
[3] thinking about something carefully, comparing
[4] study again
[5] prepare (by collecting together different elements)
[6] plan carefully
[7] be in a situation (at the end)

[8] roughly plan
[9] write (or rewrite) in full
[10] do background reading on
[11] take benefit from
[12] make a note of
[13] rewrite in full (on a computer)
[14] find out more

Exercises

33.1 **Look at A opposite. Complete the sentences using the verbs from the box and the correct particles. Put the verbs in the correct form.**

allow	carry	draw	finish	point	set	start

1 Zeyneb's experiments were mostly .... in the 19th century using much less sophisticated equipment than is available today.
2 This theory .... research from several well-known scientists.
3 I thought we could read Hayder's research for the seminar tomorrow, but my tutor .... that the original research paper is over 700 pages long!
4 Alexander Fleming didn't .... to discover penicillin when he started experimenting with bacteria, but it was one of the most important discoveries of its time.
5 He spoke for 50 minutes and then .... the lecture with a question and answer session.
6 Firstly, I'd like to .... an introduction to the subject of quantum physics, before moving on to some key definitions.
7 If we .... variations caused by weather conditions, the results are broadly in line with our predictions.

33.2 **Choose the correct alternative to complete these sentences.**

1 Our tutor asked us to put *away / together / off* a report based on what we'd discussed in the seminar.
2 The handout had a list of references so we could read *to / along / up* on the topic before the next lecture.
3 I always *jot down / type up / write out* the key points during a lecture even if there's a handout.
4 When I *sketch out / jot down / type up* my notes later, it helps me remember what I learned.
5 I'm just going to *sketch out / bring up / follow up* my initial ideas for the essay tonight, and then I can work on it in more detail next week.
6 *Think through / Get out of / Follow up* the essay question carefully and identify the issues you need to talk about.
7 It's really important to *end up / follow up / weigh up* all the evidence before presenting your final argument.
8 After a long discussion, we *got out of / ended up / went over* agreeing that the character of Becky Sharp was not likeable, but very interesting.
9 We're going to *end up / go over / get out of* the solutions to the problems in last week's exam and discuss any questions.
10 If you want to *think through / go over / follow up* on the question Jemma asked about game theory, I can recommend a couple of interesting books on the subject.

33.3 **Rewrite each sentence using a phrasal verb based on the word in brackets in an appropriate form.**

1 This morning we're going to focus on Maslow's 'Hierarchy of Needs'. (LOOK)
2 The lecturer highlighted the fact that this research is still in its very early stages. (POINT)
3 To begin, I want to talk about the background to the research. (START)
4 In order to make the most of the seminar, it's a good idea to do the suggested reading beforehand. (GET)
5 Can I borrow your lecture notes? I didn't manage to write down the last few points. (GET)
6 Don't worry about writing every word; just make a note of the key points. (JOT)
7 For next week's seminar, I'd like you all to research one aspect of this theory. (LOOK)
8 I'd like to finish the lecture today with a short video. (ROUND)

33.4 **Correct the mistakes with the particles in these sentences.**

1 The biology department needs undergraduates to help carry through research on plant cells over the summer, and I'm going to apply.
2 The department has just received some funding to look through the links between diet and certain types of cancer.
3 He spent most of the summer working on his thesis but ended out having to change it when some new research came out.
4 The discussion we had last week brought into some very interesting questions about US foreign policy in the 1950s.
5 As you read for on the subject for your essay, don't forget to make a note of useful sources as you go.
6 A group of engineering students from Bristol have set off to prove the strength of plastic by building the largest Lego structure in the world.

This unit contains phrasal verbs which are all suitable for use in formal essays.

A

Read Rebecca's notes for an essay she is going to write on the subject of 'Globalisation'. Her notes contain useful phrasal verbs for essay-writing.

Plan:

Devote a paragraph each **to** opposing arguments

Mention how globalisation often **deprives** workers **of** their rights

But also mention how poorer countries can **profit from** global markets

Relate globalisation **to** other changes (mobility, Internet, etc.)

Refer to recent international gatherings (G8 etc.)

Cater for non-technical readers as well as specialists

What best **sums up**[1] the present situation – give examples/quotes

Things to remember!

- **Aim at** being neutral
- **Base** opinions **on** sound evidence
- Don't let irrelevant details **detract from**[2] the main argument

[1] represents the most typical qualities of something (Note that this is the only verb on this page where the particle can come either before or after the object.)
[2] make something seem less good than it really is or than it was thought to be

B

Look at these extracts from essays where phrasal verbs have been used successfully, helping to create a good written style.

Furthermore, it is a quiet village and basically **consists of** families with very young children.

Democracy is **founded on** the ideal of equality for all citizens. [(always passive) based on a particular idea or belief]

The people have many difficulties to **contend with**: poor soil, inadequate roads and lack of investment. [have to deal with a difficult or unpleasant situation]

Government economic policies have **resulted in** an improved standard of living in the region.

We need to find ways to **improve on** the current system of distribution of goods. [do something in a better way or with better results than when it was done before]

Efforts to **interest** young people **in** the political process often fail. We need to **invest** more thought **in** finding ways of involving young people in politics.

Many people **object to** their leaders treating them as if they were not capable of running their own lives. (Note the -ing form of the verb after **object to**.)

The university has always **insisted on** a high standard of teaching and research.

Exercises

34.1 Look at A. Complete this paragraph with the correct particles.

> 4:21PM
>
> In this essay I intend to discuss the advantages and disadvantages of the information revolution. I shall relate technological change ………… (1) other changes in society, referring extensively ………… (2) the literature in the field. I shall consider how some people, particularly those in wealthier countries, have profited enormously ………… (3) the information revolution. However, I shall also devote considerable attention ………… (4) the way in which some people in poorer societies suffer by being deprived ………… (5) access to the information which others enjoy. I shall then present the mobile phone as the device which seems to sum ………… (6) the essence of the information revolution, basing my opinions ………… (7) the evidence I have presented and aiming always ………… (8) objectivity.

34.2 Complete these sentences using the correct particle and an appropriate ending.

1 The research team consists ....
2 Immigrants to the UK have to contend ....
3 The headteacher would like to interest more pupils ....
4 The examinations board insists ....
5 It is essential that society should invest ....
6 The change in the law resulted ....
7 The government is keen to improve ....
8 The writer's philosophy is founded ....
9 Some critics have objected ....

34.3 Find the only example sentence on the opposite page where the particle could be in a different place. Rewrite that example sentence putting the particle in the alternative position.

34.4 Rewrite each sentence using a word from the box so that it keeps the same meaning. Use each word only once.

| aimed | cater | consists | deprived | detract | devoted | objected | refers | resulted | sum |

1 The teaching materials will bear historians as well as economists in mind.
2 The recent problems in the company are bound to make its reputation less favourable.
3 The policy of clearing the hillsides of trees appears to have led to an increased danger of flooding.
4 There are three players from France, one from Sweden and two from Russia in the football team.
5 Many people did not like being moved from their houses to high-rise flats.
6 Having your freedom taken away from you is a very difficult punishment to endure.
7 In her article, the writer frequently quotes a research study carried out in Canada in 2015.
8 The book has been written for undergraduate students who have little previous knowledge of the subject.
9 For me, this song captures the atmosphere in rural England in the 1980s.
10 Much of the book deals with the writer's experiences in the United States.

> ## Over to you
>
> Choose a subject that you specialise in or are particularly interested in and write a paragraph relating to that subject. Use as many of the phrasal verbs from this unit as you can in your paragraph.

A Structuring a business

Business News in Brief

- Howard Green of M and Q is moving to Paris to **head up**[1] the company's new French operations. Green will also be **looking after**[2] M and Q's interests in Francophone Africa.

- There are growing rumours, as yet unconfirmed, that Scottish Mobiles is planning to **buy out**[3] its rival Celtic Telecom.

- 20-year-old pop star Anastasia is reported to have **set** her parents **up**[4] with the restaurant business they have always dreamed of.

[1] be in charge of (or, simply, head)
[2] responsible for
[3] buy a company (or part of a company) so that you own all of it
[4] given them the money they need to start a business

B Doing business

Here are some useful business collocations or common word combinations using phrasal verbs.

phrasal verb	collocating words	definition of phrasal verb
aim sth **at** sb	a product / programme / magazine at women / young people / students	intend something to influence someone, or be noticed or bought by someone
break into sth	a new market / work in the media / Hollywood	become involved in a type of business or activity that is difficult to become involved in
bring in sb/sth or **bring** sb/sth **in**	customers / clients / new business	attract people, encouraging them to buy products or services
bring out sth or **bring** sth **out**	a new product / a book	produce something to sell to the public
deal in sth	art / shares / drugs	buy and sell particular goods as a business
firm up sth or **firm** sth **up**	arrangements / prices / details	make something more definite or precise or less likely to change
sign up sb or **sign** sb **up**	a new employee / a model / a film star / a basketball player	get someone to sign a document stating they will work for you
turn out sth or **turn** sth **out**	cars / films / computers	make or produce something for sale
turn over sth or **turn** sth **over**	$6 million / £100,000	generate a specific amount of money in a particular period of time

Tip

When you come across a new phrasal verb in a business context – or indeed in any context – it can be useful to note it down with two or three collocating nouns.

Exercises

35.1 Complete this radio interview using words from the box. Use each verb in the correct form only once, unless otherwise indicated.

aim	deal	firm	set	break	head	turn (use twice)	look	bring (use twice)	buy

Interviewer Welcome to our weekly spot 'The two-minute interview'. My guest this week is Gordon Flockheart, chairman and CEO of the Kiros group. Gordon Flockheart, you've .... (1) up several major companies during your long career, most recently the Kiros empire, which .... (2) over more than £500 million last year. What's the secret of your success?

Flockheart Well, first and foremost, I owe a huge debt of gratitude to my grandfather, who .... (3) me up in business at the young age of 24. Since then I have been very fortunate in getting the right people to .... (4) after my interests. Secondly, we .... (5) in high-value, luxury personal goods and we've succeeded in .... (6) into markets where other companies thought they had a monopoly. We've .... (7) out new products at the right time and at the right price, and we've .... (8) them at the higher end of the market.

Interviewer There are rumours that you would like to .... (9) out one of your main rivals, Lasaque. Any truth in that?

Flockheart We are in negotiations with Lasaque, there's no secret about that, but nothing has been .... (10) up yet. The markets will just have to wait and see.

Interviewer There have also been rumours that you are considering selling off your clothing range and focusing on accessories and electronics. Is that true?

Flockheart No, that's just a silly rumour! We're actually .... (11) out more clothing items than ever and have .... (12) in a lot of new customers thanks to our latest range of menswear.

Interviewer There we must leave it. Gordon Flockheart, thank you.

35.2 Complete each of the sentences below with an object from the box. Put it in the correct place or places in the sentence.

10,000 pairs of shoes	a new sports car	modern art	the USA	arrangements
the new department	a young Brazilian footballer		the lower end of the market	

1 Our business has had lots of success in Europe, but now we'd like to break into.
2 Have you heard? Latifa has been asked to head up.
3 Arsenal has signed up.
4 Her father made his fortune by dealing in.
5 Get your people to call my people to firm up.
6 The new factory is already turning out a week.
7 The Alpha model is aimed at.
8 The company is planning to bring out soon.

35.3 Many phrasal verbs can have different meanings in other contexts. Write two sentences illustrating two different ways in which each of these phrasal verbs can be used. Use a dictionary if necessary.

set up	break into	bring in	bring out	turn out

A Coping with money

● ● ●   ✉   Reply   Forward

Hi Sara,

How are you coping financially this term? My parents had to **bail** me **out**[1] last week. I'd **run through**[2] a huge amount of money without realising it and I couldn't pay my fees. But they **coughed up**[3] without a protest. I guess I'll have to **work off**[4] the debt in the holidays. Expensive being a student, isn't it?

Freyda

[1] help a person or organisation to get out of difficulty by giving them money
[2] spent a lot very quickly

[3] (informal) provided money, often unwillingly
[4] reduce the size of a debt by earning money to pay for it

 I can't believe my mobile phone bill. It **gobbles up**[5] a large part of my salary every month. And I've had so many other bills! I've had to **break into**[6] my savings and use money I'd **put by**[7] for the holidays.

[5] (informal) uses a lot of something, especially money

[6] start to use an amount of money that you have been saving
[7] saved in order to use it later

● ● ●   ✉   Reply   Forward

Hi Matthew,

Just back from my trip to South America, which was fantastic, but it **set** me **back**[8] €8,000 and **cleaned** me **out**[9] completely. I was just wondering if you could lend me a couple of hundred euros? I'll **square up**[10] with you when I get my next pay cheque.

Robert

[8] (informal) cost a particular amount of money, usually a large amount
[9] (informal) you used all the money you had on it
[10] (informal) pay somebody the money that you owe them

I **came into**[11] some money recently. My great aunt died and left me a very generous sum and I got a big bonus at work last month, too, so the money's been **rolling in**![12] I'm seriously considering buying a flat and **renting** it **out**.

[11] got money from someone who died
[12] (informal) arriving in large amounts

B Financial services

If you are unable to pay everything in the same month, we'll arrange for your payments to be **carried forward** to the next month.

What are the best ways of **ploughing back**[1] profits into a small business? Call us for advice.

[1] putting money that you have earned into a business in order to make the business bigger or better

If your aim is to **put aside**[2] money regularly, our monthly savings plan enables you to **pay** a regular sum **into** your bank account each month.

[2] save money for a particular purpose

Exercises

36.1 **Answer these questions about the verbs on the opposite page.**

1 Which five verbs in A suggest that a large amount of money is being spent or received?
2 Which three verbs suggest that someone is putting money into a bank account or saving it in some other way?
3 Which two verbs in A suggest that someone is paying back a debt in some way?
4 Which verbs are more informal ways of saying:
a) settle a debt
b) give someone money to help them
c) make someone spend all their money
d) use a lot of money rapidly
5 Which verb relates to earning money from property?

36.2 **Complete these sentences using phrasal verbs from the opposite page.**

1 My parents told me not to rely on them to .... me out if I got into debt.
2 I couldn't pay everything this month, but I've been allowed to carry the remainder .... to next month.
3 The burglars took everything I had; they totally .... me out.
4 Have you managed to .... any money by for the holidays?
5 My car is terribly expensive – it seems to gobble .... all the money I earn.
6 If you can lend me £100, I'll .... up with you when I get paid.
7 Buying property and then .... it out is supposed to be a very good investment.
8 Every birthday, Grandpa gives me some money to .... into my savings account.
9 For the first couple of years, we ploughed our profits .... into the business.

36.3 **Match the beginning of each sentence with its ending, completing each sentence with the correct particle.**

1 It is going to take me ages to work	a) .... more than I had anticipated.
2 For the first few years, we ploughed	b) .... some money on your gran's death.
3 Do try to put a little bit of money	c) .... my student debts.
4 I'm grateful to my mum for coughing	d) .... my savings for as long as I can.
5 You will certainly come	e) .... enormous sums of money.
6 Buying a car unfortunately set me	f) .... enough money for me to buy a car.
7 I want to put off breaking	g) .... all our profits into the business.
8 Chris started gambling and he ran	h) .... each month for a rainy day.

36.4 **Here are some more phrasal verbs relating to money. Work out from the context what they mean and rewrite the sentences replacing the underlined verbs with a word or phrase that means the same.**

1 I never had much money when I was a student but I managed to <u>scrape by</u> somehow.
2 If everyone <u>chips in</u>, then we should be able to afford a nice leaving present for Beth.
3 Rashid's been <u>raking in</u> money ever since he had that brilliant idea for a website.
4 At the bakery it was Amanda's job to <u>cash up</u> at the end of every day.
5 Jason <u>staked</u> a ridiculous amount <u>on</u> a horse race and, needless to say, he lost it all.

36.5 **Answer these questions.**

1 How much did your last holiday set you back?
2 What kinds of things do people usually put money aside for?
3 What, apart from a flat, might gobble up your money?
4 What do you think it is worth breaking into savings for?
5 Who would you ask to bail you out if you had financial problems?

Moving house

● ● ●   ✉   Reply   Forward

Hi Freddie,

I'm just **settling in**[1] to the new house now and beginning to enjoy it. There were so many things that needed doing in the first few days. I had to **chuck away**[2] some old bits of furniture that belonged to the previous owner, **put up**[3] my bookshelves in the study, **smarten up**[4] the living room with a coat of white paint, **wash down** the kitchen walls and units, **put away** all the kitchen things that were still in boxes, **mop up**[5] a pool of oil in the garage, **block up**[6] a suspicious-looking hole that could have been a mouse hole (aargh!) and **put** all the empty boxes **out**[7] in the rubbish. I thought I'd never finish! As I'm writing this I'**ve got** the TV **on** and one of those home-improvement programmes is just about to start. I'm going to switch it off – I can't take any more!

Once I've got the place **straightened up**[8], I'll invite you over for a meal.

Love,

Abigail

[1] becoming relaxed and happy in new surroundings
[2] (informal) get rid of something that is not needed any more (also **chuck out**)
[3] fasten a piece of furniture (e.g. shelves, cupboard) to a wall or assemble something
[4] make a place (or a person) look tidier
[5] use a cloth or a mop to remove a liquid that has been dropped or that has spread
[6] fill a hole so that nothing can pass through it
[7] (common collocation: put the rubbish out)
[8] made tidy

At home

Pull up a chair and come and sit next to me. I want to show you something. [move a piece of furniture (especially a chair) near to something or someone]

The last person to leave has to **lock up**. [lock all the doors and windows of a building when you leave it]

We were sorry to **part with** our old sofa, but our son needed one for his flat. [give something away, usually when you do not want to]

Pull/push the door **to**, will you? It's cold in here. [only used of doors and windows: close or almost close a door or window by pulling it towards you / pushing it]

Here, let me **plump up** this cushion; then you can rest your head on it and relax. [make something (e.g. cushion, pillow) rounder and softer, especially by shaking it]

We'll have to move those bags and shoes; they're just **cluttering up** the hallway. [fill something in an untidy or badly organised way]

We've had the bedroom **done out** in pale green. It's a nice relaxing colour. [decorated (also **done up**)]

This morning I forgot to **clear away** the breakfast things before leaving the house. [remove in order to make a place tidy]

I'm fed up with having to **clean up after** / **clear up after** my flatmates. [remove dirt someone has made / make the place tidy by putting things back where they belong]

> ### Tip
>
> Associating a set of phrasal verbs with a place or a situation (e.g. your house or flat) will help you remember them better.

Exercises

37.1 Look at the pictures and complete the descriptions below with verbs from the opposite page.

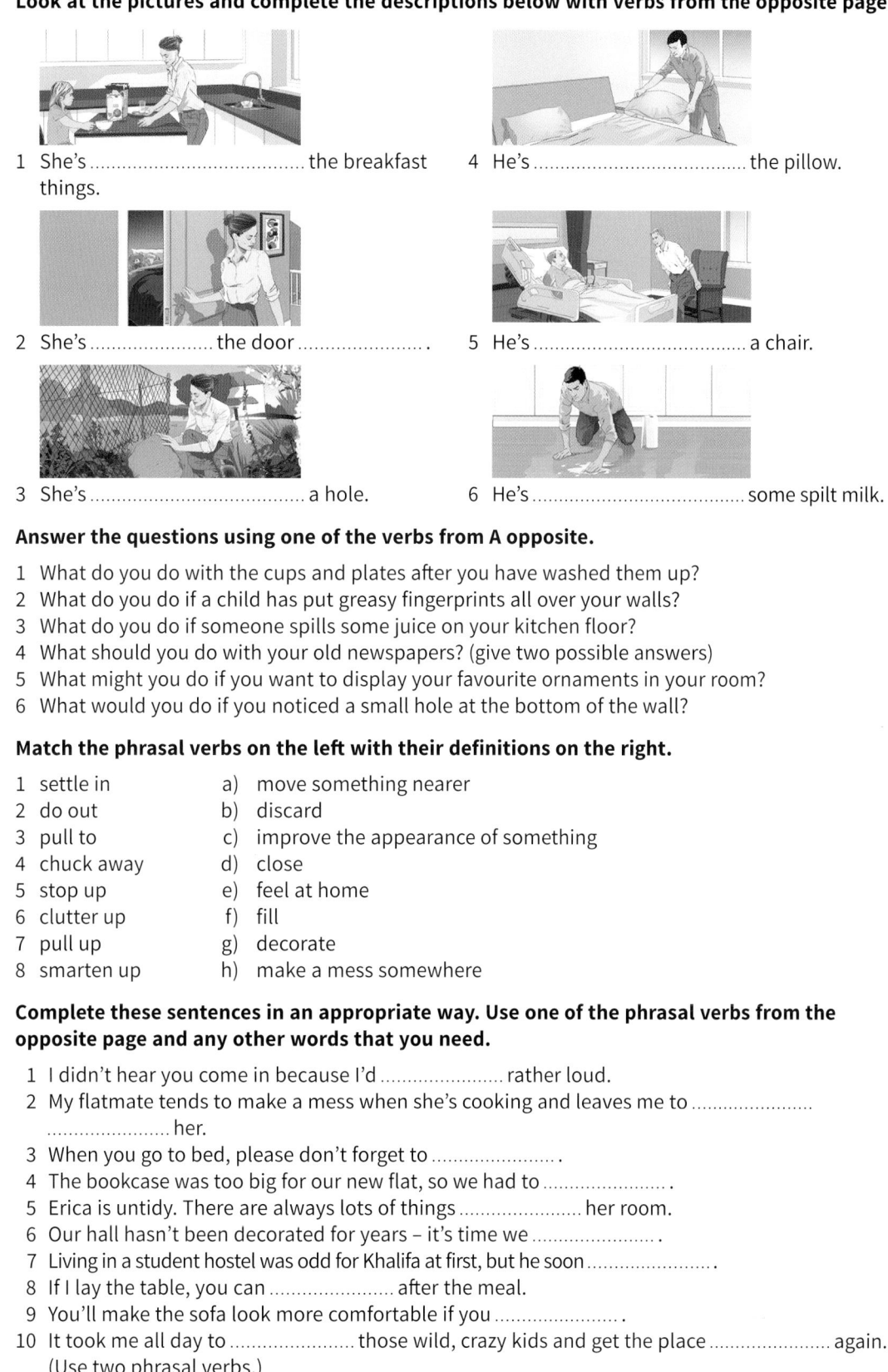

1 She's .... the breakfast things.

2 She's .... the door ....

3 She's .... a hole.

4 He's .... the pillow.

5 He's .... a chair.

6 He's .... some spilt milk.

37.2 Answer the questions using one of the verbs from A opposite.

1 What do you do with the cups and plates after you have washed them up?
2 What do you do if a child has put greasy fingerprints all over your walls?
3 What do you do if someone spills some juice on your kitchen floor?
4 What should you do with your old newspapers? (give two possible answers)
5 What might you do if you want to display your favourite ornaments in your room?
6 What would you do if you noticed a small hole at the bottom of the wall?

37.3 Match the phrasal verbs on the left with their definitions on the right.

1	settle in	a)	move something nearer
2	do out	b)	discard
3	pull to	c)	improve the appearance of something
4	chuck away	d)	close
5	stop up	e)	feel at home
6	clutter up	f)	fill
7	pull up	g)	decorate
8	smarten up	h)	make a mess somewhere

37.4 Complete these sentences in an appropriate way. Use one of the phrasal verbs from the opposite page and any other words that you need.

1 I didn't hear you come in because I'd .... rather loud.
2 My flatmate tends to make a mess when she's cooking and leaves me to ....
   .... her.
3 When you go to bed, please don't forget to ....
4 The bookcase was too big for our new flat, so we had to ....
5 Erica is untidy. There are always lots of things .... her room.
6 Our hall hasn't been decorated for years – it's time we ....
7 Living in a student hostel was odd for Khalifa at first, but he soon ....
8 If I lay the table, you can .... after the meal.
9 You'll make the sofa look more comfortable if you ....
10 It took me all day to .... those wild, crazy kids and get the place .... again. (Use two phrasal verbs.)

38 Clothing and appearance

Actions connected with clothing and appearance

roll up one's sleeves

zip up a jacket

The trousers are too short, so **let** them **down**.

tie back your hair

The trousers are too long, so **take** them **up**.

The children love **dressing up**.

B Dressing up to go out

Lottie is telling Alice about a party she went to.

Lottie	Most people looked really smart – there were some amazing designer outfits – but there was one man in a weird **getup**[1] with a red wig. It looked as if he thought it was a fancy-dress party!
Alice	(laughs) What did you wear?
Lottie	Well, to tell you the truth, it was rather a disaster. I wanted to wear my little black dress, but I had trouble **getting into**[2] it. I didn't realise how much weight I've put on over the past few months. I'll have to **let** it **out**[3] or else lose some weight! When I'd finally squeezed into it, I looked so awful in the mirror I just took it straight off again and **pulled on**[4] my boring old brown dress. You know, the wool one with the full skirt that I've worn a million times.
Alice	Oh, I like that dress.
Lottie	Well, so do I, but it was all creased and I didn't have time to iron it, so I just **smoothed it down**[5] with my hands and hoped for the best. I was so late by this time, I didn't realise till I got to the party that I **had** the wrong colour shoes **on**. I was still wearing my sister's **cast-offs**[6], which go perfectly with my black dress but not with my brown one! But it didn't really matter because when the music started, I **flung** my shoes **off**[7] to dance anyway.

[1] the particular clothing, especially when strange or unusual, that someone is wearing
[2] be thin enough to be able to put your clothes on
[3] make a piece of clothing wider by removing the sewing from the side edges and then sewing closer to the edge of the material

[4] put on clothes quickly
[5] press with your hands in order to make something flat
[6] clothes which have been given to somebody else because the first owner cannot use them any more
[7] removed very quickly

> **Tip**
>
> Remembering a story and the verbs used to describe the events is a good way of learning a series of verbs at the same time.

English Phrasal Verbs in Use Advanced

Exercises

38.1 Answer these questions.

1 What other item of clothing can you roll up apart from your sleeves?
2 What else can you zip up apart from a jacket?
3 Do you know the opposite of zip up? (Clue: it is not a phrasal verb.)
4 Can you think of anything else you might tie back apart from hair? (Clue: don't think of clothing – think of something that might hang down or grow too much.)
5 What other things apart from trousers can be let down or taken up?
6 What do you think you are doing to trousers if you (a) let them out or (b) take them in?
7 What sort of clothes do people put on when they dress up, for example as a famous person, or as someone from another historical age?

38.2 Choose the correct word to complete these sentences.

1 I had no time to think about what I looked like, so I .... on my old jeans.
  a) rolled   b) pulled   c) let   d) took
2 Come on – time to .... up your sleeves and get down to work.
  a) pull   b) zip   c) roll   d) tie
3 Sienna stood up, ... down her skirt and began to address the audience.
  a) smoothed   b) got   c) tied   d) zipped
4 To my embarrassment I suddenly realised that I .... my T-shirt on backwards.
  a) took   b) had   c) got   d) let
5 I ate so much on holiday that I had difficulty .... into my suit today.
  a) pulling   b) dressing   c) getting   d) zipping
6 Do we need to .... up for the party tomorrow?
  a) zip   b) fling   c) tie   d) dress
7 I was so tired that I just .... off my clothes and fell into bed.
  a) rolled   b) got   c) flung   d) let
8 When I was a child I always hated wearing my older brother's ....-offs.
  a) let   b) cast   c) get   d) zip

38.3 Complete these sentences with the correct phrasal verb expression from the opposite page.

1 We were surprised when we arrived at the party because the host was wearing a kind of Superman .... with a mask, cape and blue bodysuit.
2 My ten-year-old daughter loves getting .... in my dresses and high-heeled shoes.
3 Now that I'm pregnant I can't .... any of my clothes.
4 Those trousers look a little tight around the waist. Shall I .... a bit for you?
5 (Father to young child) You'd better .... your jacket .... It's cold outside.

38.4 Answer these questions.

1 Who do children often get cast-offs from?
2 Have you ever gone out with the wrong shoes on?
3 Have you ever had difficulty getting into something you haven't worn for a long time?
4 Do you think a lot about what to put on or do you just pull on the first thing you find?
5 If your jeans needed to be taken up, would you do it yourself or get it done for you?
6 Have you ever had to dress up in fancy dress for a party? If so, who or what did you dress up as?

A Getting to know someone

Daisy   You and Lucas have been **going out together**[1] for ages now, haven't you?

Isabelle   Yes, we have. Longer than I'd ever have imagined when we first met.

Daisy   Why, didn't you like him much at first?

Isabelle   No, I **warmed to**[2] him at once – it was just the odd way we met.

Daisy   Oh, how was that? At a club or at work?

Isabelle   No, we got stuck together in a lift that broke down. That's what **brought** us **together**[3]! We were the only people there, so we soon **struck up**[4] a conversation. We discovered we'd got a mutual friend – Martha Gordon. You know her, don't you?

Daisy   I **know of**[5] her. I've **heard of**[6] her because my brother used to talk about her a lot, but I've never actually met her. She went to work in Australia, didn't she?

Isabelle   That's right. Lucas had just **heard from** her, so he told me all her news and then we got on to all sorts of other things. Anyway, I thought he was really nice.

Daisy   So, you **flirted with**[7] him, no doubt!

Isabelle   Just a little, perhaps. Anyway, by the time they'd repaired the lift he'd asked me to **go out with** him. And that was six months ago!

[1] having a romantic relationship
[2] started to like
[3] caused us to be friendly with each other
[4] started (collocates with *conversation*, *friendship*)
[5] have heard of her but don't know her personally
[6] know a little about her because of being told about her
[7] talked and behaved in a way which shows someone that you are sexually attracted to them

B Relationship problems

○ ● ● ●   ↻ 🔍 🏠

Advice: Relationships

I really like a girl in my English class. I'd love to ask her to **come out** for a coffee, but should I wait for her to make the first move? – Alfie, London   ⊞

I am worried about my partner. He got **mixed up with** some untrustworthy people when he started a new job six months ago. Should I say anything to him? – Grace, Dundee   ⊞

I have been happily married for ten years. However, lately, my wife has been getting more and more distant with me. I now suspect she may be **cheating on**[1] me. What should I do? – Connor, Belfast   ⊞

Last week I made the mistake of telling my daughter-in-law that she **fusses** too much **over**[2] her children. I didn't mean to upset her, just to help. But it has caused a major **bust-up**[3] in our relationship and it's **come between**[4] me and my son too. How can I **patch** things **up**[5]? – Isla, Glasgow   ⊞

My best friend is always **sucking up to**[6] our lecturer. I think she's trying to **butter** her **up**[7] so she gets better grades. It's annoying and unfair. Should I say anything? – Megan, Cardiff   ⊞

[1] (informal) having a sexual relationship with someone else
[2] pays too much attention to
[3] (informal) break (in a relationship)
[4] spoilt the relationship
[5] improve the situation
[6] (informal) trying to make the lecturer like her by doing and saying things that will please her
[7] (informal) be very nice to someone so they will do what you want

Exercises

39.1 **Rewrite the underlined part of each sentence using a phrasal verb from A opposite. Make any other necessary changes.**

1   Marwa   Do you know the novelist Madeleine Parker?

     Alex   No, but I <u>know a bit about her from what one or two people have told me</u>.

2   Robert   I was surprised to hear Nick and Polly have got engaged.

     Anna   I wasn't. They've been <u>having a romantic relationship</u> for two years.

3   Max   Did you see Tim talking to that American girl at the party?

     Will   Yeah, he was <u>chatting to her and behaving in a way which showed he was attracted to her</u> all evening.

4   Harriet   Did you have any success getting to know that dark-haired guy?

     Katie   No. I tried to <u>start</u> a conversation with him, but he wasn't very friendly.

5   Jason   You seem to like the new boss, anyway.

     Andrew   Yes, I <u>started to like him</u> straight away in fact. He's very nice.

6   Sara   Did you and Liam first meet at the tennis club?

     Amber   Yes, you could say it was tennis that <u>caused us to be friendly with each other</u>.

39.2 **Correct the mistakes with the particles in these sentences.**

1   I've never met Antonia Goff, but I know with her because Charles works with her.
2   I had an email last month from Dominic, but I haven't heard to him since then.
3   I think Joe is cheating to me. Somebody saw him out with another girl.
4   Mrs Butler fusses ever so much on her two sons, even though they're adults.
5   Daria spent all evening flirting to her friend's brother.
6   I'm afraid my son is getting mixed up of some bad company at university.
7   Majid struck off a conversation with the person sitting next to him, and the flight passed quickly.
8   Rosa told me about your bust-out with Sebastian.

39.3 **Answer these questions.**

1   Michael and Ella are trying to patch things up. Are things good or bad between them at the moment?
2   If you warm to somebody, do you feel (a) anger towards them, (b) in love with them, (c) a liking for them?
3   If a discussion about money comes between two people, what does it do to them?
4   If you suck up to your teacher, do you (a) say things to annoy him/her, (b) say things to please him/her, (c) respect him/her?
5   If you want someone to do something for you, what could you do to encourage them?
6   If you have a bust-up with someone, do you have (a) a big party to celebrate something, (b) a match or competition to see who's best, (c) an argument causing a break in your relationship?
7   If someone says 'Mary got mixed up with some guy from London', do they think Mary was in a good relationship or an undesirable one?
8   Which is correct in this sentence, *go* or *come*, or both?
    I really like Josh; I wish I had the courage to ask him to .... out with me.

> ## Over to you
>
> Find an example of an article about relationships in a magazine. Make a note of any phrasal verbs that you find in the article and write them down in their context.

A   Talking about negative qualities

Leah   What do you make of Natasha's new boyfriend? He's **getting on**[1] a bit, isn't he?!

Naomi   Yes. He must be at least 20 years older than her. I must say I didn't like him very much. His eyes were **boring into**[2] me and it made me feel uncomfortable.

Leah   I'm glad you felt like that too. He really scared me.

Naomi   Scared you? You need to **toughen up**[3] a bit! You shouldn't let anyone scare you. It's not just his eyes, though, is it? He's so **outspoken**[4]! In fact, he's rude.

Leah   He swore at me the other day. I didn't answer back though. I wouldn't **descend to**[5] his level. And how about the way he speaks about his sister?

Naomi   No wonder she's a bit odd. Having a brother like that would **screw** me **up**[6]!

Leah   I'm amazed Natasha's so keen on him. I **had** her **down as**[7] a sensible person.

Naomi   You know, sometimes I think she's like a teenage girl who needs to **grow out of**[8] needing a father figure. I mean, she's 30, not 13!

[1] (informal, always continuous) becoming old
[2] looking very hard at
[3] become stronger and more able to deal with problems (also transitive: **toughen** sb **up**)
[4] having a tendency to express opinions even though they may offend people
[5] behave so badly

[6] (informal) make someone feel confused and unhappy about their life
[7] (informal) thought that they were a particular type of person (especially when they are not in fact like that)
[8] stop doing something as you get older

B   Talking about positive qualities

Look at this speech by a company manager at a party for a colleague who is retiring.

Jack is leaving us today and I want to wish him a happy retirement. Having worked closely with him, I can personally **vouch for**[1] his unswerving loyalty to the company over the last 21 years and his extraordinary skills as a personnel manager. Right from the beginning, his ability to handle people **shone through**[2]. He **prided** himself **on**[3] the good relations he enjoyed with junior staff; he knew that good relationships mean everything in the workplace. It was always such a pleasure to see how his face would **light up**[4] whenever he managed to solve a tricky personnel issue; for him, resolving a difficult situation was its own reward. Jack was also excellent at **drawing out**[5] younger, less experienced members of staff, and he showed that rare talent for **bringing out**[6] the best in all his colleagues. I'm sure everyone would agree that he always **came across**[7] as calm, professional and committed to his staff. His departure will be a great loss to the company.

[1] say that you know someone and that you can promise that they have a good character or good skills
[2] became apparent
[3] took pride in

[4] look very happy
[5] helping people to feel more confident
[6] making qualities more noticeable
[7] appeared to be

> ### Tip
>
> Note how the meaning of a phrasal verb can sometimes vary depending on whether it is used with an object or not. For example, **come across** (see above), when it is used with an object means 'find or meet something/somebody by chance': *I **came across** an old photo of us when we were at university the other night.* Make a note of any verbs whose meanings change in this way.

Exercises

40.1 Look at these pages from Georgia's private diary, where she writes about people she knows and works with. Complete the text using phrasal verbs or adjectives from A opposite.

MON 17

The affair with Chloe seems to have .... (1) Hugo up quite badly – he seems so unhappy and confused. He'll have to .... (2) up if he's to cope with life and all the horrible things that can happen when you're in love. Poor man.

WED 19

Funny, I .... (5) Ava down as a fairly .... (6) person, but she's actually the complete opposite, quite shy and quiet when you get to know her better. The good thing is she seems to have .... (7) out of her girlish infatuation with that stupid man Henry at last. I guess she's more mature now she's turned 30!

TUE 18

Spent the evening with Victoria and her new partner. I don't know how old Simon is, but he's definitely .... (3) on a bit and his hair's going grey.

Bad day at the office – some documents got lost. The boss suspected me and Evie. His eyes just .... (4) into us in a very accusing way and he questioned us for a long time.

THU 20

Lydia and I almost had a serious row last night. She insulted me a couple of times and I felt furious, but I refuse to .... (8) to her level, even though it would be easy enough!

40.2 Complete these annual appraisal summaries, written by a personnel manager, with the correct particles.

1 Zoe sometimes comes .... as a little aggressive, but in general she has good relations with her colleagues and seems to bring .... the best in the staff she manages.
2 Elizabeth has had to overcome a great deal due to her physical disability, but her determination and will to succeed always shine .... despite the difficulties.
3 Luke prides himself .... his ability to cope with huge amounts of stress and to meet deadlines. He has always met deadlines, though I can't personally vouch .... his ability to deal with a major crisis.
4 It's always so nice to see how Cameron's face lights .... whenever he is praised for his achievements, and he has had some notable successes in the last 12 months. Let's hope it continues that way.
5 Louis is very good at drawing .... the shyer and less confident members of staff. He seems like an excellent candidate for promotion in the next round.

Over to you

Try and find some job advertisements in English. Job descriptions often refer to personal qualities needed for the job. Note any phrasal verbs you find.

41 Feelings

A

Note the phrasal verbs connected with feelings.

● ● ●　　✉　Reply　Forward

Hi Francesca

I don't know what I'd do without your support. At the moment, I'm finding it hard to **summon up**[1] the energy to get out of bed in the morning. I don't know if I've **gone off**[2] the idea of making a career as a singer or if I just **don't care for**[3] the type of music the band is playing now. I feel as if the band leader **has got** something **against**[4] me and is trying to **turn** the other members of the band **against**[5] me too. I know I need to **loosen up**[6] and that I mustn't **work** myself **into**[7] a state about it – staying calm and confronting him is the only way to resolve the situation – but I feel so low, I can't face it.

Love Phoebe

● ● ●　　✉　Reply　Forward

Hi Phoebe

I understand just how low you're feeling, but you can **snap out of**[8] it and not **give in to**[9] all these negative thoughts! I know you, and I know you can get through this. I think you're secretly **hankering after**[10] a change and perhaps leaving the band would be a good idea. If you do decide that's the best way forward, I'm sure you'll soon **perk up**[11] and be your usual self, **brimming with**[12] enthusiasm for everything!

Love Francesca

[1] find (used about someone trying hard to find a quality that is needed)
[2] (UK, Aus) stopped liking
[3] don't like
[4] dislikes for some reason
[5] make others dislike
[6] relax mentally
[7] make myself feel very upset

[8] (informal) force yourself to stop feeling sad or upset
[9] if you give in to an emotion, you stop trying not to feel it and you allow your actions to be controlled by that emotion
[10] wanting very much
[11] become happier or more energetic
[12] filled to capacity with

B

Note how the second speaker uses a phrasal verb to paraphrase the first.

Erica	Bella was very angry. She was almost crying.
Julian	Yes, it was obvious she was **choking back**[1] her anger and **fighting back**[2] the tears.

[1] forcing herself not to show her feelings　　[2] trying hard not to show an emotion

Will	Armand looked so surprised when he received his leaving gift, didn't he?
Paula	Yes, I think he was **bowled over** by everyone's generosity.
Zara	Molly suddenly started talking uncontrollably about her emotions.
Luke	Yes, she let it all **spill out**, didn't she?
Ellie	You didn't look physically and mentally able to tolerate such a long meeting.
Rosie	No, I wasn't **feeling up to** it. I'd had a cold and was feeling tired and weak.
Aisha	I was very sorry to hear that Isaac's mother has died.
Natalie	Yes, poor man. My sympathies **go out** to him and his family.
Salim	I think the news shocked Imogen and really upset her.
Ollie	Yes, it obviously **shook** her **up** a lot.
Ruby	I felt so sad as I stood at the War Memorial.
Evelyn	Yes, an overwhelming feeling of sadness **came over** everyone.
Emma	We should stay calm and not do or say anything stupid.
Jack	Yes, we mustn't let our emotions **run away with** us.

Exercises

41.1 Complete these sentences with a verb from A.

1 When you came for the job interview, you were .... with self-confidence.
2 I just couldn't .... up the courage to tell my boss I wanted a pay rise.
3 Please try to .... up and look a bit more cheerful before our visitors arrive.
4 Mia has a nervous disposition but usually manages not to .... in to her fears.
5 She's .... after a major career change, so she might go back to university.
6 Try not to .... yourself into a state about everything; calm down.
7 I've really .... off football recently. I used to love it, but now it just bores me.
8 Stop being so bad-tempered. Just .... out of it!
9 He was very nervous at the beginning of his presentation, but he .... up after a minute or two.

41.2 Which verb in B matches each definition?

1 force yourself not to show some feeling ....
2 begin to affect ....
3 surprise or please a lot ....
4 make someone feel shocked or upset ....
5 encourage us to do foolish things ....
6 feel physically and mentally strong enough to do something ....

41.3 Which phrasal verb from the opposite page fits each set of collocations?

1			3	
to	anger		to	an easy life
	tears			(a) change
	disappointment			a fast car

2			4	
	charm			excitement
to be .... by someone's beauty			to	enthusiasm
	generosity			self-confidence

41.4 Read the remarks about different people and then answer the questions below.

Keira doesn't care for her boss.   Felix can't snap out of his bad mood.

Joel was quite bowled over by the news.   Hannah tried her best to choke back her tears.

Harvey ought to perk up a bit.   Sofia is turning people against the boss.

Poppy is brimming with anticipation.   Aaron has something against his teacher.

1 Who is feeling down?
2 Who is finding it hard to change how he feels?
3 Who is feeling dislike?
4 Who is making people dislike someone?
5 Who wanted to cry?
6 Who dislikes someone for a reason that is not apparent?
7 Who was very surprised about something?
8 Who is really looking forward to something?

41.5 Rewrite each sentence using the word in brackets.

1 Layla let her feelings become very obvious. (SPILL)
2 Grandma doesn't think she could manage a long flight. (FEEL)
3 We must not allow our feelings to make us do something we'll regret. (RUN)
4 You mustn't let those feelings of insecurity take over. (GIVE)
5 Everyone suddenly felt very tired. (CAME)
6 We extend our sympathies to all the victims of the disaster. (GO)

Social and emotional commitments

● ● ●   ✉   Reply   Forward

Hi Nicholas,

What did you **get up to**[1] at the weekend, anything exciting? We had quite a nice weekend here. It was my mum's birthday, so my sister and I **treated** her **to**[2] a night out. We **took** her **out** for dinner on Saturday, and then we **went on to** a jazz club because she's a great jazz fan.

Mansour

[1] (informal) do   [2] paid for her to do something pleasant

● ● ●   ✉   Reply   Forward

Hi Mansour,

Glad to hear you had a nice weekend. I did too. I was passing by an old friend's place on Sunday, so I **called in on**[3] him. Luckily he was at home. We didn't do anything special, just **hung out**[4] and chatted.

Nicholas

[3] visited for a short time, usually   [4] spent time together not doing anything special
on your way to somewhere else

● ● ●   ✉   Reply   Forward

Hi Holly,

It's just one big **letdown**[5] after another in my love life at the moment. The day after we had that terrible row, Kian **dropped by**[6] and persuaded me to agree to him **taking** me **out**[7] for a meal last night. I thought it would be a chance for us to forget everything, you know, and **move on**[8]. I should have refused, but I said yes, and then he stood me up again. He phoned afterwards and gave some feeble excuse and now he's all romantic again and wants to meet up. I know what you're going to say – it's your fault, **deal with** it, and say no. Is that right?

Flora

[5] disappointment   [7] going somewhere and doing something with someone,
[6] made a short visit to someone,   usually something you have planned or paid for
    usually without arranging it   [8] go forward in one's life and not look back to the past

Other aspects of social life

We're having a small **get-together** at our place on Saturday night. Would you like to come? [informal social gathering]

Shall I call Amelia and see if we can **hook up with** her and Nancy and go clubbing? [(informal) meet someone for a particular purpose]

It's six o'clock. I'd better **shoot off** or I'll be late for dinner. [(informal) leave]

Wow, that was a fantastic meal. I'll need a couple of days to **sleep** it **off** now, though! [sleep until you feel better, especially after too much alcohol or food]

Loads of people **rolled up** to see Theo's band at Zino's last night. [arrived at a particular place or event – when people **roll up** somewhere, they often arrive late] They had to **turn** people **away** as there wasn't enough room. [refuse to allow them to enter]

I'm really **getting into** snowboarding. It's amazing. [becoming involved in an activity]

Let's invite Dan too. We mustn't forget him just because he's **moved away** from the village.

Exercises

42.1 Complete the phrasal verbs or phrasal expressions in the second speaker's answers.

1 **Mark** Do you still find it difficult living on your own?

   Jules Well, I've just got to .... with it and .... on. It's no good living in the past.

2 **Hamza** Was the concert as good as you expected?

   Steve No, it was a big .... Very poor. A complete disappointment.

3 **Maksim** Can't you stay for dinner? We've got loads of food.

   Archie No, I'd better .... off now; I've got a report to do for tomorrow morning.

4 **Eliza** Seth, how nice to see you! I wasn't expecting a visit!

   Seth Well, I was just .... by so I thought I'd come and say hello.

5 **David** How was Henry's birthday celebration?

   Rachel Well, we all .... up expecting a big party, but there were only a few members of his family there.

42.2 Answer these questions.

1 If someone says they've been getting seriously into bird-watching, what do they mean?
2 If someone asks you what you got up to over the summer, what do they want to know?
3 If someone said they were having a family get-together, what would be happening?
4 If someone says to you, 'Let's just hang out', what do they want to do?
5 If someone said they wanted to take you out, is it likely they want to (a) kill you, (b) go out with you and pay for you, (c) go with you to show you the way out of a building?

42.3 Read these remarks by different people and then answer the questions below.

Hessa Alexander dropped by the other day.

Lara It would be nice to hook up with Jake and Liam.

Amy Mum and Dad treated me to a wonderful weekend in Paris.

Callum I'll need a week to sleep off that dinner!

Ivy I got turned away from that restaurant once.

Thomas I moved away from Hobblethorpe because I needed a change.

Jessica It'd be nice to call in on Alejandro when we're in town.

Ronnie After the meal we went on to a really great club.

1 Who had far too much of something?
2 Who was not allowed to enter somewhere?
3 Who wants to visit someone?
4 Who went to live in a different place?
5 Who was visited by someone?
6 Who was already out somewhere and then went somewhere else?
7 Who wants to meet someone?
8 Who had a nice time and didn't have to pay?

A   Talking about how you are

Mrs Smith   How are you these days? Have you managed to **throw off**[1] that cold you had when we last met?

Mr Jones   Well, yes, it **cleared up** after a couple of days, but I'd no sooner **got over** that than I **picked up** another one. It's horrible. I keep **breaking out in**[2] a sweat and my nose is completely **bunged-up**[3].

Mrs Smith   Well, I hope you don't **pass** it **on** to me. I'm feeling bad enough as it is. My arthritis has **flared up**[4] again. And you know I fell and cut my hand a week ago? It's only just started to **heal up**[5] and the swelling hasn't **gone down**[6] yet.

Mr Jones   I think we should both go to the doctor's again, don't you?

[1] (informal) get rid of a slight illness
[2] (of sweat, spots, rash) suddenly appears on the skin
[3] (informal) blocked

[4] (of illness) returned
[5] become covered by new skin
[6] returned to its normal size

B   Feeling tired

There are a lot of phrasal verbs in English relating to the idea of sleep and feeling tired. For example, **drop off** and **nod off** are both informal and both mean fall asleep, but **nod off** is used particularly about situations when you did not intend to fall asleep.

Here are some more phrasal verbs relating to being very tired.

phrasal verb	phrasal adjective/noun	definition of phrasal verb	example
wear out sb or **wear** sb **out**	**worn out**	make someone very tired	Going round the shops all day has **worn/tired/wiped** me **out** / **done** me **in**.
tire out sb or **tire** sb **out**	**tired out**		What a day I've had! I am **worn out** / **tired out** / **done in** / **wiped out**!
do in sb or **do** sb **in** (informal)	**done in** (informal)		
wipe out sb or **wipe** sb **out** (informal)	**wiped out** (informal)		
burn out	**burnt-out** (noun = **burnout**)	become so ill or tired that you can't work creatively, because of overwork	Don't work too hard – or you'll **burn out** before you're 30!
	washed out	tired, pale and ill	What's the matter with Kay? She looks **washed out**.

C   At the doctor's

Don't worry. There's a lot of it **going around**[1]. I'll put you on some tablets to help you sleep. They should **knock** you **out**[2]. Keep taking them for at least a fortnight – you shouldn't **come off** them until I say so. This particular bug **takes** a lot **out of**[3] you, so when you begin to feel better, make sure you eat lots of fruit and vegetables to **build** yourself **up**[4].

[1] a lot of people are complaining of this
[2] make you sleep heavily

[3] makes you feel very weak
[4] make yourself stronger

Exercises

43.1 **Rewrite the underlined parts of these sentences using a phrasal verb or phrasal expression from the opposite page. Make any other necessary changes.**

1   Doctor   So, how can I help you today?

       Patient   I think I've <u>caught</u> a chest infection. I'm coughing and wheezing a lot.

2   Doctor   When did you first notice the problem?

       Patient   Well, <u>a rash suddenly appeared</u> on my neck about a week ago.

3   Doctor   And what's troubling you, Mrs James?

       Patient   Well, I had an ear infection about a month ago. It seemed to <u>disappear</u> when I took the antibiotics you gave me but now it's <u>returned</u> again.

4   Doctor   Mr Kelly, hello, how are things?

       Patient   Well, OK, but my nose is <u>blocked</u> all the time. Can you give me something for it?

5   Doctor   Miss Peters, what can I do for you?

       Patient   Well, I sprained my ankle a week ago, but the swelling hasn't <u>diminished</u> and it's still painful.

6   Doctor   Right, Mr Troy, what's troubling you?

       Patient   Well, I just feel absolutely <u>exhausted</u> all the time. I have no energy at all.

43.2 **Read the remarks about different people and then answer the questions below.**

Bethany   I just can't seem to throw off this cold.

Teddy   I hope Bethany doesn't pass on her cold to me.

Grace   I'm getting over the flu now.

William   My scar is healing over nicely now.

Natasha   This bronchitis is taking a lot out of me.

Elliot   I know I look really washed out.

Harry   I feel totally burnt out.

Daniel   I keep nodding off and missing parts of the TV show.

1   Who is feeling weak because of an illness?
2   Who is ill but getting better?
3   Who is feeling sleepy?
4   Who is finding it difficult to get better?
5   Who is completely exhausted from overwork?
6   Who is pale, ill and tired?
7   Whose skin is looking better?
8   Who is keen not to catch someone else's illness?

43.3 **Match the beginning of each sentence with its ending.**

1   The doctor put me
2   I've come
3   The tablet knocked me
4   I found it difficult to
5   There's a lot of flu going
6   I'm quite weak, so I need to build
7   I feel worn

a) out and I slept deeply.
b) out from all that work.
c) off the antibiotics.
d) myself up a bit.
e) on a course of antibiotics.
f) drop off last night.
g) around right now.

> ## Over to you
> Find a magazine article on a health issue and make a note of any phrasal verbs that are used in it.

A Phrasal verbs referring to actions or positions of the body

It was very cold and we **huddled up** together to keep warm.

Dylan **stuck** his head **out** of the window to see what was happening in the street below.

During the dance we had to **spread** our arms **out** and go round in a circle.

She **stretched out** her hand to try to reach the fruit.

The cat **curled up** on the sofa and went to sleep.

Molly **bent down** to pick up the puppy.

B More phrasal verbs connected with the body

phrasal verb	definition of phrasal verb	example
loosen up / warm up	prepare your muscles for a physical activity by stretching and doing simple exercises	We always do exercises to **loosen up / warm up** before playing tennis.
swing around/ round	suddenly turn around so that you can see someone or something behind you	I **swung round** when I heard my name and saw Jude running towards me.
tense up	if you tense up, your muscles stiffen because you are not relaxed	'Relax! Don't **tense up** and you'll float!' said the swimming instructor.
thaw out	(slightly informal, metaphorical) become warmer after getting very cold	'Oooh! It was freezing outside! Turn the heater on! I need to **thaw out**.'
waste away	gradually get thinner and weaker, usually because of illness	Poor old Mrs Jones is just **wasting away**. She's been so ill, poor woman.
pick yourself **up**	stand up again after you have fallen	(Parent to child who has just fallen) 'Come on, **pick** yourself **up**! Don't cry! You're OK.'
double up **double over**	suddenly bend your body forwards because you are laughing a lot or in a lot of pain	When she told me, it was so funny I just **doubled up** laughing.
turn around/ round (sb/sth) or **turn** (sb/sth) **around/round**	turn so that you are facing the opposite direction, or make someone or something do this	(to somebody who is trying on a skirt) '**Turn around**, let me see it from behind.' He **turned** the car **around** and drove back home.

Exercises

44.1 **Look at A. Match the beginning of each sentence with its ending.**

1 If you all huddle up together
2 If you stretch out your arm
3 Spread out your arms
4 Now bend down
5 If you stick your head out of the window
6 You can curl up in the armchair

a) the horse will take the carrot from your hand.
b) you'll be able to see our car.
c) and go to sleep if you like.
d) you'll feel a bit warmer.
e) and move them in circles.
f) and touch your toes.

44.2 **Answer these questions using one of the phrasal verbs from B.**

1 What do you normally need to do before starting on an exercise routine?
2 If you have been outside for a long time on a very cold day, what may it take you some time to do when you go indoors again?
3 What do you have to do if you fall over?
4 What do you do if you hear a sudden noise behind you?
5 What happens to your muscles if you are feeling very anxious?
6 What happens if someone doesn't eat enough over a long period of time?
7 If you suddenly have an excruciating pain, what may you do?

44.3 **Correct the five particle mistakes in this paragraph.**

I'm rather worried about my neighbour. I saw her the other day in the garden and she was doubled out in pain. She also looks as if she is wasting off. I asked her about it and she said she was just trying to lose some weight, but she clearly didn't like my talking about it and I could sense her tensing in. I think she's probably been doing far too much exercise. She spends hours outside bending away to touch the ground or spreading off her arms and swinging them in circles. I can see that she's in pain and I long to tell her to relax a bit.

44.4 **Rewrite each sentence using the verb in brackets in an appropriate form.**

1 You must be freezing – do come inside and get warm. (THAW)
2 Look at me – now face in the opposite direction. (TURN)
3 Their daughter was lying in a little ball on her bed with her thumb in her mouth. (CURL)
4 He put his arm out of the window and waved at us. (STICK)
5 If you don't eat more, you'll get far too skinny. (WASTE)
6 The stand-up comic was so good that we spent the evening in fits of laughter. (DOUBLE)

44.5 **Explain the play on words in these sentences.**

1 The twins doubled up laughing.
2 The rubbish collectors were wasting away.
3 The grammar teacher tensed up when Maria said 'writed' instead of 'wrote'.
4 The taxi driver picked himself up after he tripped over the suitcase.

45 How people speak

A

In these dialogues, the second speaker uses a phrasal verb in their response.

Parent Go and study! You haven't done any revision yet this week! Did you hear me?

Child OK, OK! Don't **go on at**[1] me! I'll do some work after supper.

[1] criticise someone continuously

Jackson Can you explain to me what we have to do at the meeting?

Paul OK, I'll just **run through**[2] the main points.

[2] explain or read something to someone quickly

Austin You can have two hours for your presentation.

Maya Two hours is far too long! I'd bore everyone stupid. I wouldn't want to listen to anyone **holding forth**[3] for that long.

[3] talking about a particular subject for a long time, often in a way that other people find boring

Archie How do you think we should present our case to the committee?

Eloise I think we should emphasise the good things and perhaps just **gloss over**[4] the difficult bits.

[4] avoid discussing something, or discuss something without talking about the details in order to make it seem unimportant

Albert How can we distract Richard while I bring in his present?

Lauren Well, I'll **engage** him **in conversation**[5] and you can leave the room discreetly.

[5] try to start a conversation with him

B

Look at these sentences with more phrasal verbs connected with speaking.

Mr Holroyd **reeled off** a list of names. [(informal) said a long list of things quickly and without stopping]

The detectives tried to **wring** the truth **out of** the suspect. [force or persuade someone to give you money or information]

The reporters **bombarded** the minister **with** questions. [directed a lot of something at one person]

Somebody raised their hand to **put** a question **to** the speaker.

I didn't really have a conversation with her. She just **talked at** me for an hour. [talked to someone without listening to them or allowing them to speak]

Without thinking, he **blurted out** the name of the hotel where the star was staying. [said something suddenly and without thinking, especially because you are excited or nervous]

I'll introduce the plan in general and then you can **expand on** it.

In the middle of my welcome speech I just **dried up**. [stopped speaking, especially because you suddenly forget what to say next]

The teacher kept asking him questions but he was nervous and he just **clammed up**. [(informal) became silent or refused to speak, usually because of shyness or fear]

I'd like to get a flat of my own but I'll have to **sound** my parents **out** first. [talk to someone to discover what they think about an idea or plan]

We were talking about the Olympics and that **led into** a discussion about drugs.

Are you going to tell the truth or do I have to **drag** it **out of** you? [make someone tell you something that they do not want to tell you]

Exercises

45.1 **Rewrite the underlined part of each sentence, using one of the phrasal verbs in A.**

1 It's so boring listening to Uncle Ed <u>lecturing us</u> about the problem with the youth of today.
2 I'll try to <u>get into a conversation with your father</u> so he won't notice you leaving.
3 I wish my parents would stop <u>criticising</u> me all the time.
4 OK, before everyone starts working, I'd like to quickly <u>remind you of</u> the instructions.
5 The personnel manager <u>said very little about</u> salary progression during our interview.

45.2 **Read the sentences and then answer the questions.**

1 After Josie got back from the party, her flatmates bombarded her with questions.
   Did Josie's flatmates ask her a lot of questions or a few questions?
2 Towards the end of the play, one of the main actors suddenly dried up.
   Would the actor have been pleased with his performance or not?
3 Nathan reeled off the names of all 50 states of the USA.
   Did Nathan have to pause and think of the name of each state?
4 Jensen clammed up as soon as Bobby came in the room.
   Did Jensen speak more or less after Bobby arrived?
5 The detective eventually managed to wring his attacker's name out of the boy.
   How easy was it for the detective to get the boy to tell her the truth?
6 Matt decided to sound out the editor before he started to write the article.
   What do you think Matt talked to the editor about?
7 Blake has a dreadful habit of talking at people.
   Why is this habit of Blake's dreadful?
8 Daniela glossed over the accident when she was telling her parents about her trip.
   What did Daniela tell her parents about the accident?

45.3 **Complete these sentences using a phrasal verb from the opposite page.**

1 Now, who'd like to .... the first question to our guest speaker?
2 In this essay I shall first outline three key issues. I shall then expand .... each of these in turn.
3 Our discussion of modern education soon .... into an argument about whether schools are better now than they used to be.
4 I'd love to join your expedition to the North Pole, but I should .... my boss out first.
5 My son doesn't tell us much about school. We have to drag things .... of him.
6 The children were so interested in the topic that they .... their teacher with questions.
7 Sadie just .... up whenever I tried to get her to talk about her work.
8 During the press conference, she was nervous and unintentionally .... out the name of the secret agent.

45.4 **Here are some more phrasal verbs connected with ways of speaking. Can you work out what they mean and rewrite the sentences, replacing the underlined verbs with your own words?**

1 Finn was so rude – he <u>cut in on</u> the conversation I was having with Faye about her new job and started to ask her questions about her daughter.
2 I don't know how you'll manage to <u>explain away</u> the scratch on your mother's car.
3 I wish he'd stop <u>wittering on</u> about the weather – it's so boring.

`Over to you`

Look up the verbs from exercise 45.4 in a good dictionary. Write down some more examples of how they are used.

A Coming and going

The boy **stole away** while his parents were sleeping. [left quietly without anyone knowing]

I'm sorry! I only **crept up on** you for a joke. I didn't mean to frighten you. [approached someone so quietly they did not know you were there till the last moment]

My landlord told us that if we didn't **clear out** of the flat by the end of the week, he'd contact his lawyer. [(informal) leave]

I'm terribly sorry for **walking in on** your private meeting! [going into a room and seeing what someone is doing when they do not want to be seen]

B Moving with other people

phrasal verb	definition of phrasal verb	example
drop back	move to a position nearer the back	Joseph started out in the lead in the race but soon **dropped back** to fifth place.
hang back	not move forwards with other people, usually because you are shy or afraid	The others rushed forward to see the tiger but I **hung back**.
pile into / out of	(informal) enter/leave a place or vehicle quickly and not in an organised way	The schoolchildren **piled into** / **out of** the bus.
squash up	(informal) move closer together in order to make space for someone else	If you **squash up**, there'll be room for Tim on the sofa too.
gain on sb/sth	get nearer to someone or something that you are chasing	The helicopter could see that the police car was **gaining on** the robbers' car.

C A long walk

● ● ●

✉   Reply   Forward

Hi Gemma!

We're having a great holiday. Yesterday we went for a long walk in the hills. It was longer than it needed to be because Ivan misread the map. We walked quite a long way but then came to a big cliff and had to **double back**[1]. We saw lots of wildlife. In the early evening we **stumbled on**[2] some deer. At first they were startled and **drew back**[3] from us into the forest, but we **stood** well **back** so as not to frighten them and they soon relaxed and went back to their grazing. We stood still and watched them for some time. We suddenly realised that it was starting to get dark and that we'd better **push on**[4]. We were **zipping along**[5] until I **tripped over**[6] a fallen branch. I thought I might have sprained my ankle, but we managed to get back to our cottage in time to have a late supper and it's fine today.

Seb

[1] go back in the direction we'd come from
[2] found/met by chance
[3] moved away because they were surprised or afraid

[4] continue on our walk
[5] (informal) moving very quickly
[6] fell because I accidentally hit my foot against something while walking

Exercises

46.1 **Complete these sentences using the correct particles.**

1 I accidentally walked .... Max and Isla the other day at the office, and they were having a terrible row about something!
2 They stole .... in the middle of the night; nobody knew they had left.
3 I looked in the rear-view mirror and saw that the mysterious motorcyclist was gaining .... me.
4 We all piled .... the car, but we had to squash .... as it was only small and there were five of us.
5 Oh! I didn't realise you were there! You shouldn't creep .... me like that!

46.2 **Complete these sentences with a verb from the opposite page.**

1 We all .... into the taxi and headed off to a club to end our perfect night out.
2 Old Mrs Gifford .... over the edge of the carpet and fell and hurt her ankle.
3 I don't think we have time to stop for lunch; we'd better .... on if we want to get there before it gets dark.
4 The fire chief told everyone to .... well back as there was the risk of an explosion.
5 The message warned them to .... everyone out of the building as quickly as possible.
6 When I was putting some books in the attic, I .... on an old picture I hadn't noticed before.
7 Crossing the valley, we were .... along, but then the car suddenly broke down as we went up a hill.
8 I suddenly realised I'd left my wallet in the café where we'd stopped for breakfast, so we had to .... back.

46.3 **Explain the play on words in these sentences. Use a dictionary if necessary.**

1 When he had finished his painting, the artist drew back to see his work from a distance.
2 The children's jackets were all undone as they stood in a row waiting for the photographer, so she zipped along the line to fasten them.
3 Squash up, kids, and when you're all sitting down, I'll give you some juice.
4 The twins set off in one direction but then doubled back to try to lose their pursuers.
5 The robbers stole away as soon as they heard the police car outside the bank.

46.4 **Complete the chart with four verbs which can be used with *back* to match the meanings in brackets. Then make four sentences using one of the verbs in each.**

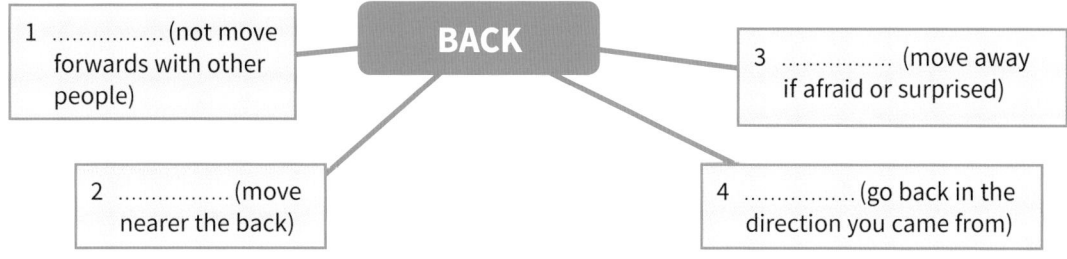

47 Nature

A Animals and plants

Elephants **feed on** plants. By **pulling down** trees to eat leaves, **breaking off** branches and **pulling up** plants, they create clearings in which new vegetation can grow to provide nutrition in the future. However, their destructive habits have meant that a number of plants are in danger of **dying out**[1].

The cherry laurel requires consistently moist soil; do not allow it to **dry out**. In favourable areas it is very invasive; if you **cut** the tree **down**, it will still **send out** limbs from the root and **offshoots**[2] from the bottom of the stem. Very hard to **dig up**. The cherry laurel has small flowers which **come out** in late spring.

The South African secretary bird **preys on**[3] insects, snakes, tortoises and rats. Small prey are **picked up** in the bill and swallowed. Larger prey are first stamped to death and then eaten. The secretary bird also stamps its feet on the ground to **flush out**[4] prey.

[1] becoming more and more rare and eventually disappearing completely
[2] plants which have developed from a larger plant
[3] catches for food
[4] force an animal to come out of its hiding place

B Water and sky

phrasal verb	definition of phrasal verb	example
dry up	disappear (used about water)	The river is in flood now – it's hard to believe it completely **dried up** six months ago.
freeze over	become covered with ice	In the far north, the sea **freezes over** for several months each year.
go out / come in	move further away from the beach / nearer the beach	When the tide **goes out**, we can look for shellfish. But we'll have to be careful as the tide **comes in** quickly here.
come out	appear in the sky (used of the sun, moon or stars)	It is spectacular here at night when the stars **come out**.
go in	become hidden by a cloud	Let's go indoors now – the sun has **gone in** and it's getting chilly.
overcast	grey, covered in cloud (used about the sky)	I don't want to go to the beach today as it is so **overcast**.
wash away	carry away by water	An old boat abandoned on the beach was **washed away** by the unusually high tide.
eat away at	gradually destroy by taking little bits at a time	The sea is **eating away at** the cliff, and houses close to the edge are at risk.

Exercises

47.1 Complete these commentaries from television nature documentaries with the correct phrasal verbs. You are given the first letter each time.

Here in this cold landscape of cliffs and stony beaches, these birds f................ .... (1) the many fish which are found offshore. Seals also p................ .... (2) the abundant fish stocks. It is hard to imagine that if global warming increases, these wonderful creatures may d................ .... (3) and never be seen again at this latitude. Sea levels will rise and e................ .... (4) the cliffs and rocky shores, w................ .... (5) their natural habitats forever. And, paradoxically, as the temperature and sea levels rise, some of the inland lakes may d................ .... (6) altogether, leaving an arid landscape.

These elegant creatures p................ .... (7) the higher branches of trees and eat the succulent leaves. In the course of their feeding, they often b................ the branches .... (8) causing damage to the trees, and even more so by p................ .... (9) the youngest saplings altogether. Fortunately, nature always revives, and the destroyed and damaged trees s................ .... (10) new o................ (11) so that, in time, the forest renews itself. Only humans are the real enemy, c................ .... (12) the trees and d................ .... (13) the most precious plants to collect specimens, denuding the forest forever, and all for commercial gain.

47.2 Answer these questions using phrasal verbs or phrasal adjectives from the opposite page.

1 What would happen to a pond if the temperature dropped to –10°C?
2 What might happen to a shallow lake if the weather is very hot and there is no rain for a long time?
3 What adjective can describe the sky when it is grey and covered in cloud?
4 Why is the sea not always at the same place on a beach?
5 If the police suspect that bank robbers are hiding in a forest, what might dogs help them to do?

47.3 Rewrite these sentences using phrasal verbs or phrasal adjectives from the opposite page.

1 As night fell, the stars appeared.
2 The sun became hidden by a cloud and the temperature fell suddenly.
3 Cats (both large and small) lift their young with their teeth to move them around.
4 It was lovely and sunny this morning but now the sky is grey.
5 Many wild animals and plants are on the verge of becoming extinct.

47.4 Complete these encyclopaedia entries using phrasal verbs from the box in the correct form. Use a dictionary if necessary.

watch over	take over	move in	bring up	fend for	chase out

In many places, grey squirrels have .... (1) and .... the native red squirrels .... (2). They have then .... (3) their territory.

Many animals .... (4) their young in a similar way to human parents, ... (5) them till they are mature; others leave their young to .... (6) themselves shortly after birth.

48 Weather

A Rain and snow

phrasal verb	definition of phrasal verb	example
beat down	come down in large amounts with force	Lying in bed, I could hear the rain **beating down**.
pelt down	(informal) fall very heavily	The rain was **pelting down** by the time we got to the top of the mountain.
hold off	not start, although you expect it to	Fortunately the snow **held off** until we had got safely home.
freeze up	become blocked with ice and stop working	It was a very hard winter last year and many people had problems with pipes **freezing up**.

B Sun and clouds

If the sun **breaks through** (the clouds), it starts to appear from behind the clouds.

If the sun **beats down**, it shines very strongly and makes the air hot.

If some kind of bad weather such as clouds or fog **rolls in**, it appears in a large amount.

If cloud or smoke **blots out** the sun, it covers it and prevents it from being seen.

If windows or glasses **fog/mist/steam up**, they become covered with small drops of water and you can't see through them.

C Metaphors

I suspected there would be trouble at the office as soon as the new boss **breezed in**[1] on his first day. He was very competent and he'd **breezed through**[2] the job interview, but he had no patience at all for anyone less able and he had a very sharp tongue. I noticed that as soon as he spoke to his PA, her face **clouded over**[3] in anger. He asked the sales manager to explain some contradictory figures in such an aggressive manner that she **froze up**[4] and couldn't say a word. I could see her eyes **misting over**[5]. By the end of that first day, his PA had **stormed out**[6], saying she would never return. The rest of us got together after work and decided that we had no choice but to try to **freeze** him **out**[7]. We agreed only to speak to him if we absolutely had to.

[1] walked in quickly and confidently (breeze = light wind)
[2] (slightly informal) succeeded very easily
[3] suddenly looked unhappy
[4] became so afraid she couldn't do or say anything
[5] filling with tears
[6] left in an angry way
[7] make him feel that he is not welcome by being unfriendly

Exercises

48.1 Complete the text below using the correct particles from A opposite.

The weather forecast said that there would be rain later on, but we were all hoping that it would hold .... (1) until Julia's birthday barbecue was over. When we first arrived, the sun was beating .... (2) and some people were too hot. But then grey clouds appeared and the rain started. At first it was quite light but then it began to pelt .... (3). We had to cook indoors but Julia wasn't too disappointed.

48.2 Mark these sentences with a 😊 if you are happy in this situation or a 🙁 if you are not happy in this situation. Explain your answers.

1 Your pipes at home freeze up while you are on a skiing holiday.
2 You receive a letter that makes your face cloud over.
3 You are walking by the sea when fog rolls in.
4 You can hear the rain beating down outside as you sit by a big log fire.
5 You are on a long country walk and the rain holds off.
6 You have to give a speech at a friend's wedding and you freeze up.
7 You breeze through an important exam.
8 You storm out of a meeting.
9 A group of friends start to freeze you out.
10 You are sitting on the beach and the sun is beating down.

48.3 Write a sentence about each picture using a phrasal verb from the opposite page.

1 ....
....
2 ....
....
3 ....
....
4 ....
....
5 ....
....
6 ....
....

48.4 Complete these sentences using a phrasal verb from the opposite page in an appropriate form. Add any other words that are needed.

1 Ellis arrived an hour late but he didn't seem worried; he just ....
2 It was such a sad film. When the hero died I could feel my eyes ....
3 Whenever I go from a cold street into a heated shop, my glasses ....
4 I can see a little bit of blue sky. I think the sun is trying to ....
5 We're going to an open air concert tonight. I hope the rain ....
6 I think the weather's changing for the worse. Look at those clouds ....
7 Don't worry about your driving test. I'm sure you'll ....
8 I always get really nervous before oral exams. I'm afraid I'll ....

Travel websites

> ● ● ● ‹ ›   ↻ 🔍 🏠
>
> **Destination of the week**   Steeple Bunting
>
>
>
> The unspoilt little market town of Steeple Bunting **stretches out** along the winding River Tare. The town is **steeped in**[1] history, and great care has been taken to ensure that modern buildings **blend in**[2] well and do not **encroach on**[3] the 16th-century centre. A particularly well-preserved building from that period is Elderflower Cottage, a delightful half-timbered house **set back**[4] from the High Street. The beauty of this white-walled cottage is **set off**[5] by the colourful flower gardens which surround it, and visitors must also not miss the walled herb garden which **opens off** the rose garden. There are many other must-see sights in Steeple Bunting and the town is **dotted with**[6] pleasant cafés where you can relax if you just want to sit and **soak up**[7] the atmosphere. The town is **bursting with**[8] tourists at the weekend, so visitors who prefer to avoid crowds are advised to come during the week.

[1] has a lot of (collocates strongly with *history*, also with *tradition*)
[2] look similar, do not seem very different
[3] advance beyond proper limits
[4] a little distance from
[5] made to look even more attractive
[6] has many, all over the place
[7] enjoy an experience
[8] very full with (only used in continuous form)

Improving houses and towns

Kingsmill renovations to begin next week

The **run-down**[1] Kingsmill area near the city's football ground is at last about to be **done up**[2]. Signs have **gone up**[3] around the area indicating that work will start next Monday. The first stage of the the work will affect the buildings which **back onto** the football ground, and Stadium Road will be **closed off** from Monday morning while the area is **reduced to rubble**[4]. Drivers wishing to access the stadium car park will need to approach it by Grant Lane, which **branches off** Rampart Street just after the petrol station.

Local resident Maisie James (74) told us, 'I'll be glad to see the back of the **boarded-up**[5] windows in the area. It's very dangerous – a ceiling **fell in** once when some children got into one of the abandoned buildings.'

Local architects Taylor and Summers have been employed to design the reconstruction, and readers can visit their office or look online to see the plans showing how the area will be **laid out**[6] and a large-scale **mock-up**[7]. Richard Taylor commented, 'The renovations will inevitably be expensive, but we hope that the costs will to some extent be **offset**[8] by the use of reclaimed sandstone and slate, and also the reclaimed rubble.'

[1] shabby, in disrepair
[2] repaired, improved
[3] been fixed into position
[4] made into a pile of bricks and stones (a strong collocation but note also: Toby was **reduced to tears** = Toby started crying)
[5] covered with pieces of wood
[6] arranged, structured
[7] model showing how something will look when it is built
[8] compensated for

> **Tip**
>
> If you notice a phrasal verb in a text, it may be useful to copy out the whole sentence. This can help you to be able to use it as well as understand it.

Exercises

49.1 Complete these two emails using phrasal verbs or adjectives from the opposite page.

⚫ ⚫ ⚫   ✉   Reply   Forward

Hi Charlotte,

Here we are in our new home. It's in an old house .... (1) back from the road in a big garden, on the top of a hill. The town .... (2) out below us. It's an old town, ... (3) in history, but .... (4) with all the excitement of a big modern city. Sometimes we just stroll through the streets .... (5) up the atmosphere.
From the back of the house, we look up into the hills, which are .... (6) with little white houses. The road that runs past our house branches .... (7) down to the river, so it's a nice place to go for a walk. I hope you can come and see us.
All the best,
Javier

⚫ ⚫ ⚫   ✉   Reply   Forward

Hi Javier,

Now you've left university you can live in luxury, but I'm still a poor student. Jade and I have moved into our accommodation for this year. It's in a rather .... (8) part of town which was rich and prosperous years ago, but now there are lots of .... (9) shops and cheap restaurants. We're in a house that backs .... (10) an old factory whose roof has fallen .... (11), and next to that was another building which has been completely .... (12) to rubble and the area is all closed .... (13). So it couldn't be more different from your view! The flat itself is OK. There's a living room and a small kitchen which opens .... (14) it, two bedrooms and the bathroom. We've talked to the landlord and he's going to let us do it .... (15) a bit. He said he'll pay for the paint and stuff. It may not be the Mediterranean, but it's home.
Love,
Charlotte

49.2 Correct the mistakes with the phrasal verbs in these sentences.

1 New housing developments are encroaching against the countryside on the edge of town.
2 Those climbing red roses really set that old white cottage out, don't they?
3 The architects made a large-scale mock-on of the new shopping centre.
4 The plain lines of the marble walls are upset by the ornate windows; together they produce a harmonious building.
5 This plan shows how the area will be lied out when it is redeveloped.
6 Signs have gone out round the area to be demolished warning the public to keep away.
7 The 1990s buildings do not blend on very well with the older houses around them.
8 The whole area is steeped with history.

49.3 Answer these questions.

1 Can you name a modern building that blends in well with older surroundings?
2 What is the nearest place to you that is sometimes bursting with tourists?
3 To what extent do you think that the place you live in is steeped in tradition?
4 What does your own home back onto?

Over to you

Look at tourist brochures or websites written in English for any city or town you are interested in. Note any phrasal verbs you find.

A Driving

Read about Freddie's nightmare car journey and note the phrasal verbs.

The whole journey was a complete nightmare. I'd only been going five minutes on the motorway when somebody **cut in**[1] on me and I had to brake really quickly to avoid an accident, but that was only the start of it. A bit further on I **pulled out**[2] to overtake a big lorry, but as I did, my engine just died. I tried revving the engine and after a couple of seconds it started again, but I had to **change down**[3] and get back into the slow lane and go very slowly indeed. Because I was so slow, I was **flagged down**[4] by a police officer who checked the car and told me that one of my tyres was worn. He said it wasn't illegal and let me continue but warned me to get it changed. The car started again without any problems, so I set off again, **picked up speed**[5] and drove a couple of miles before, guess what, the worn tyre **blew out**[6]! So I changed the tyre, which was another half hour wasted. Then I **picked up**[7] a hitchhiker – I felt sorry for him. After a while we **branched off**[8] the motorway, and I left him where he wanted to be and went to a nearby café for a cup of tea. When I came out, the rain was pelting down and someone had **blocked** me **in**[9]. Then to cap it all, I realised the hitchhiker had taken my waterproof jacket from the back seat!

[1] suddenly drove in front of me, not leaving enough space between the two vehicles
[2] drove onto a road or onto a part of the road where the traffic is moving faster
[3] put a vehicle into a lower gear, usually in order to go slower
[4] made to stop by waving at the driver
[5] started to go faster
[6] suddenly burst
[7] to let someone get in your car with the purpose of taking them somewhere
[8] turned onto a smaller road
[9] put a car or other vehicle so close to another vehicle that it cannot drive away

B Other phrasal verbs connected with transport

Five planes were **stacked up** over the airport waiting for permission to land. [flying over an airport at different heights waiting to be told they can land]

Two young men had **stowed away** on the ferry, hoping to enter the country illegally. Police said they had already arrested more than 20 **stowaways** at the port this year. [hidden on a ship, aircraft or other vehicle in order to travel secretly or without paying; person who does this]

There's a popular programme where celebrities pretend they have been **cast away** on a desert island and have to survive. [left on an island with no other people after swimming from a ship that is sinking]

She was **knocked over** by a cyclist and broke her arm. [hit by a vehicle and injured or killed]

A police car **pulled** us **over** to the side of the road and two police officers searched the car.

The traffic lights were very slow to change and all around me impatient drivers were **revving up**. [make a car's engine work faster while the car is not moving]

Exercises

50.1 **Look at A. Choose the correct word to complete these sentences.**

1 The train started slowly but soon *revved / picked / pulled* up speed.
2 I hate drivers who *cut / block / flag* in on you when you're driving on a motorway.
3 You *pull / blow / change* down when you want to reduce your speed.
4 I wish my neighbour wouldn't *rev / blow / change* up outside my window early in the morning.
5 Take care when you *blow / change / pull* out to overtake.

50.2 **Look at these pictures, and then complete the sentences about them below using phrasal verbs from the opposite page.**

1

2

3

4

5

6

1 The police officer is ....
2 The driver is ....
3 The aeroplanes are ....
4 The tyre has ....
5 The car is ....
6 The car has been ....

50.3 **Put the words in the correct order to make sentences.**

1 down / The / flagged / on / a / police / ten / found / lorry / board / stowaways / and
2 bedroom / car / was / a / I / woken / revving / by / window / up / outside / my
3 car / on / caused / cutting / an / by / nearly / accident / in / us / That
4 very / blew / motorway / out / when / I / was / frightened / the / tyre / my / on

50.4 **Complete these sentences using a phrasal verb from the opposite page.**

1 The boy managed to .... on a plane to Australia and was only discovered when he arrived in Sydney.
2 The old man was .... by a car that was speeding away from a burglary.
3 I couldn't get out of the car park – someone had .... me ....
4 A police officer .... Elodie .... and fined her for driving too fast.
5 *Robinson Crusoe* is about someone who was .... on a desert island.
6 Take that narrow road that .... the main road just after the railway bridge.
7 I'm taking my car to work tomorrow so I can .... you .... on the way.
8 I hate it when your plane has to spend ages .... waiting to land.

> ### Over to you
>
> People often talk about journeys they have made. Write sentences about your journey to work or college or about any other interesting journeys you have made using some of the phrasal verbs on this page, together with any other phrasal verbs connected with travel that you know.

51 The news

A

How journalists get the news

Some news comes from press releases that are **put out** by companies or organisations. However, journalists also **pick up**[1] stories from their contacts. Occasionally a story **gets out**[2] when a politician or film star **confides in**[3] someone who is not discreet. Sometimes a rumour starts and journalists **sound out**[4] people in the know to check its truth. It may sometimes be difficult for them to **root out**[5] the information they want, but journalists get very good at **worming** stories **out of**[6] people who don't want to talk to them. Sometimes they may **stake out**[7] their potential subject's house until they get the story they want. In fact, the ability to **ferret out**[8] a story may be as important for a journalist as the ability to **write** it **up** well.

[1] learn by chance
[2] becomes known (of something secret)
[3] tells something private or secret to someone
[4] get an opinion from
[5] search for and find something that is difficult to find
[6] getting information from someone who does not want to give it
[7] watch continuously
[8] find out something after searching for it

B

Political news

Pensions protest

A major protest took place yesterday after news **leaked out**[1] about the government's plans to raise the retirement age further. Workers of all ages **walked out** from factories and offices to **join in** public demonstrations. Police attempts to **head off** the main protest march failed, but fortunately all the demonstrations **passed off** without any major incidents. The government has denied that it is planning to use force to **put down** any future protests.

Brookes joins influential committee

Tim Brookes has been voted on to the Environmental Committee. Brookes has been an MP since his party first **got in** in 1997, and he claims that his main ambition has always been to **get onto** this important committee. There were a number of powerful contenders for the place, but Brookes succeeded in **whipping up** considerable support and won the coveted place. Brookes' critics say that he has a tendency to **dumb down** complex issues, but he argues that anything that gets people talking about the environment is worthwhile.

[1] became known

C

The police and the army in the news

sentences from newspapers	meaning of phrasal verb
If there are not enough volunteer recruits, the government will have to **call** people **up**.	order people to join the armed forces
The new general **joined up** when he was 21.	joined the army
The enemy continues to **hold out** in the south.	defend itself against attack
The army is to be **sent in** to help earthquake victims.	(of people with special skills) sent to an area
Troops are expected to **pull out** before May.	move out of an area
Two planes were **shot down** last night.	destroyed by enemy fire
The kidnapper **gave** himself **up** last night.	allowed the police to catch him
The police will **move in** if the situation escalates.	go to a place to deal with a difficult situation

Exercises

51.1 An experienced journalist is talking to a new young reporter. Complete his advice below using phrasal verbs from A. You are given the first letter of each phrasal verb.

A lot of your time will be spent trying to r.................. .... (1) information, and that can be boring – going to record offices, surfing the Internet, reading press releases p.................. ....(2) by government departments, and that sort of thing. It's also important to hang out with other journalists and see what you can p.................. ....(3) from them. You might discover a story that has l.................. ....(4). The secret with celebrities is to get them to c.................. ....(5) you. If they just think you're trying to w.................. private information ....(6) them to create a scandal, they won't give you anything. And they hate it when journalists s.................. ....(7) their homes. With politicians, it's best to s.................. them ....(8) about various topics to find out what they want to talk about; don't be aggressive – that won't get you anywhere. Just like celebrities, if they think you're trying to f.................. ....(9) a story that's going to g.................. ....(10) and cause them embarrassment, they'll keep quiet and you'll get nothing. And take your time w.................. your stories ....(11). Don't rush the process.

51.2 Match each headline 1–7 with an extract from the article a–g.

1 OIL PROTEST PASSES OFF PEACEFULLY
2 UN TROOPS TO PULL OUT OF PHRASALIA
3 ARMY MOVES IN TO QUELL DISTURBANCES IN NORTHERN PROVINCE
4 RESERVISTS CALLED UP AS SITUATION WORSENS
5 PAINTSHOP WORKERS WALK OUT AT AUTO PLANT
6 SPECIAL FORCES ATTEMPT TO HEAD OFF REBELS IN QUESA REGION
7 UNIVERSITIES ACCUSED OF DUMBING DOWN ENTRANCE EXAMS

a) 5,000 men have been ordered to report to local bases for immediate posting to the front.
b) The aim is to push back the advance and to restore government control.
c) 2,000 people assembled calmly outside the ministry and chanted slogans.
d) The riots had reached a level which could no longer be tolerated, the defence minister said.
e) Their work was now complete and had been a success, a spokesperson said.
f) Pass rates have increased by a huge 50% this year.
g) 250 downed tools and started an unofficial strike this morning.

51.3 Rewrite the underlined parts of these sentences, using a phrasal verb from the opposite page. Make any other necessary changes.

1 The conservatives <u>won the election</u> in 2015.
2 A helicopter was <u>destroyed by enemy fire whilst in flight</u> yesterday.
3 My great-great-grandfather <u>became a soldier</u> when he was only 16.
4 The kidnappers <u>surrendered to the police</u> just after midday.
5 The rebels <u>successfully defended themselves</u> for six weeks.
6 The government has <u>ordered</u> a group of experts <u>to go</u> to assess the flood damage.
7 The government <u>crushed</u> the rebellion using massive force.
8 Mr Fleet is trying to <u>arouse</u> some enthusiasm for the concert he is trying to organise.
9 Hundreds of people <u>participated</u> in the celebrations outside the palace.
10 Theodore <u>got a place on</u> the party's national committee.

> ## Over to you
>
> Phrasal verbs are very common in newspaper headlines – perhaps because they are often short and dramatic words. See how many you can find in any one copy of a newspaper. Make a note of any interesting ones.

52 Secrets and lies

A News headlines

INVESTIGATION **BEARS OUT**[1] FRAUD CLAIM

[1] proves that something that someone has said or written is true, or say that someone is telling the truth

COMPANY **HUSHED UP**[2] FINANCIAL SCANDAL

[2] stopped the public from finding out about something bad that had happened

GOVERNMENT URGED TO **LEVEL WITH**[3] PUBLIC OVER HEALTH RISKS

[3] (informal) tell the truth about something

PRIME MINISTER ACCUSED OF **PAPERING OVER**[4] CABINET DISAGREEMENT

[4] hiding a difficulty to try to make people believe that there is no problem

MINISTERS TRIED TO **COVER UP**[5] ARMS SCANDAL, SAYS OFFICIAL REPORT

[5] stop people from discovering the truth about something bad

AGENTS **SPIED ON**[6] UN DIPLOMATS: FORMER SPY BREAKS SILENCE

[6] watched secretly in order to discover information about them

B Email gossip

● ● ●   Reply   Forward

Hi Nicole,

I wasn't at all surprised to hear that Dylan and Maria are getting engaged, were you? The way they've been looking at each other was a real **give-away**[1], wasn't it? And Maria almost **let** the secret **out** a couple of weeks ago anyway, even though they continued to **make out**[2] that they were just good friends. They seem to be crazy about each other!

Esther

[1] (informal) something that makes you aware of a fact that someone else was trying to keep secret
[2] claim falsely that something is true

● ● ●   Reply   Forward

Dear Aidan,

I need to **confide in**[3] you. I've been suspecting for a long time that one of my employees, George, has been stealing from the till at work, so I actually hired a private detective. He **dug up**[4] a few unpleasant facts, I'm afraid. George has had a number of convictions for theft already. But the detective hasn't managed to prove that he is stealing from us. So I've decided to just **play along**[5] and pretend I don't know, to see if I can **catch** him **out**[6] – you know, just see if he **gives** anything **away**[7] without realising it. Am I doing the right thing, do you think, or should I confront him?

Oscar

[3] tell someone things that you keep secret from other people
[4] discovered new facts about a person or situation after a lot of searching
[5] (informal) pretend to agree with someone, or to do what someone wants for a short time, in order to get something from them or to avoid making them angry
[6] discover that someone is lying or doing something wrong
[7] lets someone know something that should be kept secret, often by mistake

Exercises

52.1 Answer these questions about the headlines in A opposite.

1 What was the aim of the investigation and what did it discover?
2 Why might the company have wanted to hush up the scandal?
3 What is the third headline implying about the government?
4 Why might the Prime Minister want to paper over what was happening in the Cabinet?
5 Does it sound as if the report supports or condemns the ministers' behaviour?
6 What has the former spy just admitted?

52.2 Match the beginning of each sentence with its ending.

1 Fortunately, my research bore   a) in someone.
2 Please just play   b) up a good scandal.
3 I wish I could confide   c) out your secret.
4 Journalists love to dig   d) on her.
5 I'm so sorry I let   e) with her.
6 We did all we could to hush   f) out my original hypothesis.
7 My friend begged me to level   g) along with the story I tell Mary.
8 Libby accused Charles of spying   h) up the scandal in the company.

52.3 Correct the ten mistakes with particles in this paragraph.

As journalists, it is our job to try to dig off stories that dishonest people are trying to cover over. Sometimes we are accused of spying at innocent people, but surely it is our duty not to allow people to paper up their scandals. Often it is not at all difficult to learn secrets. People are often eager to confide with someone who is willing to lend a sympathetic ear. Or they let off a secret without realising it. Little things like a blush or a quick glance at someone else can be a real give-out to an experienced reporter. Of course, sometimes people try to make over that they have nothing to hide, and then it can be a good idea to play on with them up to a certain point. Then you suddenly take them by surprise with an unexpected question and in this way you can often catch them across.

52.4 Which word could fit into all the sentences in each set? Look in your dictionary for any new meanings.

1 The lawyer tried to .... the accused out in a lie.
  Be aware of exam questions designed to .... you out.
  Every year unexpected snowstorms .... people out.

2 Isabella likes to .... out that she has a very important job.
  Can you .... out that small yacht on the horizon?
  Who should I .... this cheque out to?

3 Please take care not to .... my secret out.
  This skirt is too tight – I'll have to .... it out.
  Don't forget to .... the cat out before you go to bed.

4 The way his hands were shaking .... away his nervousness.
  The company .... away six new cars as part of their advertising campaign.
  It was meant as a surprise but Kate .... the game away.

A Obeying rules and laws

Police officer	Well, Mr Smith. I am pleased to say we have **caught up with**[1] you at last.
Mr Smith	But, I'm innocent, sir. Breaking the law would be **going against** my principles.
Police officer	Well, several of your fellow criminals have **informed on**[2] you.
Mr Smith	Just wait till I see them!
Police officer	They say you make a habit of persuading old ladies to **sign over**[3] their property to you.
Mr Smith	But they did it of their own free will.
Police officer	The court is going to have to **impose** a substantial sentence **on**[4] you this time.
Mr Smith	But what if I promise to **abide by**[5] the law in the future?
Police officer	Well, you will certainly need to do that, and who knows, if you **adhere to**[6] the rules in prison, you might be **let out** early, but I'm certain the judge will give you a prison sentence – you won't be **let off** again.

[1] managed to catch
[2] given information to the police about someone who has done something wrong
[3] give someone else legal rights to something
[4] give someone a punishment
[5] (formal) obey
[6] (formal) obey

B Describing rules and laws

NEWS

Progress on tax evasion

The government has long been anxious to introduce a new law relating to tax evasion. The intention is to **toughen up**[1] the existing legislation, bringing all crimes related to the non-payment of taxes **under** the authority of the Financial Crimes Agency, giving the FCA considerable new powers and **providing for**[2] the imprisonment of serious offenders. The initial proposals for the law were **thrown out**[3] at the committee stage. However, some modifications were made and the new proposals **went through** the committee stage last week. The next step is for them to be **voted on** in Parliament. It is expected that they will **get through** without difficulty, as there is general cross-party agreement that the current laws have too many loopholes and should be **tightened up**[4]. Once passed, the new regulations will be **rolled out**[5] gradually over the coming year.

[1] make more limiting and difficult to avoid
[2] (formal) allowing to happen
[3] rejected
[4] made stricter
[5] introduced

> ### Tip
>
> Write sentences using phrasal verbs on small cards, missing out the preposition or particle. Write the missing word on the back of the card. Test yourself regularly using the cards.

Exercises

53.1 Are you a good citizen? Complete this questionnaire and then answer the questions.

HOW LAW-ABIDING ARE YOU?

Work out your score and then turn to page 157 to find out if you are a good citizen.

1 Have the police or a court ever .... (1) a fine on you?
   Yes: 0   No: 2
2 Do you .... (2) to speed limits?
   Rarely or never: 0   Mostly: 1   Always: 2
3 Would it go .... (3) your principles to take items from your place of work for your own private use?
   No: 0   Yes: 2   Depends on value: 1
4 Do you abide .... (4) parking laws?
   Rarely or never: 0   Mostly: 1   Always: 2
5 If you knew that a friend or family member had committed a crime, would you .... (5) on them?
   No: 0   Depends on how serious: 1   Yes: 2
6 If you park illegally in a foreign country because you genuinely don't understand the rules, do you think you should be .... (6) off or punished?
   Not punished: 0   Punished: 1

53.2 Correct the mistakes with the phrasal verbs in these sentences.

1 The new act went across Parliament last week and will become law on 1 January.
2 The anti-litter laws should be tightened in; as it is now, nobody is ever prosecuted.
3 He went on a two-year crime spree before the police finally caught up to him.
4 She avoided tax by signing out her property to her two sons.
5 The new law provides with jail sentences of up to ten years for repeat offenders.
6 Building regulations come by local government rather than national or European law.
7 The bill was passed by the Lower Chamber but was thrown away by the Senate and never became law.
8 The bill will be voted to in Parliament next week, and the government hopes it will get across without too much opposition. [two mistakes]
9 If trials prove successful, the government intends to roll in the scheme across the whole country next year.
10 He was sentenced to three years in prison, but he'll probably be let off in 18 months.

53.3 Rewrite the underlined parts of these sentences using a phrasal verb from the opposite page. Make any other necessary changes.

1 The former CEO of Wilson & Wallace has been <u>released from prison</u> after serving a ten-year sentence.
2 If you don't <u>follow</u> the health and safety regulations, you will be punished.
3 The government plans to <u>make</u> the existing laws <u>more strict</u>.
4 The law reforming the Health Service <u>was passed by</u> Parliament with a large majority.
5 Evan's criminal activity was discovered when his neighbours <u>told the police about</u> him.

53.4 Here are some more phrasal verbs connected with rules and laws. Work out from the context what they mean (or look them up in a dictionary) and rewrite the sentences, replacing the underlined phrasal expressions with a word or phrase that means the same.

1 He was tried last week, found guilty and <u>sent down</u> for five years.
2 This government has <u>brought in</u> more new laws than any other in the last 50 years.
3 The new law will <u>come into force</u> in March.
4 The military authorities <u>put out</u> an order banning demonstrations in the area around the parliament buildings.

A Computers

Several verbs related to computers are based on the verb *go*, meaning access or use something.

You can **go on** a computer, the Internet, a website.

You can **go to** a menu, an item on a menu, a particular web page or part of a page, or a link.

Note how phrasal verbs are used in these extracts from an online computer helpline.

> **Query** 17:02
> How do I stop **pop-up adverts**[1] from **coming up** every time I **go on** the Internet?

> **Answer** 17:03
> **Go to** the tools menu on your browser and click 'disable pop-ups'.

> **Query** 19:35
> When I try to **print off** more than one copy of a document, a warning light **comes on** on the printer or the printer just **goes off** altogether and I have to switch it on again.

> **Answer** 19:40
> Try re-installing the printer driver. You can **call up** the information you need for your printer by opening the control panel, **going to** 'printers' and then clicking 'help'.

> **Query** 9:18
> I want to **set up** a **drop-down menu**[2] on my website. How do I do it?

> **Answer** 9:25
> Go to our tutorial page, **type in** your query and follow the instructions.

> **Query** 11:57
> How can I get my photos to **fade in** and **fade out**[3] when I show them on my computer?

> **Answer** 11:59
> Just right-click on the folder and choose 'Slide show'. They'll fade in and out automatically.

> **Query** 14:10
> There was a power cut the other day while I was working on my computer and a whole load of data got **wiped off**[4] the hard drive. How can I avoid this in future?

> **Answer** 14:14
> You can buy a piece of equipment which will automatically provide **back-up** power.

[1] unwanted advertisements which suddenly appear on the screen when you are online
[2] a list of choices which appears on a computer screen
[3] become gradually louder or brighter (fade in) or quieter or darker (fade out)
[4] removed

B Other technical equipment

When the battery is low, simply **plug** the unit **into** the mains supply to recharge.

Tune into any radio station anywhere in the world with our free app. You can **pick up** hundreds of thousands of stations 24 hours a day.

Spending hours **wiring** everything **up**[1] is a distant memory. All you have to do is switch on and connect!

[1] connecting something to a piece of electrical equipment by using electrical wires

Developments in technology mean that scanners no longer need to **warm up**[2].

[2] start working so that it becomes warm enough to work well

Looking for a printer that never **seizes up**[3]? The new Jentra 850 has a unique paper feed.

[3] stop moving or working in the normal way

Exercises

54.1 **Complete these sentences with phrasal verbs from A opposite.**

1 At the end of a scene in a radio play, the actors' voices often ....
2 When you bought your new laptop, did you find it easy to ....?
3 Could you .... three copies of the document, please?
4 The network crashed and the information I'd just added got .... the system.
5 When using this program, you can instantly .... the figures you need.
6 If you click on the icon, a .... menu appears on your screen.
7 All you have to do to get an instant answer is .... your question.

54.2 **Choose the correct word to complete these sentences.**

1 With my new radio I can .... far more stations than I used to be able to get.
  a) tune in   b) pick up   c) set up
2 If a machine stops moving or working normally, you can say that it has ....
  a) cut off   b) wiped off   c) seized up
3 OK, If you want to create a template, go .... the Tools menu.
  a) on   b) in   c) to
4 I'm going to have to get my printer repaired – it keeps going .... for no apparent reason.
  a) on   b) off   c) out
5 Please could you help me .... my new computer?
  a) set up   b) tune in   c) pick up
6 Whenever Mohammed is abroad, he .... the BBC World Service to listen to the news.
  a) seizes up   b) tunes into   c) calls up

54.3 **Are these sentences true or false about the computer that you usually work on?**

1 Pop-ups come up every time you go on the Internet.
2 You create bullet points by going to the Format menu and clicking on 'Bullets' and 'Numbering'.
3 Your printer plugs into the back of your monitor.
4 You can pick up radio stations from all over the world.
5 It takes less than a minute for your machine to warm up.
6 It makes an automatic back-up of files on a regular basis.

54.4 **Complete each sentence in an appropriate way using one of the phrasal verbs from the opposite page and any other words that you need.**

1 The advantage of a wireless connection is that you don't ....
  ....
2 You can print a document by selecting the print icon or by ....
  ....
3 It's quite easy to .... a website with these step-by-step instructions.
4 Whenever I switch on my computer, it takes time ....
  ....
5 I can use this cable to listen to my MP3 player in the car by ....
  ....
6 If the printer is beginning to run out of ink, a warning light ....
  ....

> ## Over to you
>
> Find an article online about a computer, camera, mobile phone, MP3 player or other piece of technology that you are interested in. Does it contain any examples of phrasal verbs? If so, note them down in their context.

A Eating

Six easy ways to eat a healthy diet

1. It's better to have three proper meals a day rather than just **pick at**[1] things all day.

2. Don't **gobble** your food **down**[2] – take your time, enjoy it. If you **wolf** it **down**[3], you won't even taste what you're eating and you'll eat more.

3. Don't just **eat in**[4] every day; spoil yourself at least once a week by having a meal in a good wholefood restaurant. Or if you feel like staying at home, **send out for**[5] something nutritious.

4. Have friends round and **serve up** a special vegetarian dish. For an easy meal, just buy lots of vegetarian pizzas, **slice** them **up** and let everyone **help** themselves **to**[6] what they want.

5. Make sure you're aware of what foods **agree with** you and what don't. Avoid anything that **disagrees with**[7] you – even if it tastes good. You'll regret it later.

6. **Cut out**[8] **fry-ups**[9] and eat more salads – you're bound to feel healthier. Eat lots of fruit and raw vegetables – they will **fill** you **up**[10] without making you **put on** weight.

[1] eat small amounts
[2] (informal) eat very fast
[3] (informal) eat very fast
[4] eat at home
[5] phone a restaurant and ask for food to be delivered to you
[6] put on a plate for oneself
[7] makes you feel slightly ill or uncomfortable
[8] stop eating
[9] (UK, informal) quick meal made of fried food
[10] make you feel that you've eaten enough

B Drinking

phrasal verb	definition of phrasal verb	example
wash down sth or **wash** sth **down**	help you swallow it	Have a drink of milk to **wash down** the tablet.
drink to sb/sth	hold up your glass before drinking from it in order to wish someone success or happiness	Let's raise a glass and **drink to** the happy couple!
dip sth **in** (sth)	quickly put it in and take it out again	She loves **dipping** carrot sticks **in** soft blue cheese.
soak up	absorb	Cook the lentils until they **soak up** half the liquid.
water down sth or **water** sth **down**	make it less strong by adding water or other liquid	You should **water down** fruit juice for your child until he or she is five years old.
spill over	flow over the edge	Alfie, hold your juice properly. It's **spilling over** the edge of your glass.

> ### Tip
>
> A number of the words in B can also be used metaphorically. Anger can *spill over*, you can *soak up* an atmosphere and plans or suggestions can be *watered down*. Learning the literal and metaphorical uses together may help you to remember these expressions.

Exercises

55.1 Complete these dialogues using phrasal verbs from the opposite page so that the second speaker agrees with and repeats more or less what the first speaker says.

1 **Mariam** The kids eat so fast! I'm sure it can't be good for them.

   Ronnie Yes, they do tend to .... / .... their food .... (Give two possible answers.)

2 Clara Polly just eats tiny amounts – no wonder she's so thin.

   Ed Yes, she just .... her food like a bird.

3 Julian Those prawns made me feel a bit sick.

   Rebecca Yes, they .... me too. I don't feel too good either.

4 Arthur I think we should stop eating burgers; they're not good for us.

   Pippa You're right. We should .... them .... and eat more salads.

5 **Michael** These trousers don't fit me any more. They must have shrunk.

   Louise No, I'm afraid you've .... a bit of weight.

6 Tim Shall we eat at home tonight? We could order something from a takeaway.

   Harriet Yes, let's .... We can .... for a pizza or something.

55.2 Read the remarks by different people and then answer the questions below.

   Rory I enjoyed it, but I couldn't eat one bit more.

   Lizzie We toasted Matthew and wished him well in his new job.

   Grace The smoked salmon made me feel unwell. I shouldn't have eaten it.

   Oliver She gave me some raw fish. It was the first time I'd ever tasted it.

   Khadijah I took a big slice of cake.

1 Who ate something that didn't agree with them?
2 Who helped themselves to something?
3 Who ate something that filled them up?
4 Who was served up something new?
5 Who drank to someone?

55.3 Complete the word puzzle.

Across
2 Do you ever .... your biscuits in tea?
3 We .... the meal down with lemonade.
6 She's put .... a lot of weight.
7 .... the cake up and give everyone a piece.

Down
1 Stop pouring! The water's going to .... over the top of the jug!
3 This juice is too strong. I'll .... it down.
4 Have some bread to .... up the rest of the sauce.
5 Particle that goes with *water* and *wash*.

55.4 Name a food or drink that ...

1 often disagrees with people.
2 can be sliced up.
3 you often serve up.
4 fills you up.
5 you should cut down on.
6 people often send out for.

56 Come

A Typical meanings of *come* in phrasal verbs

You may have already met some phrasal verbs with *come* in this book or elsewhere. For example, **come in** [start speaking during a discussion (Unit 11) or, for the sea, come nearer to the beach or coast (Unit 47)], **come at** somebody [move towards someone in order to attack them (Unit 22)], **come at** something [think about something in a particular way (Unit 24)], **come down** [pass from one generation to another so that it continues (Unit 10) or, for a price or level, become lower (Unit 10)].

Come typically expresses movement and the particle shows the direction of the movement. **Come in** above suggests a person 'entering' a discussion. **Come at** someone suggests directing oneself at/towards someone and **come at** something suggests directing one's thoughts to a particular subject. **Come down** suggests moving through time (from the more distant past towards the present).

B More phrasal verbs with *come*

Look at these extracts from two interviews for *Policy and Finance* magazine.

Interviewer	You are often seen as a survivor. How did you survive your difficult second term in government? Was it just luck?
Politician	Luck? No, luck doesn't **come into it**[1]. You have to work in politics. As you know, the party **came in for**[2] a lot of criticism on its tax policy and was also **coming under**[3] attack from pensioners' groups. We were **coming across**[4] as insensitive to ordinary people's needs and problems, so we needed new ideas. I **came up against**[5] critics in my own party, and it was a difficult period, but we **came through**[6] it because we were strong and determined to succeed.

[1] (usually negative) have an influence
[2] received (collocates with *criticism* or *praise*)
[3] getting a lot of
[4] being seen by others

[5] faced
[6] managed to get to the end of a difficult situation

Interviewer	You once **came out with**[1] a famous remark that surprised everyone: 'Capitalism is dead.' Do you still believe that?
Economist	I was misquoted. What I said was that in a period when new technology was **coming in** and replacing traditional employment patterns in the workplace, we needed to rethink our basic economics. Other economies which have combined capitalism with a caring social framework have **come off**[2] better in the long term. If our standards of employment and social care are to **come up to**[3] those of our neighbours, then we need something other than a traditional form of capitalism. And this is where a more cooperative approach **comes in**[4]. Our workers' general life skills have **come on**[5] a long way since the days of mass manual labour, and we have to involve them and their skills in a more democratic way. A new era has to **come into**[6] being or we will simply be left behind.

[1] suddenly said
[2] ended up in a good position (**come off better**) or bad position (**come off worse**) because of an argument or some kind of struggle
[3] reach

[4] is involved
[5] improved
[6] begin

> **Tip**
>
> Look at the units which deal with the meanings conveyed by the particles (Units 9–15). These may help you learn the meanings of the phrasal verbs in Units 56–60.

Exercises

56.1 Complete these sentences with phrasal verbs from A opposite.

1 Originally stories .... from one generation to the next through the spoken word rather than in writing.
2 The tide .... and goes out twice a day.
3 Prices tend to .... when the economy is experiencing a recession.
4 Surrealist artists .... their work very differently from artists of previous generations.
5 In a formal meeting you should wait until you catch the eye of the chairperson before .... to join a discussion.
6 The Russian revolutionary Trotsky died when someone .... him with an ice axe.

56.2 Complete these sentences with the correct particles.

1 Any original idea is bound to come .... a certain amount of opposition at first.
2 I prefer not to argue with Caitlin because she usually comes .... best.
3 The new licensing laws will come .... force on 1 January.
4 The Chancellor is bound to come .... attack for putting forward such a controversial proposal.
5 Small children say the funniest things – you never know what they are going to come .... next.
6 Sometimes your brother comes .... as being a bit unfriendly.
7 I gave up football because I wanted a change. Age doesn't come .... it.
8 Now I'd like to discuss the next stage of the project and this is where your plans come ....

56.3 Rewrite the underlined parts of these sentences using a phrasal verb from the opposite page. Make any other necessary changes.

1 Álvaro's English has <u>improved</u> a lot since he met Flora.
2 <u>Most people think Hugo is</u> confident and extrovert.
3 The Prime Minister has <u>received</u> a considerable amount of criticism lately.
4 Ellen <u>makes</u> some very strange comments sometimes.
5 This history homework does not <u>meet</u> the standards we expect from our students.
6 We've had a difficult year but we've <u>survived</u> and are looking forward to the future now.
7 At this point I should like to invite Anastasia Snow to <u>enter the discussion</u>.
8 I was afraid the dog was going to <u>attack</u> me.

56.4 Which phrasal verb with come fits each set of collocations? Use a dictionary to help you if necessary.

1 to not	standard expectations scratch	3 to	scrutiny attack pressure
2 to	competition a problem prejudice	4 to	effect being force

57 Get

A

A Phrasal verbs with *get*

There are many phrasal verbs with *get*, some of which you may have already met in this book or elsewhere. For example, **get your act together** [become more organised (Unit 8)], **get around** [travel, of news or rumours (Unit 9)], **get by** [have just enough money to pay for the things you need but no more (Unit 6)], **get** someone **down** [make someone depressed (Unit 10)] and **get off** [finish work (Unit 31)].

B Phrasal verb collocations with *get*

collocation	meaning
The children are very quiet. I hope they're not **getting up to mischief**.	doing something naughty
Now we're all here, let's **get down to business**.	start our work
I wish my parents would **get off my back**! I'm studying as hard as I need to.	stop nagging me
The football coach decided it was time for his team to **get back to basics**.	start again at the beginning
The business was a little slow to **get off the ground**, but it's doing very well now.	get started
I just can't **get** the situation with Tom **out of my mind**.	stop thinking about
Doctors try to **get the message across** that too much salt is bad for you.	make people understand
You are far too soft on Holly. You let her **get away with murder**.	behave badly and not be criticised or punished
What happened between Kian and Daisy? We must try to **get to the bottom of** it.	understand properly, not superficially
They've seen how popular the product is and now other companies want to **get in on the act**.	become involved

C Getting down to a good gossip

Alice Hi, Beth! Haven't seen you for ages. What have you been **getting up to**[1] recently? Anything interesting?

Beth Well, I've been **getting around**[2] quite a lot actually, mainly for work. I've been to Italy a couple of times and Ireland, visiting our offices. But I've also been **getting into**[3] golf recently and I managed to **get in**[4] a few rounds between meetings.

Alice That's great. It's good if you can **get** something **out of**[5] the trips for yourself as well as for work.

Beth That's right. In fact, I'm finding it quite hard to **get back into**[6] the ordinary office routine now.

Alice Well, let's **get together** one evening soon and catch up properly on all the news.

[1] doing
[2] travelling to different places
[3] becoming keen on
[4] find time for
[5] get benefit from
[6] return to (after some time)

> ### Tip
>
> Many phrasal verbs have a whole range of different meanings. If you come across a phrasal verb and it doesn't make sense with any meaning that you know, look it up online at http://dictionary.cambridge.org to see if it has a different meaning in that context.

Exercises

57.1 **Put the words in the correct order to make sentences.**

1 she got / together / her act / It's time / a job / found / and
2 not looking / always / to mischief / The children / when / get up / I'm
3 the bottom / of that / I must / strange letter / get to / I received
4 down / We / business / to / got / immediately
5 is too / Modern / complicated / life / to basics / should / get / We / back (two sentences)

57.2 **Complete these dialogues using phrasal verbs from the opposite page so that the second speaker agrees with and repeats more or less what the first speaker says.**

1 Anna   Sienna always wants to be part of anything that involves publicity.

   Ella   Oh yes, if publicity's involved she always wants to
   ....

2 Alex   We'll just have to survive on less money now that I've lost my job.

   Ameena Yes, don't worry I'm sure we'll ....

3 Zara   Everyone soon found out about Harry's divorce. I'm amazed.

   Victoria Oh yes, the story soon ....

4 Lily   It's often difficult to make people understand how important it is to protect the environment.

   Callum   Yes, it's hard to ....

5 **Adam** Sarah always seems to behave badly and never get criticised by anyone.

   Antonia Yes, she seems to be able to ....

6 Emma   I just can't stop thinking about Lucía.

   Sergio I know. It's the same for me. I just can't ....

57.3 **Complete these sentences using the correct particles.**

1 Studying so hard really got me .... so I took a break to cheer myself up.
2 Look, just get .... my back, will you! I'm sick of you finding fault with me.
3 The project took a long time to get .... the ground, but we're moving now.
4 I hope I get something .... that summer course I've registered for; it's quite a lot of money to pay.
5 I'd like to get .... a game of tennis later today. Are you free around five?
6 Hi there. What have you been getting .... since I last saw you?
7 Ryan has got .... photography recently; he spends all his time editing pictures on his computer.
8 Let's get .... for lunch one day. I've got loads to tell you.

57.4 **Rewrite these questions, replacing the phrasal verbs with a word or phrase that means the same.**

1 When do you normally get off work?
2 Do you get around a lot?
3 Is there any time of the year when you find it hard to get back into the routine of your daily life?
4 What have you been getting up to recently?
5 What sorts of things get you down?
6 Where do you usually get together with your friends?

57.5 **Now answer the questions in 57.4.**

58 Go

A Typical meanings of *go* in phrasal verbs

Look at these meanings of *go down* which you may have already met. Note that what they have in common is change from a bigger or more positive state to a smaller or more negative state.

phrasal verb	meaning	unit
go down	if a computer system **goes down**, it stops working	10
	become worse in quality	58
	if part of your body that is bigger than usual because of an illness or injury **goes down**, it starts to return to its usual size	43

As these examples show, *go* typically carries meanings connected with movement, change or things happening. Here are some more examples:

We should **go back over** these figures. I think there's a mistake somewhere. [examine again]

The house **went for** €900,000, which was more than we expected. [was sold for]

The festival will **go ahead** despite the bad weather. [happen]

I've been **going over** in my mind what happened the other day. I think we have a big problem. [thinking about something that happened or that was said]

Lucas has decided to **go into** politics. I'm not sure I would vote for him! [become involved in]

Who would want to **go after/for** such a boring job? [try to get]

B Other phrasal verbs with *go*

Look at the verbs with *go* in these short news clips.

The event **went off**[1] as planned and £5,000 was raised for charity.

Mr Drake said he had decided to **go over to**[2] the Green Party as he was disillusioned with his own party's policies on the environment.

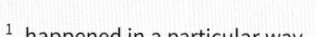

Youths who **go around**[3] vandalising property should be forced to repair the things they have damaged.

The young parents **went through**[4] agony before their missing child was found.

Going by[5] the government's own statistics, they have failed to stop the rise in drug addiction

Three candidates will **go forward** to the next round in the election for party leader.

The newspapers are really **going for**[6] Ben Rone. They seem determined to **go after**[7] him and destroy his career.

[1] happened in a particular way
[2] leave one group or organisation and join another competing group or organisation
[3] spend time (used about doing something that is unpleasant for other people)
[4] experienced (used about an unpleasant or difficult situation or event)
[5] using as a reference
[6] attacking
[7] to chase or follow someone in order to catch them

120 *English Phrasal Verbs in Use Advanced*

Exercises

58.1 **Look at A. Complete the text below using particles from the box.**

| after | ahead | down | for | into | over |

It's been a terrible week. As you know, I'm planning to go .... (1)
teaching. On Monday I went .... (2) a trainee teacher position
that was advertised at a school in town, but I didn't get it. I'm not sure
why. I've been going .... (3) the interview in my mind, but I don't
think I said anything too stupid. Then on Tuesday I fell off my bike and
managed to twist my ankle. It was terribly swollen for a day or two, but
it's beginning to go .... (4) now. It's my birthday party tomorrow.
I hope you can come. Plans are still going .... (5) for that, of
course, although I don't suppose I'll be able to dance very much. I'm
probably going to sell my bike, though. I hope it'll go .... (6) at
least £300, which will help me out till I manage to find a job.

58.2 **Match the beginning of each question with its ending.**

1 Are you planning to go after
2 Is the end-of-term concert going ahead
3 Why did you decide to go over
4 How much did their house go for
5 Did your anniversary party go off
6 Could you help me go back
7 Has the swelling on your knee gone down
8 Which teams are going forward

a) when they finally managed to sell it?
b) over our business accounts?
c) yet?
d) in the school hall as usual this year?
e) to the semi-final?
f) to a different political party?
g) the boss's job when he leaves?
h) as well as you'd hoped?

58.3 **Correct the mistakes with particles in these sentences.**

1 Lara has been promised that her name will go over for a place on the board of directors next year.
2 Going for the weather forecast, there'll be snow tomorrow.
3 They went on a terrible time during their daughter's illness.
4 You really mustn't go across telling such terrible lies.
5 Cameron has always wanted to go on law.
6 The journalists went into her wherever she went.

58.4 **Which particle fits in each of these sets of sentences? Use a dictionary if necessary.**

1 Elsa really went .... me in the office today.
   They are selling their old car but don't expect it to go .... much.
   Please be quiet, children – and that goes .... you too, Seth.
2 The standard of school-leavers' English is going ....
   The office computer system has gone .... again.
   The bump on the boy's head looked alarming, but it quickly went ....
3 Let's go .... our plan of action for tomorrow again.
   I keep going .... what I said to him, wishing I could take my words back.
   He started his political life as a Republican but later on went .... to the Democrats.
4 I was nervous about playing in the concert, but everything went .... very well.
   I didn't wake up when my alarm clock went .... this morning.
   Don't drink this milk – I think it's gone ....

59 Keep

A

A Phrasal verbs with *keep*

In this book or elsewhere, you may have already met **keep in with** someone [be friendly with someone because they can help you (Unit 5)], **keep up** with something [be able to understand or deal with something that is developing very fast (Unit 24)] and **keep it up** [don't stop doing (Unit 30)]. This unit presents more of the many other phrasal verbs with *keep*.

B Describing problems

After our son had to be **kept in**[1] hospital overnight after suspected appendicitis several months ago, the doctors explained that they thought his stomach pain was stress related. His school have always kept us informed about any concerns they have, and until recently, everything seemed to be going really well. But now I'm sure our son is **keeping** something **to**[2] himself. He normally tells us about all his worries and doesn't **keep** anything **back**. We've asked him what the problem is, but he won't tell us anything. We've got a meeting with his teacher next week, so should I **keep out of**[3] it until then and not make a fuss?

I'm a medical student and up till now I've managed to **keep ahead** of the other students in my year. I really want to do well in my exams. However, now I have a problem with my flatmate. She always wants to spend hours discussing her problems with me and this is **keeping** me **from** my studies. On top of that, she **keeps on**[4] inviting her friends to come and stay. We've only got two small bedrooms so they have to sleep on the sofa and they **keep** me **up**[5] chatting until the early hours of the morning. It's not so bad at the weekend, but they often come during the week when I've got nine o'clock lectures. I really need to speak to her about everything that is annoying me, but I don't want to add to her problems. What should I put first – work or friendship?

[1] made to stay somewhere
[2] keep something secret
[3] not become involved

[4] continues doing something repeatedly
[5] made to stay up late

C Some advice

- **Keep off** sugary drinks if you want to stay slim.
- If you are on a diet, or on a budget, a bowl of homemade soup is a good and inexpensive way to **keep** your strength **up**[1].
- **Keep** your music **down** late at night or you'll annoy your neighbours.
- When answering an exam question, you will get better marks if you **keep to**[2] the point.
- When you buy a house, remember to budget for its **upkeep**[3] as this can be very costly.

[1] not allow something that is at a high level to fall to a lower level
[2] don't start writing about other topics
[3] keeping a building in good condition

Keep at it *and you'll get on top of those phrasal verbs.*

Exercises

59.1 Complete these emails using the correct particles.

● ● ●   ✉   Reply   Forward

Hi Georgia,

Keep this .... (1) yourself, but I heard something very interesting the other day. You know
how Lydia is always trying to keep .... (2) with the boss and you know how she just tells
everyone EVERYTHING (she can never keep anything .... (3), can she?)? Well, she told
me she's actually getting married to him! Can you believe it?

Megan

● ● ●   ✉   Reply   Forward

Hi there Andrew,

Thanks for the invitation to the week in France, but I think you're trying to keep me .... (4)
my studies! Seriously, I really shouldn't take any more time off. My new year's resolution is to
keep .... (5) with my studies, so I'm trying to do five hours a day, five days a week.
If I had a week off, I think I'd find it hard to keep .... (6) the momentum.

Madeleine

● ● ●   ✉   Reply   Forward

Dear Max,

Katie's had a row with Archie and she wants me to help sort it out. I think I should keep ....
.... (7) it. What do you think? I find it hard to keep .... (8) all the ups and
downs of their love life. I think they should solve their own problems, don't you?

Naomi

59.2 Look at these brief notes giving people advice or warnings. Rewrite the underlined parts of the sentences using a phrasal verb from the opposite page. Make any other necessary changes.

1 Please <u>play</u> your music, TVs and radios <u>at a minimum volume</u> during the exam period.
2 Every household will be asked to contribute £10 a month towards the <u>maintenance</u> of the village recreation ground.
3 All team members are strongly advised to <u>refrain from eating</u> fatty foods during the training period. It is important to <u>maintain</u> your fitness to the highest level.

59.3 Which particle could fit into all the sentences in each set?

1 There is one rule which we ask all club members to keep ....
  I wish the lecturer would stop digressing and keep .... the point.
  Before your exams, make a revision timetable and try to keep .... it.

2 I wish my parents wouldn't keep .... at me about getting my hair cut.
  Keep .... going until you reach the T-junction and then turn left.
  My grandma kept .... working until she was in her 80s.

3 Why don't you go to bed now? I really don't want to keep you ....
  At university Jack did a course on ornithology, but I don't think he's kept .... his interest in birds.
  Things change so quickly in Faye's life – it's hard to keep .... with what's going on.

59.4 Answer the following questions.

1 What sort of thing has kept you up late at night?
2 Have you ever been kept in hospital overnight? If so, why?
3 What are you going to do to keep up your knowledge of phrasal verbs?

60 Take

Typical meanings of *take* in phrasal verbs

Take often carries a meaning of 'remove', as in:

> We hope you will **take** many happy memories **away** from your stay here.

> Phil's boss has agreed to **take** him **off** the night shift.

> Helena **took** her parents **out** for a meal. (Unit 42)

Take also sometimes carries a meaning of doing something quickly or something happening quickly or abruptly, for example **Take it away**! (Unit 30), **take aback** [surprise], **take off** (of a plane) and **take out** [kill or destroy in a military battle].

B

Organising a charity concert

I must say I was **taken aback**[1] when I saw the cost involved, but I wanted it to be a memorable experience for people. A huge amount of time was **taken up**[2] with phone calls persuading sponsors to be involved. The **uptake**[3] was slow at first, but bit by bit we managed to persuade local companies and individuals to support us. The work didn't end when the concert was over. We spent a whole day **taking down**[4] the stage set and lighting and so on, but none of that **took away from**[5] the pleasure we got from organising it. And I think the audience **took away**[6] something that will stay with them for a long time. Overall it was worth it – a great experience for all involved.

[1] very surprised
[2] used
[3] number of people who committed themselves
[4] removing by separating into pieces and taking the pieces away
[5] made it seem less good or successful
[6] remembered [used about e.g. a memory, an impression, a message]

C

Other phrasal verbs with *take*

phrasal verb/noun	definition of phrasal verb/noun	example
take sb **away**	take to a different place	He **took** his mum **away** for a week to the coast.
take sb **off** sth	remove from a job	He was put in charge of security, but he was **taken off** the job after a week as he was not strict enough.
	stop giving someone a particular type of medicine	The doctor **took** her **off** the pills as they were making her sick.
take up sth or **take** sth **up**	discuss something or deal with something	The tutor promised to **take** the problem **up** with the Head of Department.
take along sb/sth or **take** sb/sth **along**	take with you	I'd advise you to **take along** an umbrella.
intake	number of people that are accepted at a particular time by an organisation, especially a college or university	This year's **intake** have higher exam grades than last year's.
take-off	imitation	She does a brilliant **take-off** of Adele.

Exercises

60.1 **Which of the phrasal verbs on the opposite page can have the following meanings?**

1 surprise someone ....
2 detract from something ....
3 leave an airport (of a plane) ....
4 destroy a military target ....

60.2 **Complete these sentences with the correct particles.**

1 My Spanish cousin is coming to stay next week, so I plan to take her .... when I visit my daughter at university.
2 Personally, I took .... a very good impression of France when I went there.
3 Joel was quite taken .... to learn that his application had been unsuccessful.
4 Much of Jason's time is taken .... with dealing with customer complaints.
5 Grandma asked the doctor to take her .... those tablets as she thought they were making her feel sick.

60.3 **Rewrite the sentences using a phrasal verb or noun based on *take*. Remember to make all the changes to the sentences that are necessary.**

1 Martin does the best imitation of the Prime Minister that I have ever seen.
2 A ridiculous amount of my time is occupied by dealing with emails.
3 Even the rain could not detract from the beauty of the scene.
4 I was very surprised when I was told that I was no longer allowed to park in front of my own house.
5 Would you like me to raise your concerns with the manager?
6 We are expecting a particularly large group of students to arrive next week.
7 We decided it would be nicer to invite our aunt for a weekend in a hotel with us rather than having her stay with us.
8 The number of people wanting a place at the weekend seminar has been rather disappointing.

60.4 **Rewrite these sentences so that the underlined words have the opposite meaning. Make any other changes that are necessary.**

1 Let's put up the decorations tomorrow.
2 The doctor has agreed to put my elderly uncle on some pills for his arthritis.
3 Her parents brought her back to their holiday home.
4 My favourite part of a flight is when the plane lands.
5 Robert's being there added to our enjoyment of the evening.
6 After Stan had been working in the kitchens for a week, he was put on washing-up duties.

Over to you

If you have now finished all the units in this book, congratulations! Remember to regularly revise the new phrasal verbs you have studied and try to use them in your own speaking and writing of English.

Unit 1

1.1
1 I decided to <u>take up</u> gardening, so I <u>took out</u> a subscription to a gardening magazine and <u>read up on</u> the subject. I <u>found out</u> so many interesting things, such as the best time to <u>plant</u> flowers <u>out</u> for the summer and how to grow vegetables. I've really <u>got into</u> it now and spend hours in the garden every weekend.

2 The other day we <u>went off</u> on a hike in the mountains. We <u>put</u> our wet-weather gear <u>on</u> as the weather forecast wasn't good. We <u>set off</u> early to avoid the rush hour and soon reached the starting point for our walk. The whole walk took about four hours and when we <u>got back</u> we were exhausted.

3 I have to <u>catch up on</u> my coursework this weekend as I've <u>fallen behind</u> a bit. I <u>worked on</u> it till midnight last night, but I still have loads to do. I have to <u>hand</u> one essay <u>in</u> on Tuesday and another one on Friday. I'm not sure whether I'll make it, but I'll try.

1.2 1 out of   2 down   3 out   4 in

1.3
1 intake
2 breakout
3 off-putting
4 outspoken
5 broken-down

1.4 1 d   2 e   3 a   4 b   5 c

Unit 2

2.1
1 no object needed
2 object needed: If you're ready to leave now, I can drop **you** off at your office. Remember, without an object, *drop off* means 'fall asleep'.
3 no object needed
4 object needed: My son is so good at English that I think the teacher should move **him** up to the advanced class.
5 object needed: I associate **this music / that perfume / Juliet** with that evening we spent together in Rome.
6 no object needed

2.2
1 I can pick you up from work and then drop you off at the airport. *Or* I can pick you up from the airport and then drop you off at work.
2 The teacher said that she would not put up with such rudeness from her class.
3 The floods have cut off several villages in the mountains. *Or* (but less likely as it is quite a long object) The floods have cut several villages in the mountains off.
4 If your spelling doesn't improve, the examiners will mark you down.
5 Margot always seems to cope cheerfully with all her problems. *Or* Margot always seems to cope with all her problems cheerfully.

2.3
1 I'll have to ask my daughter to **sort** my Internet connection **out**. *Or …* to **sort out** my Internet connection.
2 I was so tired after work that I **dropped off** in the train on the way home.
3 I was **marked down** because my essay was over the word limit.
4 Jason has no right to **look down on** me – he's no better than I am.
5 Lara doesn't **get on** (well) with one of her flatmates.
6 You have to **face up to** the fact that you will probably never see each other again.
7 Maria has got a new job **looking after** an old lady.
8 If you **deprive** the children **of** sleep, they won't be able to concentrate at school.
9 In Lapland we had to **contend with** some difficult driving conditions.
10 The road to our house **branches off** (the main road) just after the service station.

2.4 *Possible answers:*
1 I'm **looking forward to** visiting my aunt in New York for a couple of weeks.
2 I've got to **catch up on** some maths I missed when I was off school on Monday.
3 My mother **picks** me **up**.
4 My favourite album is *Sergeant Pepper's Lonely Hearts Club Band*, and I like it because I **associate** it **with** being a student.
5 I feel stressed when I have too many different things to **contend with** at the same time.
6 I usually **drop off** as soon as my head touches the pillow.

Over to you

This is how the *Cambridge Advanced Learners' Dictionary* deals with these verbs:
associate *sth* **with** *sth* phrasal verb
deprive of verb [T] [T = transitive]
contend with *sth* phrasal verb
face up to *sth* phrasal verb

Collocations highlighted by examples in *Cambridge Advanced Learners' Dictionary*:
risks **associated with** smoking
deprive someone **of** freedom/rights/sleep
contend with problems / someone's death
face up to the fact that

Unit 3

3.1
1 onset
2 overkill
3 back-up
4 input
5 warm-up
6 letdown
7 standby

3.2
1 The police opened the container and arrested two **stowaways**.
2 There was a **breakdown** in negotiations with union members (after a couple of hours).
3 There was a management **buyout** of the company in 2014.
4 There was a **walkout** (by the workers) last night and the factory was forced to close.
5 The military **build-up** is continuing on both sides of the border.

3.3
1 There has been a stand-**off** for several days now in the talks between the government and the rebels. Neither side will make any concessions.
2 Last year there were 15,000 new Internet business start-**ups**, most of which only survived for a few months.
3 After years without releasing an album, Madeleine Flame has staged a come**back** with her new collection of love songs.
4 Holly: Have you decided where you're going this summer?
  Flora: Not really. It's a toss-**up** whether it'll be Italy or Greece.
5 I met Nasser and we just had a knock**about** on the college football pitch for half an hour.

3.4
1 Output	4 outbreak
2 lookout	5 Lift-off
3 downpour	6 a break-in

Unit 4

4.1
1 There was a **worn-out** carpet on the stairs.
2 The newsletter has a list of **forthcoming** activities at the tennis club.
3 What's happened? You're looking very **downcast**!
4 Unlike her sister, Emily is very **outgoing**.
5 I find the cover of this novel very **off-putting**, don't you?
6 It doesn't matter what time of day it is, Polina always looks **tired out**. *Or* … **worn out**.
7 We are not in the habit of going to such **overpriced** restaurants.
8 When you meet my boss I think you'll find her surprisingly **outspoken**. *Or* … **outgoing**.

4.2
1 a **fold-up** chair   2 a **broken-down** car   3 a **built-in** oven   4 a **foldaway** bed

4.3 *Possible answers:*
1 An advantage of having a live-in nanny might be that the children look on her as one of the family; a disadvantage might be that the parents do not get much privacy.
2 A foldaway bed would be particularly useful in a small room, especially one that is also used for entertaining visitors.
3 A job requiring tact might not be suitable for a very outspoken person – a diplomat, for example, or a beautician.
4 You might want to give a watered-down version of something that happened to you to your parents if you think they might not like the whole truth.
5 A job in show business requires you to be outgoing – an actor, singer or TV presenter, for example.
6 A difficult social problem would tend to be ongoing – for example, the problem of poverty or of discrimination.
7 If you are having a meal in a restaurant, you might find it off-putting if someone at the next table talks very loudly.
8 You might think that meals, clothes or cosmetics are often overpriced.

4.4	**broken-down**	not working
	candid	**outspoken**
	continuing	**ongoing**
	diluted	**watered-down**
	downcast	miserable
	dynamic	**go-ahead**
	exhausted	**tired out**
	extrovert	**outgoing**
	forthcoming	future
	obsolete	**outdated**
	off-putting	repellent
	shabby	**worn out**

Note that *worn out* can also mean exhausted.

4.5 *Possible answers:*
1 If the union doesn't accept our terms, what should we have as the position **that we will agree to if we cannot get our main aim**?
2 Clara always feels **ignored** / **lonely** when her brother's friends come round to play.
3 Julian is usually chatty but his sister is not very **talkative** / **communicative**.
4 You shouldn't get **so upset** / **in such a state** about every little thing.
5 Zack met me at the airport with arms **open wide ready to embrace** me.

Unit 5

5.1
1 *Collocation* means the way words combine with each other.
2 a, c and e
3 They are things that are written.
4 Because it will help you to be able to use them appropriately in your own speaking and writing.
5 You might want to note down:
whether it collocates with positive or negative things or both
whether it collocates with people or things as objects
whether it collocates with people or things as subjects
whether it collocates with particular types of situation

5.2
1 appropriate
2 appropriate
3 not appropriate – *hit on* is used about good ideas; in this context it would be better to say 'You can always rely on Joseph to **come up with an idea** that will never work.'
4 appropriate
5 not appropriate – though it would be appropriate to talk about the need to **keep in with your bank manager**

5.3
1	after	5	off
2	into; off	6	off / up
3	through	7	in with
4	with		

5.4
1 Helena **sailed through** her driving test.
2 I've really **gone off** coffee.
3 The wind is **easing off/up** now. *Or* The wind has **eased off/up** now.
4 If I have a problem, I find a walk by the sea often helps me to **hit on** a solution.
5 Masses of people **streamed into** the shop as soon as it opened, hoping to find a bargain in the sale.
6 His argument is **riddled with** holes.

Unit 6

6.1
Dear Mr Janes,

Thank you for your letter of 23 May **complaining** about the bad service you experienced at this hotel. I promise you we will **investigate** the problem at once and **respond** to you as soon as possible. We always try to **achieve/meet** the highest standards of service, and if we have failed to **meet/achieve** those standards we will immediately seek to **remedy** the situation. Meanwhile we hope you will **continue** making Miromana Hotels your first choice for all your business and leisure travel.

Yours sincerely,

G. H. Logan (General Manager)

6.2
1 Will you **look after** Aunt Jessie while I go and get the children's supper ready?
2 He **went into** the subject in great detail in his lecture.
3 When the president died his son **took on** the title of Great Leader.
4 I like her. Do you think I should **ask her out**?
5 During the war he **went over to** the enemy side and was killed in action.
6 She **bought up** all the shares in the company last year.
7 The local newspaper **put out** a story about a strange animal seen in the city park.
8 I think I'll **call in on** my grandfather on the way home from work.
9 The deal **fell through** at the last minute.
10 I managed to **get by** on about €70 a day when I was travelling.

6.3

computers and technology	academic lectures/writing	money and business
back up, hack into, log in, print off, scroll down	base on, gloss over, put forward, sum up	bail out, carry forward, sell up, square up, take over, turn over

6.4
1 Despite his family's poverty, Alfie never **wants for anything**.
2 You must inform the police if you have evidence **which bears on** the case.
3 Jack will have to **call on** all his ingenuity to resolve the situation.
4 The president **ascribes** his party's victory **to** his leadership.
5 The manager will **attend to** your enquiry without delay.

Unit 7

7.1 *Possible answers:*
1 later than expected
2 They've risen.
3 aggressively
4 He wants to read the agenda and make sure it is correct. Perhaps also prepare what they are going to say.
5 more
6 go straight into the proposal without any planning
7 not pay any attention to them, not consider their proposal

7.2
1 It's not good for children to spend too much time **glued to** a screen.
2 Choosing a university course **boils down to** deciding what you want to do with your life.
3 I arrived at the stadium early and watched the other spectators **flooding in**.
4 Laura **dragged herself away from** the window and returned to her desk.
5 Sam was staring at Megan, **drinking in** every word she said.
6 George **brushed off** / **swept aside** all objections to his plan, saying they were unimportant.

7.3
1 stands by
2 soldier on
3 fished out
4 nosing around
5 eat into
6 brushed off or swept aside
7 struck out
8 sandwiched between

7.4 *Possible answers:*
1 If someone warms up an audience, they make it more receptive and friendly, more relaxed (perhaps by telling some jokes). Coldness in English equates with unfriendliness and warmth with friendliness. Warming up people and warming up food both have the idea of making something pleasanter.
2 If someone falls into a job, they get it very easily and without making any effort. So both falling into a hole and falling into a job have the idea of something happening by chance.
3 If you climb down in an argument, you admit that you were wrong. So both uses of climb down suggest moving back to the level of other people from a position in which you were separated from others.

Unit 8

8.1
1 the baby
2 get on like a house on fire
3 let off steam
4 to spite their face
5 take the sting out of something
6 run rings round somebody; go round in circles

8.2
1 off; nose; spite; face
2 put; roots
3 ran rings
4 sting; of
5 round; circles
6 throw; baby
7 get; house
8 letting off

8.3 After a year of travelling, I decided to ~~put~~ my act together and get

a job. A friend who worked for a bank put in ~~some good words~~

for me. In fact he ~~pushed in~~ all the stops and arranged for me to

have lunch with the CEO. I got ~~on the wrong feet~~ by saying I wasn't

ready to ~~plant~~ down roots yet; I think they were looking for

someone to make a long-term commitment. I should have kept quiet!

1	get
2	a good word
3	pulled out
4	off on the wrong foot
5	put

8.4
1 her heels in
2 for lost time
3 to the fact
4 his own
5 the heat
6 your mind

Unit 9

9.1
1 banging
2 floating
3 run
4 switched
5 ask
6 fly
7 lying
8 clowning

9.2
1 ask around
2 lying around/about
3 gets around/about
4 bosses; about/around
5 clowns around/about

9.3
1 lying/pottering/playing/clowning around/about; lying around/about; switched around
2 play/clown/run around/about; bossing us around/about; run around/about
3 work around
4 skirt around (Note that **skirt around** can also be used to describe physical movement, e.g. *We decided to **skirt around** the city centre to avoid the rush-hour traffic*.)
5 banging around/about; flying around/about. (Note that it would also be possible to say that *all sorts of rumours have been going around/about among the neighbours*.)

Over to you

Possible answers:

phrasal verb	meaning	example
crowd around	surround someone or something, standing close together	Please don't **crowd around** the desk. Stand in an orderly queue.
knock sth **about/around** / **knock about/around**	if people knock a ball about, they hit or kick it to each other for fun	We knocked a ball about in the park after work.
turn around	turn so that you are facing the opposite direction	I saw him walk up to the door, but then he hesitated, **turned around** and walked away again.
turn sth **around**	make something unsuccessful (e.g. a business) become successful	Paul has made a very successful career out of **turning** failing businesses **around**.
roll about/around	laugh a lot	Kathy is very funny. Her stories had us all **rolling around**.
blunder about/around	move in an awkward way (often because you can't see where you're going)	When the lights went off, we were all **blundering around** in the darkness.

Unit 10

10.1 1 Heidi Knight   2 Lucas Hind   3 Harry Irving   4 Oliver Reece   5 Mia Calvo

10.2 *Suggested answers:*
1 The computer system suddenly **went down** this morning, so we're doing everything manually at the moment.
2 I'm sorry I'm so irritable. Things have been **getting me down** lately.
3 Shall I **put you down (**on my list**)** to sponsor me for the charity walk?
4 This event will **go down** in history as the worst catastrophe this country has ever suffered.
5 The company had to **shut down** all their machines during the 24-hour strike at the factory.
6 The salesman **came down on the price**, and after that we even managed to **knock him down** by a further 10%.
7 Many everyday remedies for minor ailments have **come down to us** from our ancestors.

10.3 1 slam the phone down
2 have it put down (rather than *put it down*, since you would probably not do it yourself)
3 tie it down
4 getting you down
5 turn it down

10.4 1 a and c   2 b and c   3 a, b and c   4 b and c

Unit 11

11.1
1 cash in on
2 come in / cut in
3 pitch in
4 usher in
5 boxed in
6 lead-in
7 factor in
8 squash in
9 build in
10 set in

11.2 1 My new curtains are excellent – they don't **let** any light in.
2 Alba, can you **show** Mr Hill in as soon as he arrives, please?
3 Having the meeting on the 28th would **fit** in better with our plans than the 30th.
4 Our office in Buenos Aires has **brought** in a lot of new business this year.
5 When you are planning the course, make sure you **build** in enough free time.
6 It's rude to **cut** in when someone else is in the middle of speaking. (Note that come in does not fit as well in this context as it does not sound so abrupt and potentially rude as cut in.)
7 If everyone **pitches** in, we'll soon get the job done.
8 If I move up, then Rachel should be able to **squash** (**fit** is also possible here) in at the end of the bench.

11.3 1 squashed   2 fitted   3 pitched   4 set   5 let

11.4 1 **bring in** customers / profits / a loss / business
2 a **lead-in** to a discussion / a bargain / a lesson
3 a recession / rain / a new product **sets in**
4 **usher in** a price increase / a new era / changes

Unit 12

12.1
1 Eliza's father to Eliza's mother: Eliza's 18 now and should make her own decisions. I think we should **back off** and let her run her own life.
2 Newsreader: The prime minister has **shrugged off** leadership threats from within his party, saying that they are only rumours.
3 Mother to father: I think we should let the kids run round in the garden for a bit and **work off** some of their energy so that they sleep tonight.
4 Mother to Imogen: Imogen, you MUST pay your electricity bill. If you don't, they'll **cut you off** and you won't have any heating.
5 Louis to Callum: Oh no! Seth wants to come back with us to Nikita's house. He's such a drag! How can we **shake him off**?
6 Chairperson: I'd like to just **round off** the meeting by giving a vote of thanks to the committee for all their work this year.
7 The last 100 metres to the top of the hill just **finished me off**. I had to sit down and rest for an hour.
8 I don't want you in my room any more, so just **shove off**!

12.2

When I come home from work, I love to just kick ~~away~~ my

shoes and relax for the evening. It's great to ~~let~~ off worrying

about work and round ~~up~~ the day with a nice meal. If I

~~have off a couple of days~~ it's even better. I usually go off to

our country cottage. I can just ~~light~~ off completely. I love it.

I never stay there long, because after a while I feel a bit ~~stood~~

off from all my friends and social life back in the city.

off
1 leave
2 off
3 have a couple of days off
4 switch
5 cut

12.3

	¹s	²t	a	r	t	e	d
		i					
		³c	o	r	d	o	n
⁴k	i	c	k				
		i		⁵s	h	o	w
		n		p			
		g		⁶l	e	a	v	e
				i			
				t			

Unit 13

13.1 1 B   2 D   3 I   4 N   5 B   6 I   7 D

13.2 1 a or b   2 b, c or d   3 a, c or d

13.3
1 Try to **focus on** what is really important and to ignore what is not essential.
2 Now we've had a bit of a rest, it's time to **press on** again.
3 I'm **counting**/**depending**/**relying on** you to let me know when my talk has gone on for long enough.
4 Your grandmother will always **live on** in your memory.
5 This is a quiet neighbourhood where noisy behaviour is **frowned (up)on**.
6 After the first few pages of the book, I decided I couldn't be bothered to **read on**.
7 Please stop **harping/going/droning on** about Lena. Your relationship is over, so just forget her.
8 I am worried about my son's behaviour. He is so easily **led on** by his friends.

13.4
1 focus
2 spring
3 dwell
4 press
5 lead (Note that **egg on** has a similar meaning.)
6 frowned
7 depend
8 going/droning/harping

13.5 *Suggested answers:*
1 You can count/rely/depend on James.
2 Dad will ramble/drone on for hours about European history.
3 Many political reputations are hanging on / riding on the outcome of next week's election.
4 Josh never stops going on (and on) / harping on about the litter in the office car park. It irritates me.
5 While tidying my room, I happened on an old diary of mine from 2001.

Unit 14

14.1
1 She shared the apples out / shared out the apples among the four children.
2 He sorted things / the situation out. *Or* He sorted out the situation.
3 She picked out the best ones / picked the best ones out.
4 He kicked Sam out of the restaurant. (Note that **He threw Sam out of the restaurant** is also possible.)
5 It juts out over the terrace.

14.2
1 I don't have any money so you can **count** me **out** from the shopping trip.
2 I **shared** the mints **out** / **shared out** the mints among my friends in the car.
3 We need to **sort out** this mess about the misprinted tickets pretty soon.
4 He really **lashed out at** me when I suggested he'd got it wrong.
5 Look at those big rocks **jutting out** from the sea.
6 **Pick out** the good strawberries and leave the rotten ones in the box.

14.3 1 I opened the door and heard somebody **yell out** from the staircase below. (Note that (**shout out** / **cry out** / **scream out** are also possible.)
   2 My position as regards the committee is that I **want out**.
   3 He always **draws out** the discussion / **draws** the discussion **out** with arguments about political ideology.
   4 When we got back to our campsite, the campfire had **gone out**.
   5 **Spread** the leaflets **out** on the table.
   6 The burglars **cleaned us out** (completely).

14.4 1 c   2 d   3 a   4 b

Unit 15

15.1 1 finish up or eat up   5 propped up
   2 pep up/jazz up   6 jazz it up
   3 shore up   7 wrap up
   4 pick them up   8 lift up

15.2 1 stand   5 bought
   2 split   6 show
   3 set   7 blown
   4 land   8 sticking

15.3 1 blow up   2 shore up   3 set up (Note that **fix up** is also possible.)   4 open up

Unit 16

16.1 1 c   2 e   3 d   4 a   5 b

16.2 1 Adriana   2 Jude   3 Mary   4 Leah   5 Jack

16.3 1 out   5 back (Note that **off** is also possible.)
   2 back   6 over
   3 along (Note that **up** is also possible.)   7 aside
   4 in   8 up

16.4 1 You'd get far more done if you didn't fritter **away** so much time.
   2 The children tried to spin their game **out** so they didn't have to go to bed.
   3 Cameron might lose his job if he doesn't pull his **socks** up.
   4 We must discuss what we need to do leading up **to** the opening of the new branch.
   5 Let's try to **set** some time apart next month to discuss progress on the project.

16.5 1 We've had to **bring** the meeting **forward** to this Tuesday as Austin will be away next week.
   2 Francesca always **drags out** any discussion. *Or* Francesca always **drags** any discussion **out**. (Note **draw out** is also possible.)
   3 I think we should **space** our meetings **out** a bit more. *Or* I think we should **space out** our meetings a bit more.
   4 I thought I had ages to prepare for my exams, but they have **crept up on** me in no time at all.
   5 I think we should try to **eke out** the printing paper. Or I think we should try to **eke** the printing paper **out**.

Unit 17

17.1 1 h 2 f 3 i 4 b 5 c 6 a 7 d 8 e 9 g

17.2 1 Theodore puts the problems down to the government, but I attribute them **to** the general world economic situation.
   2 To a large extent, how a person accounts for the problems in their lives seems to depend largely **on** their own parents' attitudes to difficult situations.
   3 I believe the new legislation will contribute to a general improvement in the standard of living, but Ben thinks it will result **in** increased poverty for most people.
   4 The desire for reform has come **out of** a general desire to improve the situation, but I suspect the proposed changes may rebound on the government.
   5 The proposals are rooted in an appropriate awareness of the problems that exist, but I do not feel that what is proposed adds up **to** a coherent programme of action.

17.3 1 The school's rituals and traditions are **rooted in** its long history.
   2 My mother **puts** the problem **down to** a decline in moral values.
   3 How do you think the changes will **impact on** your business?
   4 The economic recession inevitably **resulted in** increased unemployment.
   5 How would you **account for** the recent increase in violent crime?
   6 Joel's criticism of Erica may **rebound on** him now that she's his boss!
   7 I do not feel that the writer's analysis of the problem **adds up**.
   8 Some unforeseen problems have **come out of** the change in legislation.

17.4 *Author's answers:*
   1 I'd put global warming largely down to increased air and road travel.
   2 I think a dramatic change in social values has led to the current increase in violent crime in most societies.
   3 I'd account for it by saying that teenage girls tend to be more inclined to work harder at school than teenage boys – though of course there are plenty of exceptions.
   4 I'd attribute the success of social media sites to the fact that they are convenient, fast and efficient.
   5 I'd point to the prevalence of materialistic attitudes as one main cause of social problems today.
   6 My own interest in English stems from the fact that I had very good English teachers when I was at school.
   7 I think that mobile phones have resulted in more communication between people – it's so much easier to keep in touch with friends and family.
   8 For me the main thing that contributes to the difficulty of phrasal verbs is the fact that one verb – like, say, *make out* – can have so many different meanings.

Unit 18

18.1 1 b 2 c 3 d 4 a 5 b

18.2 1 reminds
   2 conjure/stir/summon/call
   3 flooding/coming
   4 associate
   5 coming/flooding
   6 blocked
   7 put
   8 stick (Note that **stay** is also possible.)
   9 store
   10 conjure/summon/call

18.3 In each case the play on words depends on the literal meaning of the basic verb in the phrasal verb.

1 To stir up memories means to make memories, often unpleasant ones, appear in your mind. A cook stirs ingredients, e.g. the ingredients for a cake or batter for pancakes.
2 To conjure up memories means to make you remember things from the past. A magician traditionally conjures a rabbit out of a hat.
3 To call up memories means to evoke memories or make someone remember something. Another meaning of call up is to require young men to become soldiers.
4 If a memory sticks with you, then you don't forget it. Glue is used to stick something to something else. The first meaning of stick here is metaphorical and the second is literal.
5 If memories come flooding back, you suddenly remember a lot of things very clearly. When pipes burst – this typically happens if they freeze and then the ice melts – then there will be a flood.

18.4 *Author's answers:*
1 I associate my childhood with the colour green because I spent so much time playing in the garden at home.
2 The smell of lavender reminds me of my childhood because we had a lot of lavender growing in our garden.
3 The pop music of the 1970s always conjures up memories of my youth.
4 I would like to block out the memory of school dinners, particularly of the awful macaroni cheese we were forced to eat.
5 I think that music makes memories come back to me more powerfully, although smells can also be very potent.

Unit 19

19.1 1 If your currency bottoms out, then it will become expensive to buy things in dollars, or to travel to the USA. But more tourists might come to your country because it's cheaper for them. So you might be happy or unhappy depending on your circumstances.
2 sprouting or springing
3 True. See the left-hand page, section A.
4 You begin to feel less confident.
5 It becomes less strong.

19.2 1 opens   2 apart   3 on   4 up   5 breaks   6 out

19.3 1 When you**'ve finished with** the scissors, could you pass them to me? (Note the change to present perfect tense.)
2 They **wound up** the business in 2014 after a year of low sales.
3 OK, so who's **magicked** the bottle opener **away** / **magicked away** the bottle opener? It was here a minute ago!
4 We've had some setbacks but we'll **press on**.
5 I only **got up to** page 12 of the book before I got bored and stopped reading it.

19.4 1 Wind up means to finish/terminate something. It is also what you do to a non-electric clock or watch to make it work.
2 Sprout up means to suddenly appear. A Brussels sprout is also a vegetable.
3 Press on means to continue in a determined way. Dry cleaners also press clothes (remove creases by using an iron or a pressing machine).
4 Spring up means to appear suddenly. A trampoline has springs, which contract and expand, making it possible for a person to bounce up and down on it.
5 Training shoes are worn by athletes when running. To run out of money means to have no money left.

Unit 20

20.1
1	up	5	up
2	rage	6	off
3	around	7	back
4	out (Note **over** is also possible.)	8	off

20.2 There was a terrible bust-**up** at work today. The departmental manager came into the office in a terrible temper. She flew **at** her PA and when people tried to calm her down, she rounded **on** them. I don't know what had got into her. She pushes everyone **around*** a lot, but she's not normally quite so aggressive. I tried not to get dragged **into** it at first, but she started shouting really loudly at Jessica, so I stepped in to try to break things **up**.

* push over would mean literally push people onto the floor

Possible answers:

20.3
1 When I tried to enter the house, the dog flew at **me**.
2 No object required
3 They threatened to bump **him** off if he told anyone about the robbery.
4 Because she had learned some judo as a child, Lauren found it much easier to fight off **her attacker** / to fight **her attacker** off.
5 I was completely taken by surprise when someone suddenly came at **me** from behind.
6 After only ten seconds in the ring, Henry's opponent had knocked **him** out.

20.4
1 Paul tried to **drag me into** the argument, but I managed to stay out of it.
2 The old man thought the boys were trying to break into his house, so he **set his dog on them**.
3 The aim of the organisation is to **wipe out** cruelty to children.
4 Although he is small, James is strong and he quickly managed to **knock his attacker out**.
5 Uncle Ronnie can **flare up** (very quickly) if you say the wrong thing.
6 The witness saw the thief **come at** the woman just as she was opening her car door.
7 The robbers came running out of the bank, **pushing over** an old lady who was in their path.
8 Older people often find it harder to **fight off** colds and other infections than younger people do.

Unit 21

21.1
making noise	reducing noise
belt out	die down
boom out	trail off
blast out	keep down

21.2
1 trailed	2 belting	3 blasting	4 keep	5 boomed	6 died

21.3
1 b	2 c	3 a	4 c	5 b	6 a	7 c	8 c

21.4
1 You would not enjoy it: droning on means continuing for a long time in a boring, monotonous way.
2 True
3 up
4 away
5 ring out
6 came over

Unit 22

22.1   This party **stands** for equality for all.
We do not hesitate to **come** out strongly against any case of injustice.
We **stick** by our principles at all times and never **cave** in to threats or pressure from the opposition.
We **side** with the underdog and do not **defer** to those who are wealthy and powerful.

22.2   1   The runners were cheered on by the spectators as they headed for the finishing line.
2   You can rely on Tim to stick up for his little sister. *Or* You can rely on little Tim to stick up for his sister.
3   My grandfather swears by raw garlic as a way of protecting himself from catching colds.
4   My mother would never have tried bungee jumping if we hadn't egged her on.
5   She wanted to go to an all-night party but her mother wouldn't hear of it.
6   The discovery of gas in the North Sea buoyed up the British economy for some years. *Or* The discovery of gas in the North Sea for some years buoyed up the British economy.

22.3   1   stick   2   side   3   cheer   4   buoy

22.4   1   My preferred course of action would be to **go** with what Ivan has recommended.
2   He began his political life as a Conservative but crossed **over** to the Labour Party when he realised that he would be more likely to get a seat in Parliament that way.
3   correct
4   correct
5   I shall have to defer **to** your superior knowledge of the situation.
6   My mother **swears** by a daily spoonful of honey to keep healthy all year long.
7   Josh is not usually naughty himself but he is quick to egg others **on**.
8   correct

Unit 23

23.1
1 c	3 e	5 a	7 b
2 g	4 f	6 h	8 d

23.2
1 down	3 to	5 to	7 in
2 in	4 on	6 down	

23.3   1   After two weeks of strikes, the company finally **gave in** and increased the overtime rate.
2   Our application for planning permission **went through** without any problems and so we can start building next month.
3   We've got a general agreement, but it will take some time to **hammer out** the details.
4   Chris always just **goes along with** what the manager says. He never thinks for himself.
5   It's going to be difficult to **nail down** all the details of the training day until we've chosen a date.
6   Charlie said he didn't like the new website design, but I think he'll **come round** when he sees the latest version.

23.4   1   a   2   b   3   c   4   c   5   b

Unit 24

24.1
1 grappling		7 cottoned
2 rough		8 hit
3 talk		9 break
4 bounce		10 piece
5 reflect		11 thrash
6 occurred		

24.2
1 up; on	5 around
2 out	6 with
3 up; on	7 at
4 with	8 in

24.3 *Possible answers:*
1 bounce off, bat around, play with, hit on an idea
2 piece together
3 thrash something out, grapple with, break something down

Unit 25

25.1
1 The basic meaning is collecting up animals who have ranged over a wide area of land, e.g. a sheepdog rounds up sheep or a cowboy rounds up cattle. With a different meaning, round up (a number / a total) also refers to raising a number or total to the nearest whole number, e.g. The bill was £9.20, so we rounded it up to £10 and gave the waiter a £10 note. See Unit 26.
2 a cushion
3 pile up
4 looking for something important among things which are not so important
5 Some of the uses of 'up' do have similar meanings. In *prop up*, *pile up* and *stack up* the particle suggests up rather than down. In *gather up*, *round up* and *line up*, the particle suggests 'together'.

25.2   1 stack up   2 round up   3 separate out

25.3
1 up   4 towards
2 away   5 up
3 among   6 up

25.4 *Possible answers:*
1 You would **fix up** a meeting.
2 They are required to **space out** the desks.
3 You might put a book under the short leg to **prop up** the table.
4 You might need to **separate out** paper, glass, food waste, etc. into different containers.
5 The photographer usually **lines** the pupils **up** before taking a school photo.
6 A sofa could **double up as** a bed if someone stays over.
7 You **gather** all the papers **up** and then throw or tidy them away.
8 You might agree to wear something distinctive so you will **know** each other **from** all the other people in the café.
9 Could you **see about** decorating the room, perhaps, while I get the food prepared?
10 It might be sensible to **sift through** the papers first to ensure that nothing important is thrown away.

Unit 26

26.1
1 The total cost of our holiday amounted **to** nearly £500.
2 The bill came to £22.20 each, so we rounded it **up** to £25 to include a tip.
3 Helena has **put** on a lot of weight recently.
4 It will take Joe some time to build **up** his strength again after such a long illness.
5 The college hoped that the advert would push **up** enrolments for its new course.
6 The new fertiliser claims to **bump** up agricultural yields considerably.

26.2   1 e   2 b   3 a   4 c   5 f   6 d

26.3
1 The new manager intends to cut costs by making the business smaller in some way – very possibly by sacking some staff.
2 It was a good place for a picnic because there were fewer trees there, so there might have been a bit of sunlight, more space to sit down, etc.
3 The number of hits on the website in June must have been much the same as the number of hits in May.

4 Young people are now clearly less interested in politics than they used to be.
5 The speaker seems reasonably happy about Joseph and what he does at home in that Joseph seems to do more than his share of the gardening even if he does less than his share of the housework.

26.4
1 knock down
2 fall off / tail off
3 amount to
4 tail(ing) off / fall(ing) off
5 slimming down
6 push up / build up
7 put on
8 adds up

Unit 27

27.1
1 Some people were going to buy our flat, but at the last moment the sale **fell through**.
2 Steve **prides** himself **on** his organisational skills.
3 The company was able to **capitalise on** the unusually wet weather by promoting its inexpensive umbrellas.
4 The England team lost the trophy in 2014 but **won** it **back** the following year.
5 It's been a difficult year for us, but we have **come out** of it with renewed vigour.
6 Leila **succeeded in** passing her driving test at her first attempt.
7 Hassan **lost out** to his brother in the finals of the tennis tournament.
8 They had a long battle in court to prove their innocence, but finally they **won through**.

27.2
1 doomed		5 rise	
2 carry		6 get	
3 pack		7 pulled	
4 sail		8 succeeded	

27.3   1 b   2 a   3 c   4 c   5 a   6 b

27.4 Oliver has always wanted to become an engineer, but it was quite difficult for him to get a place at college. He didn't get in at his first attempt, losing **out** to applicants with better exam grades. However, at his second try he succeeded **in winning** a place. He then sailed **through** all his first-year exams but failed some of his exams in the second year, as he started spending a lot of time on the rugby pitch, playing for the college first team, rather than in the library. Then his team fell **behind** in the college league after three games, so he wasn't too happy and did even less work, and as a result he failed three exams. However, he's always prided himself **on** being able to revise very efficiently when he's really under pressure, and in the third year he did enough to pull himself **through**. His friends were amazed that he managed to carry it **off**, as they were sure he could not have packed **in** enough study in such a short time to get **through** the exams. But Oliver knew that he had only just got **by**/**through** and he resolved to organise his life much better after leaving college.

Unit 28

28.1

1	clear	6	spill
2	hanging	7	caught
3	break	8	smooth
4	landed	9	resort
5	walk	10	make

28.2
1 When the doctors examined the dead man, they found his body was **riddled with** disease.
2 I just **grasped at** the first opportunity to get out of my boring job and do something more exciting. I wasn't prepared to just **live with** it / **resign myself to** it; I had to make a change.
3 I **fell back on** / **had to resort to** my knowledge of map reading from my days as a scout to help us find a way out of the valley.
4 I'm sorry, I've **botched things up** and caused a lot of problems for everyone.
5 A healthy diet and plenty of exercise is the best way to **safeguard against** heart disease.
6 His life is difficult. His parents died last year when he was only 16. Now he just has to **bear up** and try to carry on as best he can.
7 I'm afraid we just have to **resign ourselves to** the fact that we are going to have to sell the house.
8 She tried very hard to **clear up** / **iron out** the misunderstandings between the two groups.

Unit 29

29.1
1 toy with something
2 reason with someone
3 mull something over
4 decide on something / work something out
5 do someone out of something
6 size up someone or something
7 tie someone down
8 single someone out

29.2
1 You need a coin.
2 No, they haven't.
3 A drum is a musical instrument that is beaten. In the past the drummer in an army used to play rousing military music to encourage soldiers to fight, and this may be the origin of drum up meaning attract support or business.
4 It took them some time to arrive at that decision – often they were originally against the idea and/ or they had to be persuaded to it.

29.3

1	work; out	6	drum up
2	single; out	7	play on
3	push; through	8	toss for
4	tie; down	9	mull; over
5	arrive at	10	playing; off against

29.4
1 Everyone is trying to dissuade me from taking the job, but I'm tending **towards** accepting it.
2 You'll need to take time to **size** up the situation before you decide what to do.

3 Wicked Uncle Fred succeeded in **doing** his brother out of his rightful inheritance.
4 correct
5 It took Lily ages to get her father to **come** round to the idea of her training as a bus driver.
6 correct
7 The advert plays **on** people's desire to appear young and attractive.
8 I don't want to do the washing-up either. Get a coin and we'll **toss for** it.

Unit 30

30.1
1 Go for it!
2 Grow up!
3 Go on!
4 Come off it! / Come on!
5 Keep it up!
6 Wake up!
7 Dream on!

30.2
1 Roll	5 Shut
2 hang	6 go
3 Drink	7 eat
4 ahead	8 take

30.3
1 Go easy on them!	3 Get off!	5 Hurry up!
2 Calm down!	4 Watch out!	6 Hold on!

Unit 31

31.1
1 fling yourself into something
2 step aside, pack something in, get off
3 ease off, coast along
4 slog away, beaver away, plug away, knuckle down
5 beaver away (a beaver is an animal with sharp teeth and a large flat tail – it lives in a dam which it builds across a river)
6 farm out and get bogged down (a bog is a piece of very wet land – if you step in a bog, it can be easy to get stuck there so that you cannot move out)

31.2
1 Louise always **flings herself into** her work.
2 I really think that it is time you **knuckled down** to your studies.
3 As a research scientist, you just have to keep **plugging away** at your experiments and eventually you'll get results.
4 If this morning's meeting goes smoothly, I should be able to **get off** by 1 p.m.
5 The meeting was going well until we got **bogged down in** the details of the sales conference party.
6 I'm not sure exactly what I'm going to say in my speech, but I'm sure I'll be able to **cobble something together** by tomorrow morning.
7 There comes a time when it is best for an older manager to **step aside** and let a younger person take over.
8 I always say that if you start a job, you should **see it through**.

31.3 I'd hate a job where I could just coast **along** without needing to think about what I was doing. I'd far rather keep busy and really don't mind how much I have to slog **away** each day. I'd soon pack **in** any job that didn't keep me working hard. I fling myself **into** everything I do. Even when I was at school, I used to beaver **away** at my homework as soon as I got home from school. My sister certainly never used to knuckle **down to** work in the way I did.

31.4 1 I can't stand the sight of blood, so I'm not really **cut out for** nursing.
2 If you hate your job so much, why don't you just **hand in** your notice?
3 When several workers were unfairly dismissed, the trade union official decided it was time to **call everyone**/**people out** on strike.
4 As a PA I spend most of my time **running round** after my boss.
5 We've had a very busy few months at work but things are beginning to **ease off** now.
6 Liam is very good at his job, so I can't understand why he always gets **passed over (for promotion)** while less able people get promoted.
7 Our company has started doing a lot of outsourcing, which means that we **farm out** jobs that we previously used to do ourselves.
8 Ever since she was a child she has wanted to **go in** to medicine.

Unit 32

32.1 1 d   2 c   3 e   4 a   5 b

32.2 1 through   5 behind
2 through; through   6 towards
3 off   7 across
4 off   8 against

32.3 *Suggested answers:*
1 As each person arrived she (asked their name and) **ticked**/**checked them off** on her list.
2 She picked up her favourite novel and **buried herself in** it.
3 He decided to **major in** economics (for his degree).
4 His tutor **moved him up** to a higher class.
5 What sort of grades do you need to **get into** university in your country?
6 I applied to Oxford University but I didn't **get in**.

32.4 *Possible answers:*
1 What would you like to do when you leave/finish school?
2 Why did you give up / stop studying French/law (or the name of any other subject)?
3 Did your sister finish/complete her degree/course?
4 Do you fancy going to see a film this evening? (Or anything else suggesting a leisure activity. Note that **snowed under** is an informal way of saying that you have a huge amount of work to do.)

32.5 *Possible answers:*
1 I usually sailed through my exams – apart from maths!
2 I fell behind with my work in my final year at school when I broke my leg badly playing football.

3 Yes, teachers often used to mark me down for bad handwriting. I used to think this was really unfair and that they should just think about the content of my work. However, now I am a teacher and have to mark badly written work, I understand why they marked me down!

4 In the UK, taking part in extra-curricular activities, such as sport or music, having work experience and good references, showing you have good organisational or leadership skills, possibly also having good contacts can count towards getting into some universities.

Unit 33

33.1
1 Zeyneb's experiments were mostly **carried out** in the 19th century using much less sophisticated equipment than is available today.
2 This theory **draws on** research from several well-known scientists.
3 I thought we could read Hayder's research for the seminar tomorrow, but my tutor **pointed out** that the original research paper is over 700 pages long!
4 Alexander Fleming didn't **set out** to discover penicillin when he started experimenting with bacteria, but it was one of the most important discoveries of its time.
5 He spoke for 50 minutes and then **finished off** the lecture with a question and answer session.
6 Firstly, I'd like to **start with** an introduction to the subject of quantum physics, before moving on to some key definitions.
7 If we **allow for** variations caused by weather conditions, the results are broadly in line with our predictions.

33.2
1 together	3 jot down	5 sketch out	7 weigh up	9 go over
2 up	4 type up	6 Think through	8 ended up	10 follow up

33.3 *Suggested answers:*
1 This morning we're going to **look at** Maslow's 'Hierarchy of Needs'.
2 The lecturer **pointed out** that this research is still in its very early stages.
3 **To start with**, I want to talk about the background to the research.
4 In order to **get the most out of** the seminar, it's a good idea to do the suggested reading beforehand.
5 Can I borrow your lecture notes? I didn't **get down** the last few points.
6 Don't worry about writing every word; just **jot down** the key points.
7 For next week's seminar, I'd like you all to **look into** one aspect of this theory.
8 I'd like to **round off** the lecture today with a short video.

33.4
1 The biology department needs undergraduates to help carry **out** research on plant cells over the summer, and I'm going to apply.
2 The department has just received some funding to look **at/into** the links between diet and certain types of cancer.
3 He spent most of the summer working on his thesis but ended **up** having to change it when some new research came out.
4 The discussion we had last week brought **up** some very interesting questions about US foreign policy in the 1950s.
5 As you read **up** on the subject for your essay, don't forget to make a note of useful sources as you go.
6 A group of engineering students from Bristol have set **out** to prove the strength of plastic by building the largest Lego structure in the world.

Unit 34

34.1 1 to   2 to   3 from   4 to   5 of   6 up   7 on   8 at

34.2 *Possible answers:*
1 The research team **consists of** two Americans, two Russians and a Swede.
2 Immigrants to the UK have to **contend with** a whole range of problems.
3 The headteacher would like to **interest** more pupils **in** studying maths at university.
4 The examinations board i**nsists on** its instructions being followed to the letter.
5 It is essential that society should **invest in** the education of its future citizens.
6 The change in the law **resulted in** a more efficient welfare system.
7 The government is keen to **improve on** the country's system of transportation. (Note that it is also possible to say to improve the country's system of transportation without any preposition. Adding *on* makes the writing a little more formal and also suggests that the system of transportation is already reasonably good.)
8 The writer's philosophy is **founded on** a firm belief in socialist principles.
9 Some critics have **objected to** the poet's occasionally coarse use of English.

34.3 What best **sums the present situation up** – give examples / quotes.

34.4 1 The teaching materials will **cater for** historians as well as economists.
2 The recent problems in the company are bound to **detract from** its reputation.
3 The policy of clearing the hillsides of trees appears to have **resulted in** an increased danger of flooding.
4 The football team **consists of** three players from France, one from Sweden and two from Russia.
5 Many people **objected to** being moved from their houses to high-rise flats.
6 Being **deprived of** your freedom is a very difficult punishment to endure.
7 In her article, the writer frequently **refers to** a research study carried out in Canada in 2015.
8 The book is **aimed at** undergraduate students who have little previous knowledge of the subject.
9 For me, this song **sums up** the atmosphere in rural England in the 1980s. (Note that *up* would not be put after the object in a sentence like this becuse the object is very long.)
10 Much of the book is **devoted to** the writer's experiences in the United States.

Over to you

Possible answer:

Soviet education was **founded on** the belief that all children could succeed given the right support. The school system was **based on** the teachings of Marx and Lenin, and it **aimed at** providing the best education possible for all pupils regardless of their social background. It must be remembered that, at the beginning, Soviet education had many problems to **contend with**. As well as widespread illiteracy and a low level of resources, there were plenty of people who **objected to** the new Soviet regime, saying that citizens were being **deprived of** basic freedoms. Although many people are critical of other aspects of Soviet society, it cannot be denied, however, that the authorities **invested** a great deal **in** the education system. This **catered** well **for** Soviet youth, most of whom **profited from** the education they received. Teachers were respected professionals who **devoted** themselves **to** their pupils, doing all they could to **interest** them **in** their lessons and **insisting on** high standards in the classroom. To summarise, if we **refer to** most contemporary accounts of the Soviet education process, we find that it **resulted in** a well-educated population.

Unit 35

35.1
1	headed	7	brought
2	turned	8	aimed
3	set	9	buy
4	look	10	firmed
5	deal	11	turning
6	breaking	12	brought

35.2
1 Our business has had lots of success in Europe, but now we'd like to break into **the USA**.
2 Have you heard? Latifa has been asked to head up **the new department**.
3 Arsenal has signed up **a young Brazilian footballer**. *Or* Arsenal has signed **a young Brazilian footballer** up.
4 Her father made his fortune by dealing in **modern art**.
5 Get your people to call my people to firm up **arrangements**. (Note that 'Get your people to call my people to firm arrangements up' is also possible, though less frequent. We are more likely to use this structure when we are saying a time afterwards, e.g. We'll firm the arrangements up next week.)
6 The new factory is already turning out **10,000 pairs of shoes** a week. *Or* The new factory is already turning **10,000 pairs of shoes** out a week.
7 The Alpha model is aimed at **the lower end of the market**.
8 The company is planning to bring out **a new sports car** soon. *Or* The company is planning to bring **a new sports car** out soon.
(Note that when the object phrase is quite long, e.g. in 3 and 6, the phrasal verb is more likely to be kept together rather than separated.)

35.3 *Possible answers:*
We must **set up** a meeting early in the New Year. [make arrangements for]
Can you help me **set up** the apparatus for the experiment? [get the equipment ready]
A good breakfast **sets** you **up** for the whole day. [prepares you]

Someone **broke into** my car last night and stole the radio. [forcibly entered]
When James caught sight of the bus approaching, he b**roke into** a run. [started]
I don't want to **break into** my savings unless I really have to. [start using]

The government is hoping to **bring in** some new legislation relating to education. [introduce]
When you're writing your essay, try to **bring in** some good phrasal verbs. [include]
They **brought in** a consultancy firm to help sort out the business. [hired/involved]

That blue dress **brings out** the colour of your eyes. [makes more noticeable]
Her new friends have certainly succeeded in **bringing** her **out** of herself. [helping her to behave in a more confident, less shy way]
I think my new face wash is **bringing** me **out** in spots. [causing spots to appear on my skin]

A lot of people **turned out** to the concert. [came to]
It **turned out** that he had known the truth all the time. [happened]
His father **turned** him **out** when he heard what he'd done. [made him leave home]

Unit 36

36.1
1 run through, gobble up, set back, clean out, roll in
2 put by, put aside, pay in
3 work off, square up
4 a) square up   b) bail out   c) clean out/cough up   d) gobble up
5 rent out

36.2
1 bail
2 forward
3 cleaned
4 put
5 up
6 square
7 renting
8 pay
9 back

36.3
1 c – **off** my student debts.
2 g – **back** all our profits into the business.
3 h – **aside/by** each month for a rainy day.
4 f – **up** enough money for me to buy a car.
5 b – **into** some money on your gran's death.
6 a – **back** more than I had anticipated.
7 d – **into** my savings for as long as I can.
8 e – **through** enormous sums of money.

36.4 *Possible answers:*
1 I never had much money when I was a student but I managed to **live (spending as little as possible)** somehow.
2 If everyone **contributes**, then we should be able to afford a nice leaving present for Beth.
3 Rashid's **been receiving large quantities of** money ever since he had that brilliant idea for a website.
4 At the bakery it was Amanda's job to **count the money taken by the shop** at the end of every day.
5 Jason **risked/gambled** a ridiculous amount **of money on** a horse race and, needless to say, he lost it all.

36.5 *Possible answers:*
1 It probably set me back about €1,000.
2 They put money aside for a big expense such as a car, a house, a holiday or for a rainy day, i.e. when they might need money unexpectedly.
3 A car typically gobbles up money because you have to pay for petrol, repairs, taxes, etc.
4 I think it's worth breaking into savings for a really good holiday.
5 I'd probably ask my parents or my brother to bail me out if I had financial problems.

Unit 37

37.1
1 clearing away
2 pushing; to
3 blocking up
4 plumping up
5 pulling up
6 mopping up

37.2
1 You put them away.
2 You wash them down.
3 You mop it up.
4 You should chuck them away or put them out in the rubbish (in the recycling bin, of course).
5 You might put a shelf up / put up a shelf / put some shelves up / put up some shelves.
6 You'd block up the hole / block the hole up.

37.3
1 e   2 g   3 d   4 b   5 f   6 h   7 a   8 c

37.4 *Possible answers:*
1 I didn't hear you come in because I'd **got the TV** / **radio** / **my music on** rather loud.
2 My flatmate tends to make a mess when she's cooking and leaves me to **clean** / **clear up after** her.

3 When you go to bed, please don't forget to **lock up** / **put the rubbish out**.
4 The bookcase was too big for our new flat, so we had to **part with it** / **chuck it away**.
5 Erica is untidy. There are always lots of things **cluttering up** her room.
6 Our hall hasn't been decorated for years – it's time we **did**/**smartened it up**.
7 Living in a student hostel was odd for Khalifa at first, but he soon **settled in**.
8 If I lay the table, you can **clear away**/**clear up** after the meal.
9 You'll make the sofa look more comfortable if you **plump up the cushions**.
10 It took me all day to **clear up after** those wild, crazy kids and get the place **straightened up** again.

Unit 38

38.1
1 trousers
2 trousers, a dress, a skirt
3 unzip
4 a plant, perhaps
5 a coat, a skirt, a dress
6 a) making them looser b) making them tighter
7 fancy dress

38.2 1 b 2 c 3 a 4 b 5 c 6 d 7 c 8 b

38.3
1 We were surprised when we arrived at the party because the host was wearing a kind of Superman **getup** with a mask, cape and blue bodysuit.
2 My ten-year-old daughter loves getting **dressed up** in my dresses and high-heeled shoes.
3 Now that I'm pregnant I can't **get into** any of my clothes.
4 Those trousers look a little tight around the waist. Shall I **let them out** a bit for you?
5 (Father to child) You'd better **zip** your jacket **up**. It's cold outside. *Or* You'd better **zip up** your jacket …

38.4 *Possible answers:*
1 from older brothers or sisters or cousins
2 Once I went out with one black shoe on and one brown shoe on.
3 I'm afraid I have, especially in the spring as I often seem to put on weight in the winter.
4 It depends, but I'm probably more inclined to pull on the first thing I find.
5 I'd get them taken up because I'm not much good at sewing myself.
6 Yes, I have. Once I dressed up as a woman from the Middle Ages and once I dressed up as a character from a Chekhov play.

Unit 39

39.1
1 Alex: No, but I**'ve heard of her**.
2 Anna: I wasn't. They've been **going out together** for two years.
3 Will: Yeah, he was **flirting with her** all evening.
4 Katie: No. I tried to **strike up** a conversation with him, but he wasn't very friendly.
5 Andrew: Yes, I **warmed to him** straight away in fact. He's very nice.
6 Amber: Yes, you could say it was tennis that **brought us together**.

39.2
1 I've never met Antonia Goff, but I know **of** her because Charles works with her.
2 I had an email last month from Doninic, but I haven't heard **from** him since then.
3 I think Joe is cheating **on** me. Somebody saw him out with another girl.
4 Mrs Butler fusses ever so much **over** her two sons, even though they're adults.
5 Daria spent all evening flirting **with** her friend's brother.

6 I'm afraid my son is getting mixed up **with** some bad company at university.
7 Majid struck **up** a conversation with the person sitting next to him, and the flight passed quickly.
8 Rosa told me about your bust-**up** with Sebastian.

39.3
1 bad
2 c
3 It spoils or damages their relationship.
4 b
5 butter them up
6 c
7 an undesirable one
8 Both are possible.

Unit 40

40.1
1 screwed
2 toughen
3 getting
4 bored
5 had
6 outspoken
7 grown
8 descend

40.2
1 across; out
2 through
3 on; for
4 up
5 out

Unit 41

41.1
1 brimming
2 summon
3 perk
4 give
5 hankering
6 work
7 gone
8 snap
9 loosened

41.2
1 choke back or fight back
2 come over
3 bowl over
4 shake up
5 run away with
6 feel up to

41.3
1 choke back or fight back
2 bowled over
3 hanker after/for
4 brim with

41.4
1 Harvey
2 Felix
3 Keira
4 Sofia
5 Hannah
6 Aaron
7 Joel
8 Poppy

41.5
1 Layla let it all **spill out** / her feelings **spill out**.
2 Grandma isn't **feeling up to** a long flight.
3 We must not allow our feelings to **run away with us**.
4 You mustn't **give in to** those feelings of insecurity.
5 A feeling of tiredness suddenly **came over everyone**.
6 Our sympathies **go out** to all the victims of the disaster.

Unit 42

42.1
1 deal; move
2 letdown
3 shoot
4 passing
5 rolled

1 That they have become very involved in bird-watching and do it a lot.
2 What you did.
3 Members of the family would all come to one place and meet each other socially.
4 Just spend time together doing nothing special.
5 (b) go out with you and pay for you. *Take someone out* can mean to kill them in a military context, of war etc. If you go with someone to show them the way out of a building, *you show them out.*

1	Callum	5	Hessa
2	Ivy	6	Ronnie
3	Jessica	7	Lara
4	Thomas	8	Amy

Unit 43

43.1 1 Patient: I I think I've **picked up** a chest infection. I'm coughing and wheezing a lot.
2 Patient: Well, **I broke out in a rash** on my neck about a week ago.
3 Patient: Well, I had an ear infection about a month ago. It seemed to **clear up** when I took the antibiotics you gave me but now it's **flared up** again.
4 Patient: Well, OK, but my nose is **bunged-up** all the time. Can you give me something for it?
5 Patient: Well, I sprained my ankle a week ago, but the swelling hasn't **gone down** and it's still painful.
6 Patient: Well, I just feel absolutely **tired out** / **worn out** / **wiped out** / **done in** all the time. I have no energy at all.

43.2
1	Natasha	5	Harry
2	Grace	6	Elliot
3	Daniel	7	William
4	Bethany	8	Teddy

43.3   1 e   2 c   3 a   4 f   5 g   6 d   7 b

Unit 44

44.1   1 d   2 a   3 e   4 f   5 b   6 c

44.2   *Possible answers:*
1 You need to loosen up / warm up.
2 It may take you some time to thaw out.
3 You have to pick yourself up.
4 You turn around (or **swing around** perhaps if you do it very quickly).
5 They tense up.
6 They waste away.
7 You may double up (in pain).

44.3   I'm rather worried about my neighbour. I saw her the other day in the garden and she was doubled **up** in pain. She also looks as if she is wasting **away**. I asked her about it and she said she was just trying to lose some weight, but she clearly didn't like my talking about it and I could sense her tensing **up**. I think she's probably been doing far too much exercise. She spends hours outside bending **down** to touch the ground or spreading **out** her arms and swinging them in circles. I can see that she's in pain and I long to tell her to relax a bit.

44.4
1 You must be freezing – do come inside and **thaw out**.
2 Look at me – now **turn round/around**.
3 Their daughter was (lying) **curled up** on her bed with her thumb in her mouth.
4 He **stuck** his arm **out** of the window and waved at us.
5 If you don't eat more, you'll **waste away**.
6 The stand-up comic was so good that we spent the evening **doubled up** (laughing).

44.5
In each case the play on words depends on another meaning of the base verb.
1 Double means two or twice and obviously there are two twins.
2 The noun waste means rubbish.
3 Tense is a grammatical term which you are certainly familiar with as a student of English.
4 A taxi driver picks people up to drive them somewhere.

Unit 45

45.1
1 It's so boring listening to Uncle Ed **holding forth/going on at us** about the problem with the youth of today.
2 I'll try to **engage** your father **in** conversation so he won't notice you leaving.
3 I wish my parents would stop **going on at** me all the time.
4 OK, before everyone starts working, I'd like to quickly **run through** the instructions (again).
5 The personnel manager **glossed over** salary progression during our interview.

45.2
1 They asked her a lot of questions.
2 He would not have been pleased with his performance.
3 He didn't have to stop and think. He spoke very quickly, almost without pausing for breath.
4 He spoke less after Bobby arrived.
5 It was difficult for the detective to get the boy to tell her the truth.
6 He wanted to find out if the editor thought it would be a good idea to write the kind of article he had in mind.
7 It's dreadful because he just talks without listening to others or even giving them much chance to speak.
8 She told them a little about it but did not give them too many details, probably in case it worried them.

45.3
1	put	5	out
2	on	6	bombarded
3	led	7	clammed
4	sound	8	blurted

45.4
1 Finn was so rude – he **interrupted** the conversation I was having with Faye about her new job and started to ask her questions about her daughter.
2 I don't know how you'll manage to **give a reason for (make it appear that it was not your fault)** the scratch on your mother's car.
3 I wish he'd stop **talking endlessly about** the weather – it's so boring.

Unit 46

46.1
1 in on
2 away
3 on
4 into; up
5 up on

46.2
1 piled
2 tripped
3 push
4 stand
5 clear
6 stumbled
7 zipping
8 double

46.3
1 Draw back means to move away because you are surprised or afraid, and artists 'draw' pictures.
2 Zip along means to move very quickly, and the phrasal verb for fastening a jacket which has a zip is 'zip up'.
3 Squash up means to move closer together in order to make space for someone else, and 'squash' can also be a kind of juice drink.
4 Double back means to turn and go back in the direction you came from; identical twins could be called 'doubles'.
5 Stole is also the past tense of 'steal' meaning to take something without the owner's permission. The robbers were probably stealing money from the bank.

46.4
1 hang   2 drop   3 draw   4 double
Possible sentences:
1 I think we should **hang back** and let the family guests go into the reception first.
2 I was walking with my sister and chatting to her, but then I **dropped back** to talk with my grandfather, who was a bit behind everyone else.
3 We approached the man to help him but then **drew back** as he looked very aggressive.
4 As the mist came down, we decided it would be best to **double back** and abandon the walk.

Unit 47

47.1
1 feed on
2 prey on
3 die out
4 eat away at
5 washing away
6 dry up
7 pull down
8 break; off
9 pulling up
10 send out
11 offshoots
12 cutting down (Note **chopping down** is also possible.)
13 digging up

47.2
1 It would freeze over.
2 It might dry up.
3 overcast
4 Because the tide comes in and goes out.
5 Dogs might help them to flush the robbers out.

47.3
1 As night fell, the stars **came out**.
2 The sun **went in** and the temperature fell suddenly.
3 Cats (both large and small) **pick up** their young with their teeth to move them around.
4 It was lovely and sunny this morning but now the sky is **overcast** / it is **overcast**.
5 Many wild animals and plants are on the verge of **dying out**.

47.4
1 moved in   4 bring up
2 chased; out   5 watching over
3 taken over   6 fend for

Unit 48

48.1 1 off   2 down   3 down

48.2 How you mark these sentences will in some cases be a matter of personal preference.

1 Your pipes at home freeze up while you are on a skiing holiday.
☹ You are likely to be unhappy about this as pipes that freeze up will probably later burst and cause a lot of damage.
2 You receive a letter that makes your face cloud over.
☹ You are likely to be unhappy.
3 You are walking by the sea when fog rolls in.
😐 Most people probably don't like it when it becomes foggy because it spoils the view, but some people may enjoy it.
4 You can hear the rain beating down outside as you sit by a big log fire.
😊 You are probably happy because you are warm and cosy when it is wet outside, but you may feel unhappy if – say – you know you have to go out later on.
5 You are on a long country walk and the rain holds off.
😊 You are probably happy – unless you are the kind of person who enjoys rain.
6 You have to give a speech at a friend's wedding and you freeze up.
☹ You are unhappy because you have become too nervous or anxious to give your speech.
7 You breeze through an important exam.
😊 You are happy because you very easily manage to do well in the exam.
8 You storm out of a meeting.
☹ You are likely to be unhappy because you left the meeting in an angry manner.
9 A group of friends start to freeze you out.
😐 You are likely to be unhappy because your friends seem to want to exclude you from their group.
10 You are sitting on the beach and the sun is beating down.
😊 Most people probably like this, but I for one don't like sitting in very hot direct sunshine.

48.3 *Possible answers:*
1 The sun is breaking through the clouds.
2 The rain is pelting down (and that person will get very wet).
3 The windscreen has fogged/misted up.
4 The lock has frozen up.
5 The sun is beating down.
6 The smoke from the chimney is blotting out the sun.

48.4 *Possible answers:*
1 breezed in (as if nothing had happened)
2 misting over
3 mist/fog/steam up

4 break through (the clouds)
5 holds off
6 rolling in (from the sea/hills/moors)
7 breeze through (it)
8 freeze up

Unit 49

49.1
1	set	6	dotted	11	in
2	stretches/is stretched	7	off	12	reduced
3	steeped	8	run-down	13	off
4	bursting	9	boarded-up	14	off
5	soaking	10	onto	15	up

49.2
1 New housing developments are encroaching **on** the countryside on the edge of town.
2 Those climbing red roses really set that old white cottage **off**, don't they? *Or* … set **off** that old white cottage, don't they?
3 The architects made a large-scale mock-**up** of the new shopping centre.
4 The plain lines of the marble walls are **off**set by the ornate windows; together they produce a harmonious building.
5 This plan shows how the area will be **laid** out when it is redeveloped.
6 Signs have gone **up** round the area to be demolished warning the public to keep away.
7 The 1990s buildings do not blend **in** very well with the older houses around them.
8 The whole area is steeped **in** history.

49.3 *Possible answers:*
1 I think the Palace of Congresses in the Kremlin in Moscow blends in very well with the cathedrals and other old buildings there.
2 I live in Cambridge and the old city centre is often bursting with tourists, particularly in summer.
3 Cambridge, particularly the ancient university there, could certainly be said to be steeped in tradition.
4 My house backs onto a primary school.

Unit 50

50.1 1 picked   2 cut   3 change   4 rev   5 pull

50.2 *Possible answers:*
1 The police officer is **flagging a car down / flagging down a car**.
2 The driver is **picking up a hitchhiker / picking a hitchhiker up**.
3 The aeroplanes are **stacked up over an airport**.
4 The tyre has **blown out**.
5 The car is **branching off the main road**.
6 The car has been **blocked in**.

50.3
1 The police flagged down a lorry and found ten stowaways on board.
2 I was woken by a car revving up outside my bedroom window.
3 That car nearly caused an accident by cutting in on us.
4 I was very frightened when my tyre blew out on the motorway.

50.4
1	stow away	5	cast away
2	knocked over	6	branches off

3 blocked; in	7 pick; up
4 pulled; over / flagged; down	8 stacked up

Over to you

Author's answer:

I had a wonderful holiday once driving down the Rhone Valley with a friend and her husband. We **set off** from Switzerland, where they were living at the time, in their British car which had the steering wheel on the right-hand side. The problem was that her husband, the only driver among us, couldn't stand having another car in front of him. If a car **picked up** enough speed to pass us, he insisted on immediately **pulling out** to overtake it. Yet, because he was on the right-hand side of the car, he didn't have a clear view of the road ahead, so he'd **cut in** ahead of the car he'd overtaken in an alarming way to avoid crashing into the oncoming traffic. In the end we were **flagged down** by a policeman, who **told** him **off** for driving in such a dangerous way. Although we saw some great places, I was quite relieved when we **got back** to Switzerland without having had any serious accidents.

Unit 51

51.1

1 root out	7 stake out
2 put out	8 sound; out
3 pick up	9 ferret out
4 leaked out	10 get out
5 confide in	11 writing; up
6 worm; out of	

51.2 1 c   2 e   3 d   4 a   5 g   6 b   7 f

51.3
1 The conservatives **got in** in 2015.
2 A helicopter was **shot down** yesterday.
3 My great-great-grandfather **joined up** when he was only 16.
4 The kidnappers **gave themselves up** just after midday.
5 The rebels **held out** for six weeks.
6 The government has **sent in** a group of experts to assess the flood damage.
7 The government **put down** the rebellion using massive force.
8 Mr Fleet is trying to **whip up** some enthusiasm for the concert he is trying to organise.
9 Hundreds of people **joined in** the celebrations outside the palace.
10 Theodore **got onto** the party's national committee.

Unit 52

52.1 *Possible answers:*
1 Its aim was to find out whether claims of fraud were correct or not – and it discovered that the claims were justified.
2 By hushing up a scandal, the company is trying to keep it secret – which suggests that it is a scandal which might harm the reputation of the company in some way.
3 It is implying that the government is not being entirely honest with the public about possible health risks.
4 Because he/she does not want knowledge of the internal disagreements to become public in case the government loses public support. In other words, he/she is trying to hide this information in the same way in which wallpaper is sometimes used to paper over cracks in a wall.
5 It sounds as if it condemns their behaviour – this is suggested by 'cover up'.
6 The spy has given information about the way in which secret agents spied on diplomats.

52.2   1 f   2 g   3 a   4 b   5 c   6 h   7 e   8 d

52.3   As journalists it is our job to try to dig **up** stories that dishonest people are trying to cover **up**. Sometimes we are accused of spying **on** innocent people, but surely it is our duty not to allow people to paper **over** their scandals. Often it is not at all difficult to learn secrets. People are often eager to confide **in** someone who is willing to lend a sympathetic ear. Or they let **out** a secret without realising it. Little things like a blush or a quick glance at someone else can be a real give-**away** to an experienced reporter. Of course, sometimes people try to make **out** that they have nothing to hide, and then it can be a good idea to play **along** with them up to a certain point. Then you suddenly take them by surprise with an unexpected question and in this way you can often catch them **out**.

52.4   1 catch
2 make
3 let
4 gave
(Note that *give the game away* (= tell someone something that should be kept secret) is slightly different from the other examples in this set in that it is a fixed expression or an idiom.)

Unit 53

53.1   1 imposed
2 adhere
3 against
4 by
5 inform
6 let
[You may be curious to know how the scores were judged in the original magazine article: 0 – 3 Call yourself an outlaw!; 3 – 6 You're good, but not very good; 7 – 10 You're a model citizen. Congratulations!]

53.2   1 The new act went **through** Parliament last week and will become law on 1 January.
2 The anti-litter laws should be tightened **up**; as it is now, nobody is ever prosecuted.
3 He went on a two-year crime spree before the police finally caught up **with** him.
4 She avoided tax by signing **over** her property to her two sons.
5 The new law provides **for** jail sentences of up to ten years for repeat offenders.
6 Building regulations come **under** local government rather than national or European law.
7 The bill was passed by the Lower Chamber but was thrown **out** by the Senate and never became law.
8 The bill will be voted **on** in Parliament next week, and the government hopes it will get **through** without too much opposition.
9 If trials prove successful, the government intends to roll **out** the scheme across the whole country next year.
10 He was sentenced to three years in prison, but he'll probably be let **out** in 18 months.

53.3   1 The former CEO of Wilson & Wallace has been **let out** after serving a ten-year sentence.
2 If you don't **abide by** / **adhere to** the health and safety regulations, you will be punished.
3 The government plans to **toughen up** / **tighten up** the existing laws.
4 The law reforming the Health Service **got through** Parliament with a large majority.
5 Evan's criminal activity was discovered when his neighbours **informed on** him.

53.4   *Suggested answers:*
1 He was tried last week, found guilty and **sent to prison** for five years.
2 This government has **introduced** / **made** more new laws than any other in the last 50 years.

3 The new law will **become official** / **take effect** in March.
4 The military authorities **issued** / **made public** an order banning demonstrations in the area around the parliament buildings.

Unit 54

54.1
1 fade out
2 set up
3 print off
4 wiped off
5 call up
6 drop-down
7 type in

54.2 1 b   2 c   3 c   4 b   5 a   6 b

54.3 These statements are all true for the writer, but whether they are for you will depend on your own computer – and on how you have set it up.

54.4 *Possible answers:*
1 The advantage of a wireless connection is that you don't **have to wire everything up**.
2 You can print a document by selecting the print icon or by **going to the File menu and choosing Print**.
3 It's quite easy to **set up** a website with these step-by-step instructions.
4 Whenever I switch on my computer, it takes time **to warm up**.
5 I can use this cable to listen to my MP3 player in the car by **plugging it into the car radio**.
6 If the printer is beginning to run out of ink, a warning light **usually comes on**.

Unit 55

55.1
1 gobble/wolf; down
2 picks at
3 disagreed with
4 cut; out
5 put on
6 eat in; send out

55.2 1 Grace   2 Khadijah   3 Rory   4 Oliver   5 Lizzie

55.3

		¹s								
²d	i	p		³w	a	⁴s	h	e	⁵d	
		i			a		o		⁶o	n
		l			t		a		w	
⁷s	l	i	c	e		k			n	
		r								

55.4 *Possible answers:*
1 Shellfish often disagree with people.
2 A tart can be sliced up.
3 I often serve up roast chicken at the weekend.
4 Rice or potatoes fill you up.
5 I should cut down on cakes and biscuits.
6 In Britain people often send out for a curry or for a pizza.

Unit 56

56.1
1 came down
2 comes in
3 come down
4 came at
5 coming in
6 came at

56.2
1 up against
2 off
3 into
4 under
5 out with
6 across
7 into
8 in

56.3
1 Álvaro's English has **come on** a lot since he met Flora.
2 Hugo **comes across as** confident and extrovert.
3 The Prime Minister has **come in for** a considerable amount of criticism lately.
4 Ellen **comes out with** some very strange comments sometimes.
5 This history homework does not **come up to** the standards we expect from our students.
6 We've had a difficult year, but we've **come through (it)** and are looking forward to the future now.
7 At this point I should like to invite Anastasia Snow to **come in**.
8 I was afraid the dog was going to **come at** me.

56.4
1 come up to   2 come up against   3 come under   4 come into

Unit 57

57.1
1 It's time she got her act together and found a job.
2 The children always get up to mischief when I'm not looking.
3 I must get to the bottom of that strange letter I received.
4 We got down to business immediately. / We immediately got down to business.
5 Modern life is too complicated. We should get back to basics.

57.2
1 get in on the act
2 get by
3 got around
4 get the message across
5 get away with murder
6 get her out of my mind

57.3
1 down
2 off
3 off
4 out of
5 in
6 up to
7 into
8 together

57.4 *Possible answers:*
1 When do you normally **finish** work?
2 Do you **travel** a lot and **do things away from home or from your normal place of work**?
3 Is there any time of the year when you find it hard to **return to** the routine of your daily life?
4 What have you been **doing** recently?
5 What sort of things **make** you **feel depressed**?
6 Where do you usually **meet** your friends **socially**?

57.5 *Possible answers:*
1 I normally get off work at about 5 o'clock in the evening.
2 I get around quite a bit – particularly in the summer months.
3 I find it hard to get back into the routine of my daily life after my summer holiday.
4 I've been away on a trip to the Czech Republic.
5 Grey, damp days get me down.
6 My friends and I usually get together at a café in town.

Unit 58

58.1
1 into
2 after/for
3 over
4 down
5 ahead
6 for

58.2   1 g   2 d   3 f   4 a   5 h   6 b   7 c   8 e

58.3 1 Lara has been promised that her name will go **forward** for a place on the board of directors next year.
2 Going **by** the weather forecast, there'll be snow tomorrow.
3 They went **through** a terrible time during their daughter's illness.
4 You really mustn't go **around** telling such terrible lies.
5 Cameron has always wanted to go **into** law.
6 The journalists went **after** her wherever she went.

58.4 1 for   2 down   3 over   4 off

Unit 59

59.1 1 to   5 ahead
2 in   6 up
3 back   7 out of
4 from   8 up with

59.2 1 Please **keep your** music, TVs and radios **down** during the exam period.
2 Every household will be asked to contribute £10 a month towards the **upkeep** of the village recreation ground.
3 All team members are strongly advised to **keep off** fatty foods during the training period. It is important to **keep** your fitness **up** to the highest level.

59.3 1 to   2 on   3 up

59.1 *Possible answers:*
1 Noisy neighbours have occasionally kept me up.
2 I was once kept in hospital after being hit on the head by a football.
3 I'm going to regularly revise the units in this book and am also going to make a point of noting down any examples of phrasal verbs I find when I'm reading English.

Unit 60

60.1 1 take someone aback
2 take away from
3 take off
4 take out

60.2 1 along   4 up
2 away   5 off
3 aback

60.3 1 Martin does the best **take-off** of the Prime Minister that I have ever seen.
2 A ridiculous amount of my time is **taken up** with dealing with emails.
3 Even the rain could not **take away from** the beauty of the scene.
4 I was **taken aback** when I was told that I was no longer allowed to park in front of my own house.
5 Would you like me to **take up** your concerns **with** the manager? *Or* Would you like me to **take** your concerns **up** with the manager?
6 We are expecting a particularly large **intake** of students next week.
7 We decided it would be nicer to **take** our aunt **away** for the weekend rather than having her stay with us.
8 The **uptake** of places for the weekend seminar has been rather disappointing.

60.4 1 Let's **take down** the decorations tomorrow.
2 The doctor has agreed to **take** my elderly uncle **off those** pills for his arthritis.
3 Her parents **took** her **away** to their holiday home.
4 My favourite part of a flight is when the plane **takes off**.
5 Robert's being there **took away from** our enjoyment of the evening.
6 After Stan had been working in the kitchens for a week, he was **taken off** washing-up duties.

Mini dictionary

This Mini dictionary includes the definitions of the phrasal verbs and related noun and adjective forms that are practised in this book. Note that many of the phrasal verbs have other meanings which do not appear here. Refer to a good dictionary such as the *Cambridge Dictionary of Phrasal Verbs* for a full list of English phrasal verbs.

The numbers in the Mini dictionary are **Unit** *numbers not page numbers.*

abide by sth to accept or obey an agreement, rule, or decision *53*

accede to sth *formal* to agree to something that someone has asked for [e.g. request, demand], often after disagreeing with it *6*

account for sth to explain the reason for something or the cause of something *17*

add up to be a reasonable or likely explanation for something *17*

add up to increase and become a large number or amount *26*

add up (sth) *or* **add (sth) up** to calculate the total of two or more numbers *1*

add up to sth to have a particular result or effect *17*

adhere to sth *formal* to obey a rule or principle *53*

agree to both sides accept something *23*

(not) agree with sb if a type of food or drink does not agree with you, it makes you feel slightly ill *55*

aim at sth/doing sth to intend to achieve something, or to be intended to achieve something *34*

aim sth at sb to intend something to influence someone, or to be noticed or bought by someone *35*

allow for sth to take something into consideration *33*

amount to sth to become a particular amount *26*

arrive at sth to achieve an agreement or decision, especially after thinking about it or discussing it for a long time *29*

ascribe sth to sth *formal* to believe or say that something is caused by something else *6*

ask around to ask several people in order to try to get information or help *9*

be asking for sth *informal* to behave stupidly in a way that is likely to cause problems for you *6*

couldn't ask for sb/sth if you say that you couldn't ask for someone or something better, you mean that that person or thing is the best of their kind *6*

ask out sb *or* **ask sb out** to invite someone to come with you to a place such as the cinema or a restaurant, especially as a way of starting a romantic relationship *6*

associate sth with sth to connect someone or something in your mind with someone or something else *2, 18*

attend to sb/sth to deal with a situation or problem *6*

attribute sth to sth *slightly formal* to believe or say that something is the result of something else *17*

average out at sth to have as the average number *26*

back off to stop being involved in a situation, especially in order to allow other people to deal with it themselves *12*

back onto sth if a building backs onto something, its back faces that thing *49*

back up (sth) *or* **back (sth) up** to make a copy of computer information so that you do not lose it *6*

back-up *n* support, help or something that you have arranged in case your main plans or equipment go wrong *3, 54*

bail out sb/sth *or* **bail sb/sth out** to help a person or organisation by giving them money *6, 36*

balance out to make things equal *26*

bang about/around to move around a place, making a lot of noise *9*

bang down sth *or* **bang sth down** to put something down with force, often because you are angry *21*

base sth on sth if you base something on particular facts or ideas, you use those facts or ideas to develop that thing *6, 34*

bat around sth *or* **bat sth around** to talk about a plan or idea and to discuss different ways of dealing with it *24*

bear on sth *formal* to be directly connected to something *6*

bear out sth/sb *or* **bear sth/sb out** to prove that something that someone has said or written [e.g. claim, theory] is true, or to say that someone is telling the truth *52*

bear up to deal with a very sad or difficult situation in a brave and determined way *28*

beat down if the sun beats down, it shines strongly and makes the air very hot *48*

beat down if the rain beats down, it comes down in large amounts with force *48*

beaver away *informal* to work hard at something for a long time, especially something you are writing *31*

belt out sth *or* **belt sth out** *informal* to sing or to play a musical instrument very loudly *21*

bend down to move the top part of your body towards the ground *44*

bend to sb/sth to do something you don't want to do *23*

blast out (sth) *or* **blast (sth) out** to produce a lot of noise, especially loud music *21*

blend in/into sth if something or someone blends in, they look or seem the same as the things or people around them and so you do not notice them *49*

block in sb/sth *or* **block sb/sth in** to put a car or other vehicle so close to another vehicle that it cannot drive away *50*

block out sth *or* **block sth out** to stop yourself from thinking about something unpleasant because it upsets you *18*

block up sth *or* **block sth up** to fill a hole so that nothing can pass through it *37*

blot out sth *or* **blot sth out** if smoke or a cloud blots out the sun, it covers it and prevents it from being seen *48*

blow out if a car tyre blows out, it suddenly bursts *50*

blow up sth *or* **blow sth up** to make something seem much worse or much better than it really is *15*

blunder about/around to move in an awkward way, usually because you cannot see where you are going *9*

blurt out sth *or* **blurt sth out** to say something suddenly and without thinking, especially because you are excited or nervous *45*

boarded-up *adj* covered with pieces of wood *49*

be bogged down to become so involved in the details of something that you cannot achieve anything *31*

boil down to sth *slightly informal* if a situation or problem boils down to a particular thing, that is the main reason for it *7*

bombard sb with sth to direct a lot of something [e.g. questions, letters] at one person *45*

boom out (sth) to speak in a loud voice, or to make a loud noise *21*

bore into sb if someone's eyes bore into you, they look at you very hard and make you feel nervous *40*

boss about/around sb *or* **boss sb about/around** to tell people what they should do all the time *9*

botch up sth *or* **botch sth up** *informal* to spoil a piece of work by doing it badly *28*

bottom out if a situation, level, or rate that is getting worse bottoms out, it reaches the lowest point and remains at that level or amount, usually before improving *19*

bounce sth off sb *informal* to tell someone about an idea or plan in order to find out what they think of it *24*

bow to sb/sth to do something you don't want to do *23*

bowl over sb *or* **bowl sb over** to surprise or please someone a lot *41*

box in sb *or* **box sb in** to prevent someone from doing what they want to do *11*

branch off if a road or path branches off, it goes in another direction *2, 49*

branch off to leave a main road by turning onto a smaller road *50*

breakaway *adj* a breakaway group is a group of people that stop being part of another group, often because they disagree with them *1*

break down if a machine or vehicle breaks down, it stops working *4*

break down if a discussion, system or relationship breaks down, it fails because of a disagreement or problem *28*

break down sth *or* **break sth down** to divide information or a piece of work into smaller parts so that it is easier to understand or deal with *24*

breakdown *n* when talks between two groups of people fail because of a disagreement or problem *3*

break-in *n* when someone manages to get in a building by using force, usually in order to steal something *3*

break into sth to become involved in a type of business or activity that is difficult to become involved in *35*

break into sth to start to use an amount of money or food that you have been saving *36*

break off sth *or* **break sth off** to separate a part from a larger piece *47*

break out in/into sth if you break out in a sweat, it suddenly appears on your skin *43*

breakout *n* when someone escapes from prison *1*

breakout *n* when something dangerous and unpleasant, like war, disease or fire, suddenly starts *3*

break through (sth) if the suns breaks through or breaks through the clouds, it starts to appear from behind the clouds *48*

break up sth *or* **break sth up** if an event breaks up a period of time, it makes it more interesting by being different to what you are doing for the rest of the time *16*

break up (sth) *or* **break (sth) up** if an occasion when people meet [e.g. meeting, party] breaks up, or if someone breaks it up, it ends and people start to leave *19*

break up (sth) *or* **break (sth) up** if a fight breaks up, or if someone breaks it up, the people in it stop fighting or are made to stop fighting *20*

breeze in/into swh to walk in quickly and confidently *48*

breeze through sth *slightly informal* to succeed in something [e.g. exam] very easily *48*

brim with sth to have or show a lot of a good emotion or good quality *41*

bring forward sth *or* **bring sth forward** to change the date or time of an event so that it happens earlier than planned *16*

bring in sb/sth *or* **bring sb/sth in** if something, for example a company, brings people or business in, it attracts people, often encouraging them to buy products or services *35*

bring in sth *or* **bring sth in** to earn or make a particular amount of money *11*

bring in sth *or* **bring sth in** if a government or organisation brings in something new [e.g. law, rule], they make it exist for the first time *53*

bring out sth *or* **bring sth out** to produce something to sell to the public *35*

bring out sth *or* **bring sth out** to make a particular quality more noticeable *40*

bring together sb *or* **bring sb together** to cause people to be friendly with each other, especially people who have argued with each other or who would not usually be friendly with each other *39*

bring up sb *or* **bring sb up** to look after a child and educate them until they are old enough to look after themselves *47*

bring up sth *or* **bring sth up** to start to talk about something *33*

broken down *adj* if a machine or vehicle is broken-down it no longer works *4*

brush down/off sb/sth *or* **brush sb/sth down** to use a brush or your hand to remove something *7*

brush off sb/sth *or* **brush sb/sth off** to refuse to listen to what someone says, or to refuse to think about something seriously *7*

build in sth *or* **build sth in** to include something as part of a system *11*

build up (sth) *or* **build (sth) up** to increase in amount, size, or strength, or to make something increase in amount, size, or strength *3, 26*

build up sb *or* **build sb up** to make someone healthier and stronger after an illness, especially by making sure that they eat a lot *43*

build-up *n* when something increases in amount, size or strength *3*

built-in *adj* if something is built-in, it is made so that it fits into part of a wall or room *4*

bump sb off *or* **bump off sb** *informal* to kill someone *20*

bump up sth *or* **bump sth up** *informal* to increase the size or amount of something [e.g. price] by a large amount *26*

bunged-up *adj slightly informal* blocked nose *43*

buoy up sth *or* **buoy sth up** to support something and help to make it more successful *22*

burn out *or* **burn yourself out** *informal* to have to stop working because you have become ill or very tired from working too hard *43*

burst out sth if you burst out laughing or crying, you suddenly start to laugh or cry *21*

be bursting with sth to be very full with something *49*

bury yourself in sth to give all your attention to something *32*

bust-up *n informal* an angry argument *20*

bust-up *n informal* a break in a relationship *39*

butter up sb *or* **butter sb up** *informal* to be very nice to someone so that they will do what you want them to do *39*

buy out sb/sth *or* **buy sb/sth out** to buy part of a company or building that belonged to someone else so that you own all of it *3, 35*

buyout *n* the buying of a company, especially by the people who previously managed it or worked for it *3*

buy up sth *or* **buy sth up** to quickly buy a lot of something, often all that is available *6, 15*

call in (on) *British & Australian* to visit a place or person for a short time, usually while you are going somewhere else *6, 42*

call on sth *formal* to use something, especially a quality that you have, in order to achieve something *6*

call out sb *or* **call sb out** to order workers to strike (= to refuse to work because of an argument with an employer) *31*

call up sb *or* **call sb up** to order someone to join the army, navy, or airforce *51*

call up sth *or* **call sth up** if something calls up a memory or an idea, it makes you remember or think about it *18*

call up sth *or* **call sth up** to find and show information on a computer screen *54*

calm down (sb) *or* **calm (sb) down** to stop feeling upset, angry, or excited, or to make someone stop feeling this way *30*

capitalise on sth to use a situation in order to achieve something good for yourself *27*

not care for sth/sb *formal* to not like something or someone *41*

carry forward sth *or* **carry sth forward** to include an amount of money in a later set of calculations *6, 36*

carry off sth *or* **carry sth off** to succeed in doing or achieving something difficult *27*

carry out sth *or* **carry sth out** to complete a task *33*

cash in on sth to make money from an event or situation, or to get some other advantage from it, often in an unfair way *11*

cash up *British & Australian* to count all the money taken by a shop or business at the end of the day *36*

be cast away to be on an island with no other people after swimming from a ship that is sinking *1, 50*

cast-offs *n* clothes which have been given to somebody else because the first owner cannot use them any more *38*

catch on *slightly informal* to understand something, especially after a long time *24*

catch out sb *or* **catch sb out** to discover that someone is lying or doing something wrong *52*

catch up on/with sth to do something you did not have time to do earlier *2*

catch up with sb if someone in authority [e.g. police, tax officials] catches up with you, they discover that you have been doing something wrong and often punish you for it *53*

be caught up in sth to become involved in an activity or situation which prevents you from moving or making progress *28*

cater for sb/sth to provide all the things that people need or want in a particular situation *34*

cave in to agree to something that you were against before, after someone has persuaded you or threatened you *22, 23*

change down *British and Australian* to put a vehicle into a lower gear (= part of a machine that controls the speed of a vehicle), usually in order to go slower *50*

chase sb/sth off/out *or* **chase off/out sb/sth** to run after a person or an animal in a threatening way in order to make them leave *47*

chatter away to talk continuously *21*

cheat on sb *informal* to behave in a dishonest way towards your husband, wife, or usual sexual partner by having a sexual relationship with someone else *39*

check off sth *or* **check sth off** to look at each item on a list, or to write something next to each item on a list, in order to make sure that everything or everyone on it is correct, present, or has been dealt with *32*

cheer on sb *or* **cheer sb on** to shout encouraging words at someone, especially a person or team in a race or competition, or to receive encouraging words or shouts *22*

chip in (sth) *or* **chip (sth) in** *slightly informal* to give an amount of money, especially when a group of people are giving money to pay for something together *36*

chirp away if a bird chirps away, it sings continuously *21*

choke back/down sth *or* **choke sth back/down** to force yourself not to show your feelings *41*

chuck away/out sth *or* **chuck sth away/ out** *informal* to get rid of something that is not needed anymore *37*

clam up *informal* to become silent or to refuse to speak about something, usually because you are shy or afraid *45*

clean out sb *or* **clean sb out** *informal* if someone cleans you out, they take or use all the money you have, or if something expensive cleans you out, you spend all the money you have on it *36*

clean out sth *or* **clean sth out** to steal everything from a place *14*

clean up after sb to remove dirt someone has made, or to make a place tidy by putting things back where they belong *37*

clean up your act to start to behave better *8*

clear sth away *or* **clear away sth** to remove things in order to make a place tidy *37*

clear out *informal* to leave a place *46*

clear up if an illness clears up, or if medicine clears an illness up, the illness goes away *43*

clear up sth *or* **clear sth up** to give or find an explanation for something, or to deal with a problem or disagreement *28*

clear up after sb to remove dirt someone has made, or to make a place tidy by putting things back where they belong *37*

climb down to admit that you are wrong *7*

climb down if you climb down from a tree, you go back down to the ground *7*

close off sth *or* **close sth off** to put something across the entrance to something, in order to prevent people from entering it *49*

cloud over if someone's face clouds over, they suddenly look unhappy or worried *48*

clown about/around to act in a silly way *9*

clutter up sth *or* **clutter sth up** to fill something in an untidy or badly organised way *37*

coast along to do only the things that you have to do without trying to go faster or be more successful *31*

cobble together sth *or* **cobble sth together** to make something quickly and not very carefully *31*

come across if an idea or an emotion comes across in writing, film, music, or when someone is speaking, it is expressed clearly and people understand it or notice it *32*

come across to behave in a way which makes people believe that you have a particular characteristic *40, 56*

come across sth/sb to discover something by chance, or to meet someone by chance *1*

come along to start to exist, happen, or be available *1*

come around/round if a regular event comes around, it happens at its usual time *16*

come around/round to agree to a plan or idea that you were against, or to stop having a bad opinion about something, after thinking about it for a long time or being persuaded by other people that it is good *29*

come at sb to move towards someone in order to attack them *20, 56*

come at sth to think about something in a particular way *24, 56*

come back if something comes back to you, you remember it *18*

come between sb if an argument or other problem comes between two or more people, it spoils their relationship *39*

come down if you come down when you are suggesting a price for something, you suggest or agree to a lower price *10*

come down if a story or tradition comes down, it is passed from older people to younger people so that it continues *10, 56*

come down if a price or level comes down, it becomes lower *56*

come in to start speaking during a discussion *11, 56*

come in if the tide (= the regular change in the level of the sea) comes in, the sea comes higher up the beach *47, 56*

come in for sth if someone comes in for criticism or praise, they are criticised or praised for something they have done *56*

come into sth to get money from someone who has died *36*

come into sth to begin to exist or happen, or to begin to be fashionable *53*

come into (being) to begin *56*

come into it if you say that a particular emotion or quality [e.g. pride, love, luck] comes into it when you are describing a situation, you mean that it influences the situation *56*

come into one's own to be very successful *8*

come off sth to stop using medicine or drugs *43*

come off better/worse to end up in a good or bad position because of an argument or some kind of struggle *56*

Come off it! something that you say in order to tell someone that you do not believe them or that you disagree with them or are angry with them *30*

come on if something [e.g. lights, heating] or a supply of something [e.g. water, electricity] comes on, it starts working *54*

come on to improve in a skill, or to make progress *56*

Come on! something that you say in order to tell someone that you do not believe them or that you disagree with them or are angry with them *30*

come out if you describe how something or someone comes out at the end of a process or activity, you describe what condition they are in or what they have achieved *27*

come out to go somewhere with someone for a social event *39*

come out if the sun, the moon, or a star comes out, it appears in the sky; also applies to flowers and leaves which appear on plants in spring *47*

come out against to state publicly that you are opposed to an issue *22*

come out in favour of to state publicly that you support an issue *22*

come out of sth if something comes out of a process or an event, it is one of the results *17*

come out with sth to say something suddenly *56*

come over sb if a feeling comes over you, you suddenly experience it *41*

come over sth if an announcement comes over a public address system, people can hear the announcement *21*

come round to to agree with somebody else's idea or opinion after a long time thinking about it or discussing it *23, 29*

come through sth to manage to get to the end of a difficult situation *56*

come to (an agreement) to agree on something after discussion *23*

come under sth to be controlled or dealt with by a particular authority *53*

come under sth if something or someone comes under a particular action by other people [e.g. attack, criticism, scrutiny, review, pressure], that thing is done to them *56*

come up if an event is coming up, it will happen soon *16*

come up if information comes up on a computer screen, it appears there *54*

come up against sth/sb to have to deal with a difficult situation or someone who disagrees with you or tries to stop you doing what you want to do *56*

come up to sth to reach an acceptable or expected standard *56*

comeback *n* when a performer gives a performance he hopes will make him popular again *3*

confide in sb to tell someone things that you keep secret from other people *51, 52*

conjure up sth *or* **conjure sth up** to make something [e.g. picture, image, memory] appear in someone's mind *18*

consist of sth to be formed from two or more things *34*

contend with sth to have to deal with a difficult or unpleasant situation *2, 34*

contribute to sth to be one of the causes of an event or situation *17*

cope with sth to deal successfully with a problem or difficult situation *2*

cordon off sth *or* **cordon sth off** if people in authority [e.g. police] cordon off an area, they put something around it in order to stop people from entering it *12*

cotton on *informal* to begin to understand a situation or fact *24*

cough up (sth) *or* **cough (sth) up** *informal* to provide money for something, especially when you are not very willing to do this *36*

count against sb/sth to make someone or something more likely to fail *32*

count sb in to include a person in a plan or activity *23*

count on sth to expect something to happen, and make plans which depend on this thing happening *13*

count out sb *or* **count sb out** *informal* to not include someone in an activity *14, 23*

count towards sth to be part of what is needed in order to complete something or achieve something *32*

cover up (sth) *or* **cover (sth) up** to stop people from discovering the truth about something bad *52*

cover-up *n* if someone stops people from discovering the truth about something bad *1*

cream off sb *or* **cream sb off** to separate the cleverest or most skilful people from a group and treat them differently *32*

creep up on sb if a date or an event creeps up on someone, it seems to come or happen sooner than they were expecting *16*

creep up on sb to move closer to someone, usually from behind, without being seen by them *46*

cross off sth *or* **cross sth off (sth)** to remove a word from a list by drawing a line through it *32*

cross over to start to support a different, often opposing, person or group *22*

crowd around/round (sth/sb) to surround something or someone, standing very close to them *9*

cry out (sth) *or* **cry (sth) out** to suddenly shout something in a loud voice, especially to get someone's attention *14*

curl up to lie or sit with your back curved and your knees close to your stomach *44*

cut down sth *or* **cut sth down** if you cut down a tree or bush, you make it fall to the ground by cutting it near the bottom *47*

cut in to suddenly drive in front of someone, not leaving enough space between the two vehicles *50*

cut in (on) (sth) to interrupt what someone is saying by saying something yourself *11, 45*

cut off sth *or* **cut sth off** to stop the supply of something such as electricity, gas or water *2, 12*

cut off (from) swh to be in a separate space or area and unable to communicate with people in a different space or area *12*

cut off your nose to spite your face to do something because you are angry, though it may cause you more problems *8*

cut out sth *or* **cut sth out** to stop eating or drinking something, usually in order to improve your health *55*

be cut out for sth to have the right qualities for something, especially a job *31*

dash off *informal* to leave a place quickly *5*

deal in sth to buy and sell particular goods as a business *35*

deal with sth to take action in order to achieve something, or in order to solve a problem *42*

decide on sth/sb to choose something or someone after thinking carefully *29*

defer to sb/sth *formal* to accept someone else's opinion because they know more than you or are more important than you *22, 23*

depend on sth/sb to need the help or support of something or someone in order to survive or continue as before *13*

depend on sth/sb if something depends on a particular situation, condition, or person, it is influenced by them or cannot change without them *17*

deprive sb/sth of sth to take something important away from someone *2, 34*

descend to sth/doing sth to behave badly in a way that other people would not expect you to *40*

detract from sth to make something seem less good than it really is or than it was thought to be *34*

devote sth to sth/doing sth to use all of something, for example your life or your time, for a particular purpose *34*

die away if something, especially a sound, dies away, it gradually becomes less strong or clear and then stops *2*

die down if something, especially noise or excitement, dies down, it gradually becomes less loud or strong until it stops *21*

die out to become more and more rare and then disappear completely *47*

dig up sth *or* **dig sth up** to take something out of the ground by digging *47*

dig up sth *or* **dig sth up** to discover new facts about a person or situation after a lot of searching *52*

dig your heels in to refuse to do what others try to persuade you to do *8*

dip sth in (sth) to quickly put something into something else and then take it out again, especially biscuits in tea or coffee *55*

disagree with sb if a type of food disagrees with you, it makes you feel slightly ill or uncomfortable *55*

dive in/into sth to start doing something suddenly without thinking about it *7*

do in sb *or* **do sb in** *informal* to attack or kill someone *29*

do in sb *or* **do sb in** *informal* to make someone extremely tired *43*

do out sth *or* **do sth out** *British & Australian* to decorate or clean a room *37*

do sb out of sth *informal* to stop someone from getting or keeping something, in a dishonest or unfair way *29*

do up sth *or* **do sth up** to wrap something [esp. present] in paper *25*

do up sth *or* **do sth up** to repair something, or to improve the appearance of something, especially a building *49*

do yourself up to make yourself look more attractive *29*

do without (sth/sb) to manage without something or someone *29*

doom (sb/sth) to sth to make someone or something sure to fail or suffer in a particular way *27*

dot sth with sth if a place is dotted with something, it has many of them, all over the place *49*

double back to turn and go back in the direction that you have come from *46*

double (sb) over/up to suddenly bend your body forwards because you are laughing a lot or you are in pain *44*

double up as sth if something designed for one purpose can double up as something else, it can also be used for something else *25*

downcast *adj* sad and depressed *4*

downpour *n* a sudden, heavy fall of rain *3*

drag sb away from *informal* to make somebody stop doing something, so that they can do something else *7*

drag sb/sth into sth to talk about or bring someone or something into a difficult or unpleasant situation, especially when that person or thing is seen as being connected with the situation *20*

drag out (sth) *or* **drag (sth) out** to continue for longer than is necessary, or to make something do this *16*

drag sth out of sb to make someone tell you something that they do not want to tell you *45*

draw back to move away from someone or something, usually because you are surprised or afraid *46*

draw on sth to use information from somewhere *33*

draw out sb *or* **draw sb out** to help someone who is shy to feel more confident *40*

draw out sth *or* **draw sth out** to make something continue for longer than is usual or necessary *14*

Dream on! something that you say in order to tell someone that what they are hoping for is not possible and will not happen *30*

dress up (sb) *or* **dress (sb) up** to put on someone else's clothes to make yourself look like someone else, or to make someone do this, usually as a game *38*

drink in to look at, listen to, or experience something with all your attention and to enjoy it very much *7*

drink to sb/sth to hold up your glass before drinking from it in order to celebrate something or to wish someone success or happiness *55*

drink up (sth) *or* **drink (sth) up** to completely finish your drink *30*

drive off to leave in a vehicle *5*

drone on to talk for a long time in a very boring way *13, 21*

drop back if you are moving forward in a group of people and you drop back, you move to a position nearer the back *46*

drop by *British & Australian* informal to make a short visit to someone in their home, usually without arranging it before *42*

drop-down menu a list of choices which appears on a computer screen *54*

drop off to fall asleep *2, 43*

drop off sb/sth *or* **drop sb/sth off** to take someone to a place that they want to go to, or to deliver something to a place, usually in a car, often when you are going somewhere else *2*

drop out to not do something that you were going to do, or to stop doing something *14*

drop out if a student drops out, they stop going to classes before they have finished their course *32*

drown out sth *or* **drown sth out** if a loud noise drowns out another noise, it prevents it from being heard *21*

drum up sth to increase interest in something or support for something *29*

dry out (sth) *or* **dry (sth) out** to make something dry, or to become dry *47*

dry up if a supply of something dries up, it ends *19*

dry up to stop speaking when you are acting or making a speech, especially because you suddenly forget what to say next *45*

dry up if an area of water [esp. river, lake] dries up, the water in it disappears *47*

dumb down sth *or* **dumb sth down** to make something [e.g. textbook, curriculum] simpler and easier to understand *51*

dwell on sth to think or talk about a particular subject for too long *13*

ease off/up to gradually stop or become less *5*

ease off/up to start to work less or to do things with less energy *31*

eat away at sb if a memory or bad emotion [e.g. bitterness, shame] eats away at someone, they think about it a lot and it makes them very unhappy *18*

eat away at sth to gradually destroy something by continuously damaging it or taking little parts of it away *47*

eat in to have a meal at home, not in a restaurant *55*

eat into sth to use or take away a large part of something valuable [e.g. savings, profits, leisure time, business] *7*

eat up sth *or* **eat sth up** to eat all the food you have been given *15*

Eat up! something that you say to someone, especially a child, in order to tell them to eat their food *30*

egg on sb *or* **egg sb on** to encourage someone to do something, often something that is wrong, stupid, or dangerous, or to be encouraged to do something *22*

eke out sth *or* **eke sth out** to use something slowly or carefully because you only have a small supply of it *16*

encroach on sth to gradually cover more and more of an area of land *49*

end up to finally be in a situation *33*

engage sb in conversation if you engage someone in conversation, you try to start a conversation with them *45*

expand on sth to give more details about something you have said or written *45*

explain away sth *or* **explain sth away** to give a reason for something bad happening which makes other people think that it is not so bad or that it is not your fault *45*

face up to sth to accept that a difficult or unpleasant situation exists *2*

factor in sth *or* **factor sth in** to include something when making a calculation or when trying to understand something *11*

fade in if the sound or picture of a film or recording fades in, or if you fade it in, it becomes gradually louder or brighter so that you can hear it or see it clearly *54*

fade out if the sound or picture of a film or recording fades out, or if you fade it out, it gradually becomes quieter or less clear until you cannot hear or see it any more *54*

fall apart if an organisation, system, or agreement falls apart, it fails or stops working effectively *19*

fallback *adj* a fallback position is something you use when other things have failed, or when there are no other choices *4*

fall back on sth to use something when other things have failed, or when there are no other choices *28*

fall behind (sb) to fail to remain level with a group of people that is moving forwards *32*

fall behind (sb) to fail to score as many points as another team or player in a competition *27*

fall in if a structure [e.g. roof, ceiling] falls in, it drops to the ground because it is weak or damaged *49*

fall off if the amount, rate, or quality of something falls off, it becomes smaller or lower *26*

fall through if a plan or agreement falls through, it fails to happen *6, 27*

farm out sth *or* **farm sth out** to give work to other people instead of doing it yourself *31*

feed on sth if an animal feeds on a particular type of food, it usually eats that food *47*

feel up to sth/doing sth to feel physically and mentally strong enough to do something *41*

fend for yourself to take care of yourself without needing help from other people *47*

ferret out sth *or* **ferret sth out** to find something after searching for it *51*

fight back sth *or* **fight sth back** to try hard not to show an emotion, or to try hard not to let your emotions control what you do *41*

fight off sb/sth *or* **fight sb/sth off** to use violence so that something or someone goes away *20*

fill up sb *or* **fill sb up** if food fills someone up, it makes them feel as if they have eaten enough *55*

finish off sb *or* **finish sb off** to make someone so tired, weak, or unhappy that they are unable to continue what they were doing *12*

finish up (sth) *or* **finish (sth) up** to eat or drink all of what you are eating or drinking *15*

finish with sth to stop using or needing something *19*

firm up sth *or* **firm sth up** to make something [e.g. agreement, details, prices] more definite or less likely to change *35*

finish off to end or complete something *33*

fish out sth *or* **fish sth out** *informal* to pull or take something out of a bag or pocket, especially after searching *7*

fit in to be able to be done between other activities *16*

fit in with sth if one activity or event fits in with another, they exist or happen together in a way which is convenient *11*

fix up sth *or* **fix sth up** to arrange something [esp. meeting] *25*

flag down sth *or* **flag sth down** to make a vehicle stop by waving at the driver *50*

flare up if someone flares up, they suddenly become very angry *20*

flare up if a disease that you had before flares up, you suddenly get it again *43*

flash back if your mind or thoughts flash back to something that happened to you in the past, you suddenly remember that thing *18*

flashback *n* an occasion when you suddenly remember something vividly that happened to you in the past *18*

flatten out if the rate of something flattens out, or if something flattens it out, it stops increasing and decreasing and begins to stay at the same level *26*

fling off sth *or* **fling sth off** to remove very quickly *38*

fling yourself into to start to spend a lot of your time and energy doing something *31*

flirt with sb to talk and behave towards someone in a way that is sexually attractive and which shows that person that you are sexually attracted to them *39*

be floating about/around if you say something is floating around, you mean that you have seen it somewhere but you do not know exactly where it is *9*

flood back if memories flood back, you suddenly remember very clearly a lot of things about an experience or period in the past *18*

flood in/into sth to arrive or enter somewhere in very large numbers or amounts *7*

flush out sb/sth *or* **flush sb/sth out** to force a person or animal to come out of the place they are hiding in *47*

fly about/around (swh) if rumours fly around, they are made in a way which makes people excited *9*

fly at sb to attack someone suddenly and violently *20*

fly into sth if someone flies into a particular state [e.g. rage, temper, panic] they are suddenly in that state *20*

focus (sth) on sth to give a lot of attention to one particular activity, situation or idea *13*

fog up if something made of glass [e.g. windscreen, glasses] fogs up, or if something fogs it up, it becomes covered with small drops of water and you cannot see through it any more *48*

foldaway *adj* a foldaway bed has parts that can be folded so that it is smaller and can be stored somewhere *4*

fold up (sth) *or* **fold (sth) up** to make something [e.g. cloth, paper, chair] into a smaller, neater and usually flatter shape by folding it, or to be able to be folded in this way *25*

fold-up *adj* a fold-up chair can be made into a smaller, neater and flatter shape by folding it *4*

follow up sth *or* **follow sth up** to find out more about something *33*

forthcoming *adj* a forthcoming event, action, or product is one which will happen or become available soon *4*

be founded on sth to be based on a particular idea or belief *34*

free up sth *or* **free sth up** to make time or money available for a particular use by not using it in another way *16*

freeze out sb *or* **freeze sb out** to make someone feel that they are not part of a group by being unfriendly towards them, or to stop someone from being included in an arrangement or activity *48*

freeze over if water freezes over, it becomes covered with ice *2, 47*

freeze up become so afraid you cannot move or do anything *48*

freeze up if something [e.g. pipe, lock] freezes up, it becomes blocked with ice and stops working *48*

fritter away sth *or* **fritter sth away** to waste something [esp. money, time] by using it in a careless way for unimportant things *16*

frown on sth to believe that something is wrong and that you should not do it *13*

fry-up *n* a quick meal made of fried food *55*

fuss over sb/sth to pay too much attention to someone or something, especially because you want to show that you like them *39*

gain on sb/sth to get nearer to someone or something that you are chasing *46*

gang up *informal* to form a group to act against someone else *6*

gather up sth *or* **gather sth up** to collect several things, especially from different places, and put them together *25*

gear sth to/towards sth/sb to design something so that it is suitable for a particular purpose, situation, or group of people *25*

get across sth *or* **get sth across** to successfully communicate an idea to other people *57*

get around if news or information gets around, a lot of people hear about it *9, 57*

get around to travel to a lot of different places *57*

get away with sth/doing sth to succeed in not being criticised or punished for something wrong that you have done *57*

get away with murder to succeed in not being criticised or punished for something wrong that you have done *57*

get back into sth to begin doing something again after not doing it for a period of time *57*

get back to basics to start again at the beginning *57*

get by to have or know just enough of something to be able to deal with a particular situation but not have or know as much as you would like *1, 27*

get by to have just enough money to pay for the things that you need, but nothing more *6, 57*

get down *or* **get sth down** to manage to write down a series of spoken points *33*

get down to sth/doing sth to start doing something seriously and with a lot of your attention and effort *57*

get sb down to make someone feel unhappy *10, 57*

get in to succeed in getting a place at a school, college, or organisation *32*

get in if a political party or a politician gets in, they are elected *51*

get in sth *or* **get sth in** to manage to do something even though you do not have much time because you are busy doing other things *57*

get in on sth *informal* to start to become involved in an activity that other people are already doing, often without being invited to *57*

get into sth to succeed in getting a place at a school, college, or organisation *32*

get into sth *informal* to be thin enough to be able to put your clothes on *38*

get into sth to become interested in an activity or subject, or to start being involved in an activity *42, 57*

get off to leave the place where you work, usually at the end of the day *31, 57*

Get off (sb/sth)! something that you say in order to tell someone to stop touching someone or something *30*

get off on the wrong foot to start something badly *8*

get off sb's back to stop nagging someone *57*

get off the ground to get started *57*

be getting on *mainly British & Australian informal* when time is getting on, it is getting late *16*

be getting on *informal* if someone is getting on, they are old *40*

get on like a house on fire to immediately like each other *8*

get on to/onto sth to be elected as a member of an organisation *51*

get on (with sb) to like someone, and enjoy spending time with them *1, 2*

get out if news or information gets out, people hear about it even though someone is trying to keep it secret *51*

get sth out of sth/doing sth to enjoy something or think that something is useful *57*

get sth out of your mind to stop thinking about something *57*

get over sth to feel better after having an illness *43*

get (sb) through sth to succeed in an examination or competition, or to help someone or something do this *27, 32*

get (sth) through (sth) if a law or proposal gets through, or if someone gets a law or proposal through, it is officially accepted by a government or organisation *53*

get the most out of sb/sth to take maximum benefit from something *33*

get to the bottom of sth to understand something properly, not superficially *57*

get together if two or more people get together, or if someone gets two or more people together, they meet in order to do something or spend time together *57*

get-together *n* an informal meeting or party *42*

get up to stand up *1*

get up to sth to do something, especially something that other people think is wrong *42, 57*

get up to sth to reach a particular place in something that you are doing and to stop there *19*

getup *n informal* the particular clothing, especially when strange or unusual, that someone is wearing *38*

get your act together to organise yourself more efficiently *8, 57*

give away sth *or* **give sth away** to let someone know something that should be kept secret, often by mistake *52*

give-away *n* something that makes you aware of a fact that someone else was trying to keep secret *52*

give in to sth if you give in to an emotion or desire, you stop trying not to feel it and you allow your actions to be controlled by that emotion or desire *41*

give in to sth iwhen someone spends a long time trying to persuade you to do or agree to something, and you finally agree to it *23*

give up (sth /doing sth) *or* **give (sth) up** to stop doing an activity or piece of work before you have completed it, usually because it is too difficult *32*

give yourself up to allow the police to catch you *51*

gloss over sth to avoid discussing something, or to discuss something without talking about the details in order to make it seem unimportant *6, 45*

be glued to sth to be watching something [esp. television] with all your attention *7*

go after sb to chase or follow someone in order to catch them *58*

go after / for sth to try to get something that you want [e.g. job] *58*

go against sth if something goes against a rule or something you believe in, it does not obey it or agree with it *53*

go ahead *slightly informal* something that you say to someone to give them permission to start to do something *30*

go ahead if an event goes ahead, it happens *58*

go-ahead *adj* using new methods and ideas to succeed *4*

go along with sth/sb to agree with someone's idea or opinion *23*

go around (swh) if an illness goes around, a lot of people get it *43*

go around doing sth if someone goes around doing something, they spend their time behaving badly or doing something that is unpleasant for other people *58*

go back over sth to examine or think about something again or after it has happened *58*

go back to sth if a situation goes back to a particular state, it returns to that state *20*

go by sth to use information or experience that you have of someone or something in order to help you decide what to do or what to think about that person or thing *58*

go down if a computer system goes down, it stops working *10, 58*

go down to become worse in quality *58*

go down if part of your body that is bigger than usual because of an illness or injury goes down, it starts to return to its usual size *43, 58*

go down to be remembered as part of something *10*

go down well-received *10*

go easy on sb to treat someone in a gentle way, especially when you want to be or should be more severe *30*

go for sb to attack someone *58*

go for sth if something goes for a particular amount of money, it is sold for that amount *58*

Go for it! something that you say to encourage someone to try and achieve something *30*

go forward if someone's name goes forward, it is suggested that that person should compete for an elected position or a job *58*

go in *informal* if a fact or piece of information goes in, you understand it and remember it *24*

go in if the sun or moon goes in, it becomes hidden behind a cloud *47*

go in to sth to choose a particular type of work as your job *31*

go into sth to describe, discuss, or examine something in a detailed way *6*

go into sth to start an activity, or start to be in a particular state or condition *58*

go off if a light or machine goes off, it stops working *54*

go off to happen in a particular way *58*

go off sb/sth to stop liking someone or something *5, 41*

go on to continue to exist or happen *4*

go on to talk in an annoying way about something for a long time *13*

Go on! something that you say to tell someone that you do not believe what they have just told you *30*

go on sth to use a computer or the Internet, or to visit a website *54*

go on at sb to criticise someone continuously *45*

Go on then! something that you say to encourage someone to do something *30*

go on to sth to start to do something after you have finished something else *32*

go on to swh to go to a particular place after going somewhere else *42*

go out if something which is burning [e.g. fire] goes out, it stops burning *14*

go out if the sea or the tide (= movement of the sea in and out) goes out, it moves away from the beach *47*

go out to sb if your thoughts or sympathies go out to someone, you feel very sorry for them when they are in a difficult situation *41*

go out together to have a romantic relationship *39*

go out with sb to have a romantic relationship *39*

go over sth to think about something that has happened or something that was said *33, 58*

go over to sth to leave one group or organisation and join a group or organisation that is competing against them *6, 58*

be going round in circles to use a lot of time and effort with no results *8*

go through if a law, plan, or deal goes through, it is officially accepted or approved *23, 53*

go through sth to experience an unpleasant or difficult situation or event *58*

go to (swh) to click on a menu, a menu item, a particular web page or part of a page, or a link when using a computer *54*

go up if a shout [e.g. cheer, cry, groan] goes up, a lot of people make that noise at the same time *21*

go up if a building or sign goes up, it is built or it is fixed into position *49*

go with sth to accept a plan or an idea, or to support the person whose ideas you agree with *22, 23*

gobble down/up sth *or* gobble sth down/up *informal* to eat very quickly *55*

gobble up sth *or* gobble sth up *informal* to use a lot of something, especially money *36*

grapple with sth to try to deal with or understand a difficult problem or subject *24*

grasp at sth to quickly use or accept an opportunity to do or have something, especially because you are unhappy with the present situation *28*

grate on sb/sth if something, especially someone's voice or way of behaving, grates on you, it annoys you *21*

grow out of sth if a child grows out of an interest, way of behaving, or illness, they stop having or doing it because they have become older *40*

Grow up! *informal* something that you say to an adult in order to tell them to stop behaving stupidly *30*

gun down sb *or* gun sb down to shoot someone and kill or seriously injure them, often when they cannot defend themselves *10*

be gunning for sb informal to try to harm someone or cause trouble for them *6*

hack into sth to get into someone else's computer system without permission in order to look at information or do something illegal *6*

hammer out sth *or* hammer sth out to reach an agreement after a lot of argument or discussion *23*

hand in sth *or* **hand sth in** to tell your boss officially that you do not want to do your job anymore *31*

Hang about/on! something that you say to tell someone to stop doing or saying something *30*

hang about/around/round with sb *informal* to spend time with someone *6*

hang back to not move forwards, usually because you are shy or afraid *46*

hang on sth to depend on something *13*

hang on to/onto sth/sb to keep someone or something *19*

hang out *informal* to spend a lot of time in a particular place, or to spend a lot of time with someone *42*

hang over sb/sth if a problem or threat hangs over a person or situation, it exists and makes people worry about what is going to happen *28*

hanker after/for sth to want something very much, especially something you know you should not want *5, 41*

happen on sb/sth to find something or meet someone without planning to *13*

harp on to talk continually about something in a way that other people find boring or annoying *13*

have sth against sb/sth to dislike or disagree with someone or something for a particular reason *41*

have sb down as sth to think that someone is a particular type of person, especially when they are not in fact like that *40*

have off sth *or* **have sth off** to spend time away from work *12*

have on sth *or* **have sth on** if you have an electrical device [e.g. television, radio, iron] on, it is operating so that you can use it *37*

have on sth *or* **have sth on** if you have clothes or shoes on, you are wearing them *38*

head off swh to begin a journey or to leave *5*

head off sth *or* **head sth off** to prevent a difficult or unpleasant situation from happening *51*

head up sth *or* **head sth up** to be in charge of an organisation *35*

heal up if a wound heals over, new skin grows over it *43*

hear from sb to receive news or information from someone, usually by letter or telephone *39*

have/had heard of sb/sth to know a little about someone or something because you have read, seen, or been told something about them before *39*

not hear of sth *or* **not hear of sb doing sth** to not allow something, or not allow someone to do something *22*

help sb to sth to put food onto a plate for yourself *55*

hinge on sth to depend on something or be very influenced by it *13*

hit on sth to have a good idea, especially one that solves a problem *5, 24*

hit out to strongly criticise something or someone *7*

hoard away sth *or* **hoard sth away** to put a supply of something in a safe place so that you can use it in the future *25*

hold back sb/sth *or* **hold sb/sth back** to prevent something from working effectively, or to prevent someone or something from making progress *1*

hold down sb *or* **hold sb down** to limit the freedom of a group of people *1*

hold forth to talk about a particular subject for a long time, often in a way that other people find boring *45*

hold off to not start, although you expect it to *48*

Hold on! to tell someone to stop doing something for a very short while *30*

hold out to continue to defend yourself against an enemy or attack *51*

hold out for sth to wait until you get what you want and to refuse to accept anything less *1*

hold over sth *or* **hold sth over** to delay something and to arrange to do it at a later time *16*

hook up US informal to meet someone for a particular purpose *42*

huddle up to move closer to other people, or to hold your arms and legs close to your body, usually because you are cold or frightened *44*

hurry along to make someone do something more quickly, or to make something happen more quickly *16*

Hurry up! *informal* to tell someone to move more quickly or do a task more quickly *30*

hush up sth *or* **hush sth up** to stop the public from finding out about something bad that has happened *52*

impact on sth/sb *slightly* formal to have a noticeable effect on *17*

impose sth on sb *formal* to force a group of people to accept something, or to give someone a punishment [e.g. fine, ban] *53*

improve on sth to do something in a better way or with better results than when it was done before *34*

inform on sb to give information about someone who has done something wrong to a person in authority, especially the police *53*

input *n* contribution to a system to help it operate *3*

insist on sth/doing sth to demand something and to make it clear that you will not accept anything else *34*

intake *n* the number of people who begin to study at a school, or who join an organisation at a particular time *60*

interest sb in sth to try to persuade someone that they want something *34*

invest sth in sth to use a lot of time or effort trying to achieve something or trying to make something successful *34*

iron out sth *or* **iron sth out** to find a way of solving small difficulties or problems, or to find a way of ending a disagreement *28*

jazz up sth *or* **jazz sth up** to make something more attractive or interesting *15*

join in (sth) to become involved in an activity with other people *51*

join up to join the army, navy, or airforce *51*

jot down sth *or* **jot sth down** to write something down quickly (so that you remember it) *33*

jut out to stick out from a surface or beyond the edge of something *14*

keep (sb) ahead to continue to be more advanced and successful than other people, or to make sure that someone is more advanced or successful than other people *59*

keep at sth to continue to do something (until it is finished) *59*

keep back sth *or* **keep sth back** to not tell someone everything you know about a situation or an event that has happened *59*

keep down sth *or* **keep sth down** if you keep the noise of something [e.g. music, voice] down, you stop it from becoming too loud *21, 59*

keep sb/sth from doing sth to prevent someone from doing something, especially work, by spending time with them *59*

keep sb in to make a child stay at school or at home, especially as a punishment *59*

keep in with sb *British & Australian* to continue to be friendly with someone, especially because they can help you *5, 59*

keep (sb) off sth to not eat, drink or use something that can harm you *59*

keep on *slightly* informal to talk in an annoying way about something for a long time *13*

keep on doing sth to continue to do something, or to do something again and again *59*

keep out of sth to not become involved in something *59*

keep to sth if you keep to the point, you do not write or talk about other topics *59*

keep sth to yourself to keep something secret *59*

keep up to be able to understand or deal with something that is happening or changing very fast *24, 59*

keep it up to continue to do something, especially to work hard or to do good work *30, 59*

keep sb up to make someone go to bed later than they usually do *59*

keep up sth *or* **keep sth up** to not allow something that is at a high level to fall to a lower level *59*

kick off (sth) *informal* to start *12*

kick off sth *or* **kick sth off** to remove your shoes by shaking your feet *12*

kick out sb *or* **kick sb out** to force someone to leave a place or an organisation *14*

knock sb about/around *informal* to hit or kick someone several times *9*

knock sth about/around *informal* to consider an idea *9*

knockabout *n British informal* when two or more people kick or hit a ball to each other for pleasure but not in a serious way, sometimes to warm up before a game *3*

knock down sb *or* **knock sb down** to cause someone to fall to the ground by pushing or hitting them *2*

knock down sb/sth *or* **knock sb/sth down** *informal* to reduce a price, or to persuade someone to reduce the price of something that they are selling *10, 26*

knock down sth *or* **knock sth down** to destroy and remove a building or part of a building [esp. wall] *2*

knock out sb *or* **knock sb out** to make someone become unconscious or to make someone fall asleep *20, 43*

knock over sb *or* **knock sb over** to hit someone with a vehicle and injure or kill them *50*

know sth from sth to know the difference between something and something else, so that you can recognise either of them *25*

know of sb/sth to have heard of someone or something and to be able to give some information about them, but not very much *39*

knuckle down to start to work or study hard, especially if you have not been working very hard before *31*

land (sb) in sth to be in a difficult situation, or to cause someone to be in a difficult situation or an unpleasant place [e.g. prison] *28*

land up *informal* to finally be in a particular place, state, or situation, especially without having planned it *15*

lash out to criticise someone or something in an angry way *14*

lay out sth *or* **lay sth out** to design the way in which a house, city, or garden is built or created *49*

lead into sth if a subject you are talking about or a discussion leads into another subject or discussion, it is the reason why you start talking about the second subject or start the second discussion *45*

lead-in something that introduces something else *11*

lead on sb *or* **lead sb on** to make someone do something bad by encouraging them or annoying them until they do it *13*

lead to sth if an action or event leads to something, it causes that thing to happen or exist *17*

lead up to sth if a period of time or a series of events leads up to an event or activity, it happens until that event or activity begins *16*

leak out if secret information leaks out, people who should not know this information find out about it *51*

lean towards sth/doing sth to support, or begin to support, a particular set of ideas or a particular political party *22*

leap out at sb if something leaps out at you, you notice it immediately *24*

leave behind sb *or* **leave sb behind** to make progress much faster than someone else *32*

leave off (sth/doing sth) to stop, or to stop doing something *12*

left out *adj* if someone feels left out, they are unhappy because they have not been included in an activity or conversation *4*

let in if something lets in water, air, or light, it allows water, air, or light to enter it through a hole or opening *11*

let off sb *or* **let sb off** to not punish someone who has committed a crime or done something wrong, or to not punish someone severely *53*

let off steam to talk or act in a way that helps get rid of strong feelings *8*

let out sb/sth *or* **let sb/sth out** to allow a person or animal to leave somewhere, especially by opening a locked or closed door *53*

let out sth *or* **let sth out** to make a piece of clothing wider by removing the sewing from the side edges and then sewing closer to the edge of the material *38*

let out sth *or* **let sth out** to tell someone about something which was supposed to be a secret *52*

let down sth *or* **let sth down** to make a piece of clothing longer by removing the sewing from the bottom folded edge and then sewing closer to the edge of the material *38*

letdown *n* something which is not as good as you thought it would be *3, 42*

level off/out if a rate or amount levels off, it stops rising or falling and it stays at the same level *26*

level with sb *informal* to tell the truth about something *52*

lie about/around (swh) if things are lying around, they are untidily left in places where they should not be *9*

lift-off *n* the moment when a spacecraft leaves the ground *3*

lift up sth *or* **lift sth up** to move something from a lower to a higher position *15*

light up (sth) *or* **light (sth) up** if your face or eyes light up, or if something [e.g. smile] lights them up, you suddenly look very happy or excited *40*

line up sth *or* **line sth up** to move something in order to make it straight or level with something else *25*

listen out for sth to make an effort to hear a noise which you are expecting *21*

live-in *adj* a live-in nanny lives at the home of the children she cares for *4*

live on to continue to exist *13*

live with sth to accept a difficult or unpleasant situation and continue with your life while it exists *28*

lockout *n* when workers are prevented from entering their place of work until they agree to particular conditions given by the employer *1*

lock up (sth) *or* **lock (sth) up** to lock all the doors and windows of a building when you leave it *37*

log in/into sth to connect a computer to a system of computers by typing your name or password, usually so that you can start working *6*

look after sb/sth to take care of someone or something by doing what is needed to keep them well or in good condition *2, 6*

look after sth to be responsible for dealing with something *35*

look at sb/sth to focus on somebody/ something *33*

look down on sb/sth to think that someone is less important than you, or to think that something is not good enough quality for you to use *2*

look for sth/sb to try to find something or someone, either because you have lost them or because you need them *2*

look forward to sth/doing sth to feel pleased and excited about something that is going to happen *1, 2*

look into sth to investigate or find out about something *33*

lookout *n* a person who looks at what is happening in the area around them, especially in order to watch for any danger *3*

loosen up to relax mentally *41*

loosen up (sth) *or* **loosen (sth) up** to prepare your body muscles for a physical activity by stretching and doing simple exercises *44*

lose out to to be less successful than *27*

magic away sth *or* **magic sth away** to make something disappear so quickly that it seems as if you have used magic *19*

major in sth *US & Australia* to study something as your main subject at university *32*

make out sth to claim falsely that something is true; to pretend *52*

make up for sth if someone makes up for something bad that they have done, they do something good so that the bad thing does not cause a problem any more *28*

make up for lost time to do something to compensate for not doing it previously *8*

make up your mind to make a decision about something *8*

mark down sb *or* **mark sb down** to give someone a lower result in an exam or competition because they have made a mistake or done something wrong *2, 32*

mist over if your eyes mist over, they become filled with tears which stop you from seeing clearly *48*

mist over/up if something made of glass [e.g. windscreen, glasses] mists up, or if something mists it up, it becomes covered with small drops of water and you cannot see through it any more *48*

be mixed up with sb to be involved with someone who has a bad influence on you *39*

mock-up *n* a model showing how something will look when it is built *49*

mop up (sth) *or* **mop (sth) up** to use a cloth or a mop to remove a liquid that has been dropped or that has spread *37*

move away to leave the place or area where you live and go and live in another place *42*

move in to begin living in a new house or area *47*

move (sb) in/into (swh) to go to a place to deal with a difficult situation *51*

move on to move forward in one's life and not look back to the past *42*

move up (sb) *or* **move (sb) up** if a student moves up, or if a teacher moves them up, they are put in a higher level or class *2, 32*

muck up sth *or* **muck sth up** *informal* to do something very badly *6*

mull over sth *or* **mull sth over** to think carefully about something for a long time, often before making a decision *29*

nail down *informal* to make a decision about all the details of something *23*

nod off *informal* to fall asleep when you do not intend to go to sleep *43*

nose about/around (swh) *informal* to look around a place, often in order to find something *7*

object to sb/sth/doing sth to feel or say that you oppose or dislike something or someone *34*

occur to sb if a thought or idea occurs to you, it comes into your mind *24*

off-putting *adj* slightly unpleasant or worrying so that you are discouraged from getting involved in any way *4*

offset *adj* if something is offset by something else it is compensated for *49*

offshoot *n* plant which has developed from a larger plant *47*

ongoing *adj* if a problem is ongoing, it continues to be a problem *4*

onset *n* the moment at which something unpleasant starts *1*, *3*

open off sth if an area opens off another area, you can enter one from the other directly *49*

open up (sth) *or* open (sth) up if a country or area opens up, or is opened up, it becomes easier to travel around it or sell things to it *15*

open up (sth) *or* open (sth) up to create a new opportunity or possibility *15, 19*

outbreak *n* a sudden beginning of something, especially something unpleasant *3*

outdated *adj* old-fashioned and therefore not as good or as fashionable as something that is modern *4*

outgoing *adj* if someone is outgoing, they are friendly and energetic and find it easy and enjoyable to be with others *1, 4*

outlook *n* the likely future situation *3*

output *n* an amount of something, produced by a person, machine, factory or country *3*

outspoken *adj* if someone is outspoken, they express their opinions even though other people might be offended by them *4, 40*

outstretched *adj* if someone's arms are outstretched they are held out in front of the person's body, often in order to greet someone *4*

overcast *adj* if the sky is overcast, it is grey and covered in cloud *47*

overkill *n* when there is more of something than is needed *3*

overpriced *adj* too expensive *4*

pack in sth *or* pack sth in *informal* to manage to do a lot of activities in a period of time *27*

pack in sth *or* pack sth in *informal* to stop doing something, especially a job *31*

paper over sth to hide a disagreement or difficulty and try to make people believe that there is no problem *52*

part with sth to give something away, usually when you do not want to *37*

pass by (swh) *British* to visit somewhere for a short time, usually while you are going somewhere else *42*

pass sb by if an event or opportunity passes you by, you do not notice it or you do not get any advantage from it *16*

pass off *British & Australian* if an event passes off in a good way, it happens in that way *51*

pass on sth *or* pass sth on to give a disease to another person or animal *43*

pass over sb *or* pass sb over to not give someone a job or a higher position and give it to someone else who is younger or less experienced *31*

patch up sth *or* patch sth up to try to improve your relationship with someone after an argument *39*

pay sth into sth to put money into a bank account, often to save money for a particular purpose *36*

peal out when bells ring loudly, they peal out *21*

pelt down *informal* to rain very heavily *48*

pep up sth/sb *or* pep sth/sb up *informal* to make something more interesting or attractive, or to make someone feel more active or energetic *15*

perk up (sb) *or* perk (sb) up to suddenly become happier or more energetic, or to make someone feel this way *41*

peter out if an energetic activity or a strong emotion peters out, it gradually becomes less energetic or strong until it stops completely *19*

pick at sth to eat only a small amount of a meal because you are not hungry or because you are feeling ill *55*

pick out sth/sb *or* pick sth/sb out to choose one thing or person or several things or people from a large group *14*

pick up if the wind picks up, it becomes stronger *1*

pick up if something [e.g. business, economy, trade] picks up, it improves or increases after a bad period *1*

pick up to lift something by using a bill (birds) *47*

pick up (sth) *or* **pick (sth) up** to start something again [e.g. story, relationship] from the point where you had stopped *1*

pick up sth if you pick up speed, you suddenly start to go faster *50*

pick up sth *or* **pick sth up** to buy something cheaply *1*

pick up sth *or* **pick sth up** to learn a new skill or language by practising it rather than being taught it *1*

pick up sth *or* **pick sth up** if a device picks up a signal or programmes broadcast by a radio station, it receives them *1, 54*

pick up sth *or* **pick sth up** to learn interesting or useful information [e.g. idea, tip, gossip] from someone or something *24, 51*

pick up sth *or* **pick sth up** to get an infectious illness from someone or something *43*

pick up sth/sb *or* **pick sth/sb up** to collect someone who is waiting for you, or to collect something that you have left somewhere or that you have bought *1, 2, 50*

pick up sth/sb *or* **pick sth/sb up** to lift something or someone by using your hands *1, 15*

pick up on sth to react to something that you have noticed or something that has happened *15*

pick yourself up to stand up again after you have fallen *44*

piece together sth *or* **piece sth together** to try to understand a situation or to try to discover the truth about something by collecting different pieces of information and considering them at the same time *24*

pile into swh to enter a place or vehicle quickly and not in an organised way *46*

pile out (of) to leave a place or vehicle quickly and not in an organised way *46*

pile up (sth) *or* **pile (sth) up** to become a pile, or to make a lot of things into a pile by putting them on top of each other *25*

pin down sb *or* **pin sb down** to force someone to stay in a horizontal position by holding them *10*

pitch in to help with work that needs to be done *11*

play along to pretend to agree with someone, or to do what someone wants for a short time, in order to get something from them or to avoid making them angry *52*

play about/around to behave in a stupid way *9*

play sb off against sb to encourage one person or group to compete against or argue with another, hoping that you can get some advantage from this situation *29*

play on sth if someone plays on your fears or weaknesses, they use them to try and make you do what they want, often in a way that is unfair *29*

play with sth if you play with the idea of doing something, you consider it, but usually do not do it *24*

plough back sth *or* **plough sth back** to put money that you have earned into a business, in order to make the business bigger or better *36*

plug away *informal* to work hard at something for a long time *31*

plug into sth if a piece of electrical equipment plugs into a supply of electricity or another piece of electrical equipment, it works by being connected to that supply of electricity or that piece of equipment *54*

plump up sth *or* **plump sth up** to make something [e.g. cushion, pillow] rounder and softer, especially by shaking it *37*

point to/towards sth if one thing points to something else, it makes it seem likely that it is true *17*

point out sb/sth *or* **point sb/sth out** to highlight *33*

pop-up adverts *n* advertisements that open quickly on a computer screen in front of what you are working on *54*

pore over sth to study or look carefully at something, especially a book or a document *5, 32*

potter about/around (swh) *British & Australian* to spend time in a pleasant, relaxed way, often doing small jobs in or around the house *9*

predispose sb to/towards sth *formal* predisposing someone to something makes it more likely that that thing will happen *6*

preside over sth *formal* to be in charge of an event or situation and have official responsibility for it *6*

press on to continue doing something in a determined way *13, 19*

prey on sth to catch for food *47*

pride yourself on sth/doing sth (always reflexive) to be proud of a quality you have or of something you do *27, 40*

print off sth *or* **print sth off** to print a particular number of copies of something *6, 54*

profit from sth/doing sth to get an advantage from something *34*

prop up sth *or* **prop sth up** to make something stay in a particular position by putting something underneath or against it *25*

prop yourself up to support yourself by leaning on or against something *15*

provide for sth *formal* if a law or agreement provides for something, it allows it to happen or exist *53*

pull down sth *or* **pull sth down** to destroy a structure because it is not wanted anymore *47*

pull on sth to put on clothes quickly *38*

pull out to drive to a different part of the road, usually a part where the vehicles are travelling faster *50*

pull out all the stops to do everything you can *8*

pull out to move military troops to a different area *51*

pull over sb/sth *or* **pull sb/sth over** if the police pull someone who is driving a car over, they order them to drive the car to the side of the road and stop *50*

pull (sb) through (sth) to succeed in dealing with a difficult period of your life, or to help someone else to do this *27*

pull sth to to close a door or window by pulling it towards you *37*

pull up to move a piece of furniture [esp. chair] near to something or someone *37*

pull up sth *or* **pull sth up** to remove something from the ground *47*

pull your socks up to make an effort to improve *16*

push sb about/around/round to tell someone what to do in a rude or threatening way *20*

push on to continue travelling somewhere *46*

push over sb/sth *or* **push sb/sth over** to push someone or something so that they fall to the ground *20*

push through sth *or* **push sth through** to make a plan or suggestion be officially accepted *29*

push sth to to close a door or window by pushing it *37*

push up sth *or* **push sth up** to increase the amount, number, or value of something *26*

put aside sth/sb *or* **push sth/sb** to save money for a particular purpose *36*

put away sth *or* **put sth away** to put something in the place where it is usually kept *37*

put back sth *or* **put sth back** to change the date or time of an event so that it happens later than planned *16*

put sth behind sb if you put an unpleasant experience behind you, you forget it so that it does not affect your life *18*

put by sth *or* **put sth by** to save an amount of money in order to use it later *36*

put down sb *or* **put sb down** to put someone's name on a list or document, usually in order to arrange for them to do something *10*

put down sth *or* **put sth down** to kill an animal because it is very old or very ill *10*

put down sth *or* **put sth down** to use force to stop people opposing the government *51*

put down roots to settle down and make a relationship more permanent *8*

put sth down to sth to think that a problem or bad experience is caused by something else *17*

put forward sth *or* **put sth forward** to state an idea or opinion, or to suggest a plan, so that it can be considered or discussed *6*

put in a good word for someone to say good things about someone to people in authority *8*

put on sth *or* **put sth on** if a person or animal puts on weight, they become heavier *26, 55*

put sb on sth to give someone a particular type of medical treatment or food *43*

put out sth *or* **put sth out** to produce information [e.g. statement, warning, press release] and make it available for everyone to read or hear *6, 51, 53*

put out sth *or* **put sth out** to put something outside the house, especially so that it can be collected *37*

put sb through sth to pay for someone to study at college or university *32*

put sth to sb to ask someone a question, or to state an opinion to someone which they are likely to disagree with *45*

put together sth *or* **put sth together** to prepare, or organise something *33*

put up sth *or* **put sth up** to fasten a piece of furniture [e.g. shelves, cupboard] to a wall or assemble something *37*

put up with sb/sth to tolerate unpleasant behaviour or an unpleasant situation *2*

ramble on to talk or write for a long time about things that are not interesting to other people *13*

rank (sth) among sth to have a particular position in a list that has been arranged in order of quality *25*

read on to continue reading and read the next part of something *13*

read up on sb/sth to do background reading on *33*

reason with sb to try to persuade someone not to do something stupid by giving them good reasons not to *29*

rebound on sb if a negative action rebounds on someone, it has a bad effect on the person who did it and they do not achieve what they were trying to achieve *17*

reduce sth to sth to destroy something that has been built [e.g. building, city] *49*

reel off sth *or* **reel sth off** to say a long list of things quickly and without stopping *45*

refer to sb/sth if writing or information refers to someone or something, it describes or is about that person or thing *34*

reflect on sth *slightly* formal to think very hard about something, or to express your thoughts about something in what you say or write *24*

relate to sth to be connected to a particular subject, or to be about a particular subject *34*

rely on sth/sb to need something or someone in order to survive, be successful, or work correctly *13*

remind sb of sb/sth to cause someone to think of someone or something *18*

rent out sth *or* **rent sth out** if you rent out something that you own [e.g. house], you allow someone to pay you money so that they can use it *36*

resign yourself to sth to accept that something we do not want to happen will happen *28*

resort to sth/doing sth to do something bad in order to achieve what you want, often because it is the only thing you can do to achieve it *28*

result in sth to cause something to happen, or to make a situation exist *17, 34*

rev up sth *or* **rev sth up** to make a vehicle's engine work faster while the vehicle is not moving *50*

be riddled with sth be full of something, especially something bad or unpleasant *5, 28*

ride on sth if something important [e.g. reputation, money] rides on something else, it depends on it *13*

rise above sth to not allow something bad that is happening or being done to you to upset you or to affect your behaviour *27*

roll about/around *informal* to laugh a lot about something *9*

roll in if money or requests for money [e.g. bills] roll in, they arrive in large numbers *36*

roll in if bad weather [e.g. clouds, fog] rolls in, it appears in large amounts *48*

Roll on sth! *British informal* something that you say in order to show that you are looking forward to a time or event *30*

roll out sth *or* **roll sth out** to make a new product, service or system available for the first time *53*

roll (sb/sth) over to turn from lying on one side of your body to the other side, or to make someone or something turn from one side to the other *1*

roll up to arrive at a particular place or event, usually late *42*

roll up sth *or* **roll sth up** to fold the edges of a piece of clothing that you are wearing [e.g. sleeves, trousers] in order to make them shorter *38*

be rooted in sth to be based on, or caused by *17*

root out sth/sb *or* **root sth/sb out** *informal* to search and find something or someone that is difficult to find *51*

rough out sth *or* **rough sth out** if you rough out a drawing or an idea, you draw or write the main parts of it without showing the details *24*

round down sth *or* **round sth down** to decrease a number to the nearest whole amount *26*

round off sth *or* **round sth off** to do something as a way of finishing an event or activity in a satisfactory way *12, 33*

round on sb to suddenly turn and attack someone, or shout at them angrily *20*

round up sb/sth *or* round sb/sth up to find and gather together a group of people or animals *25*

round up sth *or* round sth up to increase a number to the nearest whole amount *26*

rule out sth *or* rule sth out to say no to something *23*

run about/around to run and play *9*

run around/round after sb *informal* to do a lot of things for someone else, especially when they should be able to do more for themselves *9, 31*

run away with sb if something [e.g. emotions, imagination, enthusiasm] runs away with someone, it makes them do or think stupid things *41*

run-down *adj* shabby, in disrepair *49*

run into sth if you run into difficulties or problems, you begin to experience them *28*

run out if a supply of something runs out, there is none left because it has all been used *19*

run over to continue past the expected finishing time *7*

run over sb/sth *or* run sb/sth over to hit someone or something with a vehicle and drive over them, injuring or killing them *7*

run over sth to quickly read something or repeat something in order to remember it or to make sure that it is correct *7*

run rings round to outwit and be cleverer than people *8*

run through sth if you run through money, you spend a lot of it very quickly *36*

run through sth to explain or read something to someone quickly *45*

safeguard against sth to do things that you hope will stop something unpleasant happening *28*

sail through (sth) to succeed very easily, especially in a test, examination etc. *5, 27, 32*

be sandwiched between sb/sth *informal* to be in a small space in the middle of two people or things *7*

scrape by to manage to live when you do not have much money *36*

scrape through (sth) to manage with a lot of difficulty to succeed in something [e.g. exam] *32*

scream out (sth) *or* scream (sth) out to suddenly shout something in a loud voice, especially to get someone's attention *14*

screw up sb *or* screw sb up *informal* to make someone feel confused or unhappy about themselves and their life *40*

scroll down/up to move text or other information on a computer screen, in order to view a different part of it *6*

see about sth to deal with something, or to arrange for something to be done *25*

see sth through to continue doing a job or activity until it is finished, especially when it is difficult *31*

seize up if part of your body or a machine seizes up, it stops moving or working in the normal way *54*

sell up (sth) *or* sell (sth) up *British & Australian* to sell your house or business in order to go somewhere else or do something else *6*

send in sb *or* send sb in to send a group of people with special skills [e.g. police, troops] to deal with a difficult situation *1, 51*

send out sth *or* send sth out if a plant sends out something [e.g. roots, shoots], it grows *47*

send out for sth to telephone a restaurant and ask for food to be delivered to your home *55*

separate off sth *or* separate sth off to remove something from a large group of things *25*

separate out sb/sth *or* separate sb/sth out to divide a group of people or things into smaller groups *25*

serve up sth *or* serve sth up to put food on plates and in dishes for people to eat *55*

set aside sth *or* set sth aside to use something, especially time, for one purpose and no other purpose *16*

set back sb/sth *or* set sb/sth back to make something happen more slowly, or to make something happen later than it should happen *16*

set sb back (sth) *informal* to cost someone a particular amount of money, usually a large amount of money *36*

be set back if a building is set back, it is a little distance from the road *49*

set in if something unpleasant sets in, it begins and seems likely to continue *3, 11*

set off sth *or* set sth off to make something look attractive, usually by providing a very different colour *49*

set (sth/sb) on sb to attack someone, or to make a person or animal attack someone *3, 20*

set out to begin something with a specific aim *33*

set up (sth) or set (sth) up to get all the necessary equipment ready for a particular activity *54*

set up sth or set sth up to make arrangements so that something can happen or exist *15*

set up sb or set sb up to give someone the money that they need to start a business *35*

settle in (sth/swh) or settle (sb) in to begin to feel relaxed and happy in new surroundings *37*

settle for to agree to something which isn't your first choice *23*

settle on sth to agree on something *23*

shake off sb or shake sb off to succeed in escaping from someone who is following you *12*

shake up sb or shake sb up if an unpleasant experience shakes someone up, it makes them feel shocked and upset *41*

shake-up *n* when big changes are made to an organisation in order to improve it *1*

share out sth or share sth out to divide something into smaller amounts and give one amount to each person or thing in a group *14*

shine through (sth) if a quality that someone has shines through or shines through something, that quality is very easily noticed *40*

shoot down sb/sth or shoot sb/sth down *informal* to criticise someone's ideas or suggestions and refuse to consider them *6*

shoot down sb/sth or shoot sb/sth down to destroy an aircraft or make it fall to the ground by firing bullets or weapons at it *51*

shoot off *British & Australian informal* to leave somewhere very quickly *42*

shoot up if the number, amount, or rate of something shoots up, it increases very quickly *7*

shore up sth or shore sth up to strengthen or improve an organisation, agreement, or system that is not working effectively or that is likely to fail *15*

shout down sb or shout sb down to shout in order to prevent someone who is saying something that you disagree with from being heard *10*

shout out (sth) or shout (sth) out to suddenly shout something in a loud voice, especially to get someone's attention *14*

Shove off! something that you say when you are angry to tell someone to go away *12*

show in sb or show sb in to lead a visitor into a room where they have arranged to meet or wait for someone *11*

show off to show someone or something that you are proud of to a group of people *12*

show up if something shows up, it can be seen clearly or easily *15*

shrug off sth or shrug sth off to not worry about something and treat it as unimportant *12*

shut down (sth) or shut (sth) down if a machine shuts down or someone shuts it down, it stops operating *10*

shutdown *n* when a factory or business closes and stops working *1*

shut out sth or shut sth out to prevent a sound or light from being heard or seen *21*

shut (sb) up to stop talking or making a noise, or to make someone do this *30*

Shut up! to tell someone to stop talking *30*

side against sb to oppose a person or group in an argument *22*

side with sb to support a person or group in an argument *22*

sift through sth to examine a large collection of something, especially papers, usually in order to discover something or to decide what is important *25*

sign over sth or sign sth over to give someone else your property or legal rights to something by signing an official document *53*

sign up sb or sign sb up to arrange for someone to sign a document stating that they will work for you *35*

single out sb/sth or single sb/sth out to choose one person or thing from a large group in order to criticise or praise them *29*

size up sb/sth or size sb/sth up to carefully examine a situation or person in order to make a judgement *29*

sketch out sth or sketch sth out to roughly plan something *33*

skim through sth to read quickly without studying the details *32*

skirt around/round sth to avoid discussing a difficult subject or problem 9

slam down sth *or* **slam sth** down to put something down with a lot of force 10

sleep off sth *or* **sleep sth off** to sleep until you feel better, especially after too much alcohol 42

slice up sth *or* **slice sth up** to cut or divide something into parts 55

slim down (sth) *or* **slim (sth) down** to become smaller in size, often by employing fewer people, or to make something smaller 26

slip away if a period of time slips away, it seems to pass quickly 16

slog away *informal* to keep working very hard, usually for a long time 31

smarten up (sb/sth) *or* **smarten sb/sth up** to make a person or a place look tidier 37

smash up sth *or* **smash sth up** to badly damage or destroy something by hitting it many times 20

smooth down sth *or* **smooth sth down** to press your hair or your clothes with your hands in order to make them flat 38

smooth over sth *or* **smooth sth over** to settle a disagreement so that it's no longer a problem 23

smooth over sth *or* **smooth sth over** to make a disagreement or problem seem less serious or more easy to deal with, especially by talking to the people involved in it 28

snap out of sth *informal* to force yourself to stop feeling sad and upset 41

be snowed under *informal* to have so much work that you have problems dealing with it 32

oak up sth *or* **soak sth up** to enjoy the effects of an experience 49

soak up sth *or* **soak sth up** if a dry substance soaks up a liquid, it absorbs it 55

soldier on to continue doing something, although it is difficult or unpleasant 7

sort out sth *or* **sort sth out** to successfully deal with a problem or difficult situation 2, 14

sort out sth *or* **sort sth out** to arrange or organise things which are untidy 14

sound out sb/sth *or* **sound sb/sth out** to talk to someone in order to discover what they think about an idea or plan 45, 51

space out sth *or* **space sth out** to arrange things so that there is enough space or time between them 16, 25

spill out (sth) *or* **spill (sth) out** if you spill out an emotion or if emotion spills out, you express it, usually by talking in an uncontrolled way 41

spill over if a bad situation or problem spills over, it begins to have an unpleasant effect on another situation or group of people 28

spill over (sth) if the liquid in a container spills over, it flows over the edge of the container 55

spin out sth *or* **spin sth out** to make something continue for as long as possible 16

split off to stop belonging to a particular group or political party and form a separate one 12

split up (sth) *or* **split (sth) up** to divide into smaller parts or groups, or to divide something into smaller parts or groups 15

spread out sth *or* **spread sth out** to open something that is folded [e.g. map, towel] and put it down flat on a surface 14

spread out sth *or* **spread sth out** if you spread out your arms, legs, or fingers, you stretch them so that there are wide spaces between them 44

spring sth on sb to tell someone some news that surprises them 13

spring up if something springs up, it suddenly appears or begins to exist 19

sprout up if a large number of things sprout up, they suddenly appear or begin to exist 19

spur on sb *or* **spur sb on** to encourage someone to try harder in order to achieve something 7

spy on sb/sth to watch secretly in order to discover information about them 52

square up *informal* to pay someone the money you owe them 6, 36

squash (sb) in to manage to get yourself or someone else into a very small space, or place that is full of people 11

squash up if people who are sitting or standing together squash up, they move closer together in order to make space for someone else 46

stack up if aircraft stack up, they fly over an airport at different heights waiting to be told they can land 50

stack up sth *or* **stack sth up** to arrange things in a tall pile 25

stake sth on sth/doing sth to risk losing money or harming something important [e.g. reputation] if a plan does not succeed 36

stake out sth *or* **stake sth out** if the police or reporters stake out a building where someone is living or hiding, they watch the building continuously in order to see who is leaving or entering it *51*

stand back to move a short distance away from something or someone *46*

stand by to do nothing to prevent something unpleasant from happening *7*

standby *n* a person or thing that can be used if someone or something else is not available or cannot be used *1, 3*

stand for sth if a group of people stand for a set of ideas, they support those ideas, or if something stands for a particular idea, it represents that idea *22*

stand-off *n* when two groups fail to reach an agreement in talks *3*

stand up to rise from a sitting or lying position to a standing position *1*

stand up if an idea or claim stands up, it is proved to be correct when it is examined carefully *15*

start sb off to help someone to start an activity, especially a piece of work *12*

to start with to begin *33*

start-up *n* when a business or organisation is created and starts to operate *3*

steal away to leave a place quietly without anyone knowing *46*

steam up (sth) *or* **steam (sth) up** if a glass surface steams up, or if something steams it up, it becomes covered with very small drops of water *48*

be steeped in sth to have a lot of (particularly tradition or history) *49*

stem from sth if a problem or difficult situation stems from something, it is caused by it *17*

step aside to leave a job or position, especially so that someone else can do it *31*

stick by sth to continue to support or use a decision, opinion, or plan *22*

stick out sth *or* **stick sth out** to push part of your body forward or out from the rest of your body *44*

stick up if part of something sticks up, it comes up above the surface of something, or it points upwards *15*

stick up for sth to defend or fight for something important [e.g. rights] *22*

stick with sb if something sticks with you, you remember it *18*

stir up sth *or* **stir sth up** if something stirs up memories, it makes you remember events in the past, usually ones that make you feel sad *18*

store up sth *or* **store sth up** to remember things, usually so that you can tell people about them later *18*

storm out to leave a place in an angry way *48*

stow away to hide on a ship, aircraft, or other vehicle, in order to travel secretly or without paying *3, 50*

stowaway *n* a person who stows away *3, 50*

straighten up sth *or* **straighten sth up** to make a place tidy *37*

stream into swh to move continuously in one direction, especially if a lot of people do this at the same time *5*

stretch out if an area of land stretches out, it continues over a long distance *49*

stretch out sth *or* **stretch sth out** to hold a part of your body straight out in front of you *44*

strike back (at) to attack someone who has attacked you *1, 20*

strike out to start doing something that you have not done before *7*

strike up sth to start a conversation or relationship with someone *39*

stumble on sth/sb to find or meet by chance *46*

succeed in sth/doing sth to achieve something that you have been trying to get or do *27*

suck up to sb *informal* to try to make someone who is in a position of authority like you by doing and saying things that will please them *39*

sum up (sth/sb) *or* **sum (sth/sb) up** to describe briefly the most important facts or characteristics of something or someone *6*

sum up sb/sth *or* **sum sth/sb up** if something sums up someone or something, it represents the most typical qualities of that person or thing *34*

summon up sth *or* **summon sth up** if something summons up a memory or an image, it makes you remember something or think about something *18*

summon up sth *or* **summon sth up** to try hard to find a particular quality [e.g. courage, energy] in yourself because you need it in order to do something *41*

swear by sth to believe that something is very effective and that it will always work well *22*

sweep aside sth *or* **sweep sth aside** to refuse to think about something or let it affect your performance *7*

swing around/round to suddenly turn around so that you can see someone or something behind you *44*

switch around/round to move two or more things, so that each of them is now in the place that one of the others was in before *9*

switch off to stop giving your attention to something or someone *12*

tail off to decrease in amount or level *26*

take sb aback if something takes you aback, you are very surprised by it *60*

take along sb/sth *or* **take sb/sth along** to take someone or something with you when you go somewhere *60*

take away sb *or* **take sb away** to take someone with you when you stay somewhere for a short time *60*

take away sth *or* **take sth away** if you take away something [e.g. memory, impression, message] from an event or performance, you remember or think about that thing after the event or performance has finished *60*

take away from sth to make something seem less good or successful *60*

Take it away! something that you say in musical contexts to tell someone to start playing or singing *30, 60*

take down sth *or* **take sth down** to remove a large temporary structure from a place by separating it into pieces and taking the pieces away *60*

take down sth *or* **take sth down** to write something, especially something that someone says *10*

take off if an aircraft, bird, or insect takes off, it moves from the ground and begins to fly *60*

take off sth *or* **take sth off** to spend time away from your work *60*

take sb off sth to stop giving someone a particular type of medical treatment or food *60*

take sb off sth to stop someone doing a particular task *60*

take-off *n* imitation *60*

take on sth *or* **take sth on** to accept a particular job or responsibility and begin to do what is needed *6*

take out sb *or* **take sb out** to go somewhere and do something with someone, usually something that you have planned or paid for *42, 60*

take out sb/sth *or* **take sb/sth out** to kill someone, or to destroy something *60*

take sth out of sb *informal* to make someone feel very tired *43*

take over sth *or* **take sth over** to get control of a company by buying most of its shares (= the equal parts into which the ownership of the company is divided) *6*

take over sth *or* **take sth over** to get control of an area of land or a political organisation, usually by using force *47*

take the sting out of something to make something that is unpleasant less so *8*

take up sth *or* **take sth up** to start doing a particular job or activity *32*

take up sth *or* **take sth up** to shorten a piece of clothing [e.g. skirt, trousers] *38*

take up sth (with) *or* **take sth up (with)** to discuss something or deal with something *60*

take up sth *or* **take sth up** to use a particular amount of time, space or effort *60*

talk at sb to talk to someone without listening to them or allowing them to speak *45*

talk sb out of sth to persuade someone not to do something *23*

talk round sb *or* **talk sb round** to convince somebody to agree to your idea or opinion through a long discussion *23*

talk through sth *or* **talk sth through** to discuss all the details of something so that you can understand it or make a decision about it *24*

tend towards sth to be likely to choose a particular thing *29*

tense up if you tense up or your muscles tense up, your muscles stiffen because you are not relaxed *44*

test out sth *or* **test sth out** to test a theory or new idea by seeing how it works in a practical situation or by finding out what other people think of it *14*

thaw out if someone thaws out, they become warmer after they have been outside and have got very cold *44*

thin out if a large number of people or things thin out, they become fewer in number *26*

think through sth *or* **think sth through** to plan carefully *33*

think up sth *or* **think sth up** to create an idea or plan by using your imagination and intelligence *24*

thrash out sth *or* **thrash sth out** to discuss a problem, idea, or plan in detail until you find a solution, reach an agreement, or make a decision *24*

throw off sth *or* **throw sth off** to succeed in getting rid of a slight illness *43*

throw out sth *or* **throw sth out** if people in authority throw out a plan or idea [e.g. bill, proposal] they refuse to accept or use it *53*

throw the baby out with the bathwater to get rid of the good parts of something as well as the bad parts *8*

tick off sb *or* **tick sb off** *British & Australian* to tell someone that they have done something wrong and that you are angry about it *12*

tick off sth *or* **tick sth off** to mark something with a tick *32*

tie back sth *or* **tie sth back** to fasten something that usually hangs down [esp. hair] so that it is fixed in position and not hanging down *2, 38*

tie down sth/sb *or* **tie sth/sb down** to fasten something or someone in a particular position, especially by using ropes *10*

tie sb down to stop someone from being free to do what they want to do *10, 29*

tighten up sth *or* **tighten sth up** to make rules more limiting and more difficult to avoid *53*

tire out sb *or* **tire sb out** to make someone very tired *43*

tired out *adj* completely exhausted *4*

toss (sb) for sth to decide which person or team can do something or have something by throwing a coin in the air and guessing which side of the coin will be on top when it lands *29*

toss-up *n informal* a situation in which two people or things seem equally likely to be chosen or two possible results seem equally likely to happen *3*

toughen up to become stronger and more able to deal with problems, or to make someone become this way *40*

toughen up sth *or* **toughen sth up** to make rules more limiting and more difficult to avoid *53*

toy with sth to consider something or doing something, but not in a very serious way and without making a decision *29*

trail off to gradually become quieter and then stop *21*

treat sb to sth to buy or pay for something for someone else *42*

trip over (sth) to fall or almost fall because you have accidentally hit your foot against something while walking or running *46*

tune into sth to turn on the radio or television in order to listen to or watch a particular programme *54*

turn (sb) against sth/sb to decide not to like or agree with someone or something, or to make someone do this *41*

turn around/round (sb/sth) *or* **turn (sth/sb) around/round** to turn so that you are facing the opposite direction, or to make someone or something do this *9, 44*

turn around/round sth *or* **turn sth around** change an unsuccessful business, plan or system so that it becomes successful *9*

turn away sb *or* **turn sb away** to refuse to allow someone to enter a place, usually because there is no more space *42*

turn down sth *or* **turn sth down** to reduce the amount of sound or heat that is produced by a device [e.g. television, radio, oven] *10*

turn out sth *or* **turn sth out** if a company or business turns out something, they make or produce it *35*

turn over sth *or* **turn sth over** if a business or a company turns over an amount of money, it makes that amount in a particular period of time *6, 35*

turn up the heat to make a relationship more intense *8*

type in to write something using a computer *54*

type up sth *or* **type sth up** to rewrite in full using a computer *33*

upkeep *n* keeping a building in good condition, usually by providing money to repair it *59*

uptake *n* the number of people who have committed themselves to something *60*

usher in sth *formal* if an event ushers in a period of time in which new things or changes happen, it is at the beginning of that period or it causes those things to happen *11*

vote on sth to make a decision about something [e.g. proposal, motion] by counting the number of people for and against it *53*

vouch for sb to say that you know someone and that you can promise that they have a good character or good skills *40*

Wake up! *informal* something you say to tell someone to listen to what you are saying when they have not been listening *30*

wake up to the fact to be realistic *8*

walk away to stop being involved in a situation that is difficult to deal with or that does not give you any advantages *28*

walk in on sb to go into a room and see what someone is doing when they did not want anyone to see them *46*

walk-on *adj* a walk-on part in a play is a very small part with no words for the actor to speak *3*

walk out to stop working because of a disagreement with your employer *3, 51*

walkout *n* when workers stop working because of a disagreement with their employer *3*

want for *formal* if someone does not want for anything, they have everything they need in order to have a satisfactory life *6*

want out *informal* to want to leave a place *14*

warm to sb to start to like someone *39*

warm up to prepare your body muscles for a physical activity by stretching and doing simple exercises *44*

warm up (sth) *or* **warm (sth) up** if an engine or machine warms up, or if you warm it up, it starts working so that it becomes warm enough to work well *54*

warm up sb *or* **warm sb up** to make a group of people who are going to watch a performance start to enjoy themselves by entertaining them for a short time before the performance *7*

warm up sth *or* **warm sth up** to heat food that has already been cooked *7*

warm-up *n* when a performer makes a group of people who are going to watch a performance start to enjoy themselves by entertaining them for a short time before the performance *3*

wash away sth *or* **wash sth away** if water [e.g. rain, flood] washes something away, it carries it away *47*

wash down sth *or* **wash sth down** to clean a large object or surface [e.g. floor, walls] with a liquid *37*

wash down sth *or* **wash sth down** to drink something while you are eating food or taking medicine in order to help you swallow it *55*

washed out *adj* if someone looks washed out, they look tired, pale and ill *43*

waste away to gradually get thinner and weaker, usually because of illness *44*

Watch out! something you say to tell someone to be careful so that they can avoid danger or an accident *30*

watch over sb/sth to protect or take care of a person or animal *47*

water down sth *or* **water sth down** to add water to a drink, especially an alcoholic drink *10, 55*

water down sth *or* **water sth down** to make an idea or opinion less strong in order to make more people agree with it, or to make a plan or suggestion more acceptable *10, 55*

watered-down *adj* when something is made less strong in order to make people agree with it *4*

wear out (sth) *or* **wear (sth) out** to use something so much that it becomes weak or damaged and cannot be used any more, or to become weak and damaged in this way *4*

wear out sb *or* **wear sb out** to make someone very tired *1, 43*

weigh up sth *or* **weigh sth up** to thinking about something carefully, comparing *33*

whip up sth to try to make people feel strongly about something *51*

whittle away sth *or* **whittle sth away** *or* **whittle away at sth** to gradually reduce the size or importance of something until it does not exist any more *19*

win back sb/sth *or* **win sb/sth back** to persuade customers to return to using your company rather than competing companies because your company has improved *27*

win out if a particular emotion or type of behaviour wins out, it is stronger than other emotions or types of behaviour *27*

win round sb *or* **win sb round** to get other people to agree with your idea after a long discussion or argument *23*

win through to finally succeed after trying hard to achieve something *27*

wind up (sth) *or* **wind (sth) up** to finish an activity *19*

wipe off sth *or* **wipe sth off** to remove information stored on part of a computer [esp. memory, hard drive] *54*

wipe out sb *or* **wipe sb** out *informal* to make someone extremely tired *43*

wipe out sth *or* **wipe sth out** to destroy or get rid of something *20*

wire up sth/sb *or* **wire sth/sb up** to connect something or someone to a piece of electrical equipment by using electrical wires *54*

witter on *British informal* to talk for a long time about unimportant things *45*

wolf down sth *or* **wolf sth down** to eat something very quickly because you are very hungry *55*

work around/round sth to organise activities to ensure that a problem does not prevent you from doing what you want to do *9*

work yourself into sth to make yourself become very angry or upset *41*

work off sth *or* **work sth off** to do something energetic to stop yourself becoming fat after eating a lot of food *12*

work off sth *or* **work sth off** to reduce the size of a debt, either by earning money to pay for it or by working for the person you owe money to *36*

work out sth *or* **work sth out** to think carefully about how you are going to do something and to make a plan or decision *1, 29*

worked up *adj* if you are worked-up, you feel very upset, nervous or excited about something *4*

worm sth out of sb to manage to get information from someone which they are trying to keep secret *51*

worn-out *adj* weak and damaged through much use *1, 4*

wrap up sth *or* **wrap sth up** to complete an activity, especially successfully *15*

wring sth out of sb to force or persuade someone to give you money or information *45*

write out sth *or* **write sth out** to write (or rewrite) in full *33*

write up sth *or* **write sth up** to write something on paper or on a computer in a complete or final form, often using notes you have made *15, 51*

yell out (sth) *or* **yell (sth) out** to suddenly shout something in a loud voice, especially to get someone's attention *14*

zip along (sth) *informal* to move very quickly *46*

zip up sth *or* **zip sth up** to fasten a piece of clothing by using its zip (= a long metal or plastic fastener), or to help someone close the zip on a piece of clothing they are wearing *38*